CO-CEP-542

FLORIDA STATE
UNIVERSITY LIBRARIES

JAN 1 9 2001

TTALLAHASSEE, FLORIDA

# Trade, Development and the Environment

# Trade, Development and the Environment

Edited by
*WTO Secretariat*

**KLUWER LAW INTERNATIONAL**
LONDON / THE HAGUE / BOSTON

WORLD TRADE
ORGANIZATION

Published by
Kluwer Law International Ltd
Sterling House
66 Wilton Road
London SW1V 1DE
United Kingdom

Kluwer Law International incorporates
the publishing programmes of
Graham & Trotman Ltd,
Kluwer Law & Taxation Publishers
and Martinus Nijhoff Publishers

Sold and distributed in
the USA and Canada by
Kluwer Law International
675 Massachusetts Avenue
Cambridge MA 02139
USA

In all other countries, sold and distributed by
Kluwer Law International
PO Box 322
3300 AH Dordrecht
The Netherlands

ISBN 90-411-9804-0
© Kluwer Law International 2000
First published 2000

**Library of Congress Cataloging-in-Publication Data**
Trade, development, and the environment/edited by WTO Secretariat
    p. cm.
  Papers from the High Level Symposium on Trade and Environment from 15–16 March
1999 and the High Level Symposium on Trade and Development from 17–18 March
1999 in Geneva.
  Includes index.
  ISBN 9041198040 (hardcover: alk. paper)
    1. Free trade–Environmental aspects–Congresses. 2. International trade–Environmental aspects–
Congresses. 3. Environmental policy–Economic aspects–Congresses. 4. Economic development–
Congresses. 5. Sustainable development–Environmental aspects–Congresses. 6. Free trade–
Environmental aspects–Developing countries–Congresses. 7. Developing countries–Economic
integration–Congresses. I. World Trade Organization. Secretariat. II. High Level Symposium on
Trade and Environment (1999: Geneva, Switzerland) III. High Level Symposium on Trade and
Development (1999: Geneva, Switzerland)

HF1703 .T725 2000
333.7–dc21

00-059312

This publication is protected by international copyright law. All rights reserved. No part of this
publication may be reproduced, stored in a retrieval system, or transmitted in any form or by
any means, electronic, mechanical, photocopying, recording or otherwise, without the prior
permission of the publisher.

Typeset in 10/11 pt Times New Roman by Newgen Imaging Systems (P) Ltd, Chennai
Printed and bound in Great Britain by Antony Rowe Limited.

# CONTENTS

# Part II.  Trade and Development

## Introduction

## 1.  Linkages between trade and development policies

## 2.  Trade and development prospects of developing countries

## 3.  Further integration of developing countries, including least-developed countries (LDCs), in the multilateral trading system

## Conclusion

# Chapter 1

## THE WORLD TRADE ORGANIZATION – A BRIEF INTRODUCTION

The World Trade Organization (WTO) is the legal and institutional foundation of the multilateral trading system. It provides the principal contractual obligations determining how governments frame and implement domestic trade legislation and regulations. It also serves as the platform on which trade relations among its Member States and customs territories evolve through collective debate, negotiation, consultation and dispute settlement.

The WTO, established on 1 January 1995, is the embodiment of the Uruguay Round results and the successor to the General Agreement on Tariffs and Trade (GATT). Governments concluded the Uruguay Round negotiations on 15 December 1993 and Ministers gave their political backing to the results by signing the Final Act in Marrakesh, Morocco, on 14 April 1994. The "Marrakesh Declaration" affirmed that the results of the Uruguay Round would "strengthen the world economy and lead to more trade, investment, employment and income growth throughout the world".

The WTO held its first Ministerial Conference in Singapore from 9 to 13 December 1996. The second was in Geneva on 18 and 20 May 1998. The third was held in Seattle, United States, from 30 November to 3 December 1999. At mid-November 1999, 135 countries and territories were members of the WTO. Another 33 governments were engaged in negotiating their terms of entry with other WTO Members.

The essential functions of the WTO are:

- administering and implementing the multilateral and plurilateral trade agreements which together make up the WTO;
- acting as a forum for multilateral trade negotiations;
- seeking to resolve trade disputes;
- reviewing national trade policies; and
- cooperating with other international institutions involved in global economic policy making.

The WTO Agreement contains 29 individual legal texts which lay out the procedures and rules for trade in goods and services and for enforcing intellectual property rights. The structure of the WTO is dominated by its highest authority, the Ministerial Conference, composed of representatives of all the WTO Members. It is required to meet at least every two years and can take decisions on all matters under any of the multilateral trade agreements.

The day-to-day work of the WTO, however, falls to a number of subsidiary bodies, principally the General Council. The latter is composed of all WTO Members and reports to the Ministerial Conference. The General Council also convenes in two other forms – as the Dispute Settlement Body, to oversee the dispute settlement procedures, and as the Trade Policy Review Body, which conducts regular reviews

1

of WTO Members' trade policies and practices. Other main bodies which report to the General Council are the Committee on Trade and Development, the Committee on Trade and Environment, Council for Trade in Goods, the Council for Trade in Services and the Council for Trade-Related Aspects of Intellectual Property Rights. Under these Councils are various committees, responsible for administering specific agreements.

# HIGH LEVEL SYMPOSIUM ON TRADE AND ENVIRONMENT

The World Trade Organization hosted a High Level Symposium on Trade and Environment on 15 and 16 March 1999. Although the WTO has held trade and environment symposia in the past with non-governmental organizations (NGOs), this was the first time that the WTO brought together high level government representatives from capitals of its Member States, in some cases at ministerial level. Previous symposia were not held on such a grand scale, but this meeting attracted 850 participants, from trade ministries, environment ministries, development ministries and other government agencies dealing with trade, environment and sustainable development matters. From the NGO community, 87 environment-related NGOs participated as well as academia, 40 industry federations and consumer groups. For two days, these representatives discussed and debated areas relevant to trade and environment.

The symposium was broadcast live over the internet, where it remained for public viewing for months after the symposium ended. To additionally facilitate public interest in the debate, a report of the Symposium was generated by the International Institute for Sustainable Development (IISD). This report was made available on the WTO and the IISD website.

The symposium was opened by Mr Renato Ruggiero, the former Director General of the World Trade Organization. He thanked the governments whose generous contributions made this event possible – Australia, Canada, the European Union, Finland, Greece, Iceland, Italy, Japan, Korea, Norway, Portugal, Sweden, the United Kingdom, and the United States.

Other key note speakers included: Sir Leon Brittan, Vice-President of the European Commission at the time, who originally proposed such an event, an idea which was subsequently supported by President Clinton, who sent a message to the symposium; Mr Klaus Töpfer, Executive Director of UNEP; Mr Ian Johnson, Vice-President of Environmentally and Socially Sustainable Development at the World Bank; and Ms Maritta Koch-Weser, the Director General of IUCN, the World Conservation Union. Moderators and Speakers for the panel discussions included internationally renowned economists, environmental lawyers, as well as government and non-governmental representatives from developing and developed nations. The speakers were carefully chosen to allow for the different and sometimes controversial viewpoints arising within this debate to be heard.

The first panel discussion addressed the "Linkages between Trade and Environment Policies" which included the discussion of the fundamental environmental and developmental challenges facing the global community, the role of the WTO and other institutions in addressing these challenges and the relationship between WTO provisions and environment measures, including those pursuant to multilateral agreements (MEAs). On the second day, one panel debated the "Synergies between Trade Liberalization, Environmental Protection, Sustained Economic Growth and Sustainable Development", focusing on how the removal of trade distortions could have a positive impact and create "win-win" solutions. The second panel dealt with the "Interaction between Trade and Environment Communities", looking at the coordination between trade and environment policymakers, the contribution of NGOs and the private sector and transparency and consultative mechanisms.

More than 100 interventions were made over the two-day period. A number of governments and various interest groups distributed relevant papers. The large and high level of attendance and the quality and diversity of views, all contributed to the importance of the event. In his summing up, Mr Ruggiero noted that while the meeting was closed a new dialogue was now open.

# HIGH LEVEL SYMPOSIUM ON TRADE AND DEVELOPMENT

The WTO High Level Symposium on Trade and Development was held at the WTO headquarters in Geneva on 17 and 18 March 1999. Renato Ruggiero, former WTO Director-General, introducing the Symposium, said that in some ways the dialogue on trade and development was an old one, because development was one of the central goals of the GATT. However, the dialogue was also new because, in the age of globalization, interdependence and instantaneous communications, the level of inequality between countries and people was becoming increasingly unacceptable. Noting that more than two billion people – a third of humanity – lived on less than 2 dollars a day, 1.5 billion people lacked access to fresh water, and 130 million children had never gone to school, Mr Ruggiero said that the idea that billions are mired in poverty, while others grow richer, was not just unsustainable; it was unconscionable. Mr Ruggiero also noted that the role of developing countries in the trading system had changed profoundly. Developing countries were becoming more and more important to the health of the world economy. Between 1973 and 1997 developing countries' share of manufactured imports into developed markets tripled, from 7.5 to 23 per cent. Mr Ruggiero stated that this reflected the reality that the development challenge is no longer a challenge only for developing countries but should be a concern of the advanced economies as well.

The two-day symposium, which was attended by the majority of WTO Members and Observers, as well as 81 organizations and NGOs, consisted of: an introductory session, addressed by the Chairman of the WTO General Council, the Secretary-General of UNCTAD, the President of ECOSOC, the Managing-Director (operations) of the World Bank, the Deputy Managing-Director of the IMF, and Professor T.N. Srinivasan, Chair of the Department of Economics at Yale University; and three panels:

- Panel I – Linkages between trade and development policies;
- Panel II – Trade and development prospects of developing countries; and
- Panel III – Further integration of developing countries, including least-developed countries (LDCs) in the multilateral trading system.

# Part I.
# Trade and the Environment

# Chapter 2

# Part I.  Trade and the environment

## Introduction

*Renato Ruggiero**

I very much hope that this symposium will mark a new departure, not only in the relationship between the WTO and civil society, but also – and especially – in the way our dialogue is carried forward. By this I mean that – while it is certainly very important to draw attention to the serious problems we face in both the environmental and development areas, and while there is certainly cause for complaint about the time we have lost and the increasing dangers and inequalities of our world – these comments alone will not move us towards the new solutions we need.

The opponents we face are certainly not the international institutions where the great majority of the nations of the world are represented. Our enemies are outside – they are environmental degradation, poverty, inequality of access to health care, to education, even to the basic requirements of food and fresh water.

What must emerge is a new message of determination and hope. A message to indicate that the globality of the challenges we face calls for global answers and global policies.

We are here, first and foremost, to improve the increasingly critical relationship between trade and the environment. We need to know each other better, because there are too many misunderstandings that need to be clarified. We need, in particular, a better understanding of the objectives and functions of the first international organization of the post-Cold War era – the WTO.

One objective is to lower barriers, not only between economies, but also between nations and people. By creating interdependence – and in turn, shared responsibility – this system is strengthening the foundations of international peace. A second objective is to avoid discrimination – to ensure that the access which a country extends to one trade partner is also extended to all other partners, developing and developed alike. This is a major achievement for international solidarity as well as for international trade. Our third objective is to create a trading system where all nations asking to join can find a place – a truly global trading system that is rules-based not power-based.

We are not a closed organization. Just the opposite. We are an organization whose fundamental objective is greater international openness and cooperation – whose goal is to lower the barriers between us, not increase them. We have 134 Members, 80 per cent of which are developing, least-developed or transition

---

* Director-General, World Trade Organization.

economies. We have 30 candidates asking to join, and practically all are developing economies or economies in transition. This is a referendum on the global appeal of this organization. We take our decisions by consensus. And our decisions are ratified by the national parliaments of all our Members. These are not opinions. They are facts, and they should not be ignored or overlooked.

Certainly we are far from perfect. Certainly we can further improve our transparency and the way we function. This meeting is the most obvious example of our will to strengthen – in the most open way – our dialogue with civil society. I will not list the many initiatives we have recently undertaken, except to mention our very successful Internet site through which we are reaching out to a much broader audience world-wide.

## NEED FOR SUSTAINABLE DEVELOPMENT

My first point is that the WTO is a strong ally of sustainable development – not an opponent. The preamble to the Marrakesh Agreement establishing the WTO states that our goals include "the optimal use of the world's resources in accordance with the principles of sustainable development, seeking both to protect and preserve the environment and to enhance the means for doing so". These are not empty words. This is a statement of real intent and realizable goals.

In fact, the trade system not only takes environmental concerns into account, but – if they are implemented in an appropriately non-discriminatory way – in such a way that these concerns can prevail. In a recent case, the Appellate Body was able to rule clearly that the WTO does not stand in the way of the environment:

"We have not decided that the protection and preservation of the environment is of no significance to Members of the WTO. Clearly it is. We have not decided that the sovereign nations that are Members of the WTO cannot adopt effective measures to protect endangered species, such as sea turtles. Clearly, they can and should. And we have not decided that sovereign states should not act together bilaterally, plurilaterally or multilaterally, either within the WTO or in other international fora, to protect endangered species or to otherwise protect the environment. Clearly, they should and do."

This appeal makes it impossible to say that trade policy does not consider environmental issues.

The framework to improve our relationship already exists. The real objective is to work together as partners, not as opponents. The priorities are many and they are important. We need to accelerate the work of the Committee on Trade and the Environment. We need to give serious consideration to current proposals for environmental assessments of the WTO's work. The issue of trade barriers and subsidies, which waste precious resources and harm the environment, is clearly one problem which must be addressed. And most important of all, we need to tackle the problem of poverty – a major cause of the environmental crisis we all face. We must focus on the real concerns of developing countries and guarantee that the fight against environmental degradation has no protectionist implications.

# TRADE AND ENVIRONMENT TOGETHER

My second point is that the trade and environment communities are not divided over objectives. We both want a strong, rules-based trading system as well as a strong and effective environmental system, and we both want the two systems to support one another. The question is how do we arrive at these objectives. We will not arrive there through unilateralism, through discriminatory actions and protectionism, with each nation free to impose its standards and priorities on the other following its own perceptions of the problem. On the contrary, we will only arrive at our shared objectives through consensus, through negotiations, by working towards a much broader vision of a rules-based international order where trade and the environment fit together as two key pieces of a much larger puzzle.

I do not believe that the issue of sovereignty is at stake in this debate. On the contrary, consensus-based multilateral rules – for trade as for the environment – by definition only extend national sovereignty beyond borders. The reality is that in today's interdependent world it is only by remaining isolated – and by turning away from international cooperation – that countries surrender their sovereignty. We all need to work towards stronger multilateral institutions, not weaker ones, if we want the rule of law and not the law of the jungle.

# CONSENSUS ON ENVIRONMENTAL ISSUES

Which brings me to my third point – the urgent need to reach global consensus on all environmental issues, and to give this consensus a stronger institutional voice. If we want to strengthen the bridge between trade and the environment then this bridge needs two pillars. This will not be the case as long as responsibility for environmental issues is scattered among a multitude of organizations and agreements, and as long as there is no global consensus about environmental priorities and answers.

With the WTO we are poised to create something truly revolutionary – a universal trading system bringing together developed, developing, and least-developed countries under one set of international rules, with a binding dispute settlement mechanism. I would suggest that we need a similar multilateral rules-based system for the environment: a World Environment Organization which would be an institutional and legal counterpart to the World Trade Organization.

Trade and the environment are important elements of a much broader reality, which is our ever-growing interdependence. To improve their relationship requires us to also improve the management of the world economy as a whole, in all its dimensions. More and more, public opinion would like to include in global economic management subjects which go beyond the traditional parameters of trade and finance – not only the environment or social and employment concerns, but also human rights, gender equality, labour standards, health issues, education, poverty, cultural diversity, ethical concerns, corruption, even security and peace. More and more our peoples are asking for globalization with a "human face". They are right, and we must meet their demands in the appropriate fora.

It would be wrong for the trading system to ignore these global concerns, and to hide from these pressures. But it would be equally wrong to pretend that the trading system can find an answer to each and every one of the challenges we face on this ever-smaller planet. Our main mission is to lower barriers in order to generate more growth. We have been successfully pursuing that objective for 50 years, and trade liberalization will continue to be a main engine for growth and development over the next 50 years.

I believe our organization, the WTO, is important to the environmental community because we have demonstrated how – through consensus – we can build a rules-based international trading system where all countries, large and small, developing and developed, can find a place. We are important, in other words, because we offer a model of the kind of new international order that is possible – and I would say imperative – for the next century.

The reality is that interdependence and globalization have a new dimension – a human dimension – that goes well beyond trade and capital flows. Many are the critics of globalization today but no one can offer a rational alternative. By weakening our interdependence and rebuilding walls we would only weaken our ability to cooperate and to share responsibility. Instead of tackling environmental and development challenges as an international community, we would be tackling them as 180 separate nations, each according to its own interests and priorities. Our world would be more divided, not more united – where in place of freedom, cooperation and solidarity, we would find nationalism and racism flourishing. It would be a world where new walls would be erected between developed and developing nations, the rich and the poor – and where, as a result, all of us would be the poorer. Is this the alternative world we want? Is this the human face we are looking for?

Let me conclude with this observation. The real challenge we face is the challenge of managing globalization – not rejecting it. I believe that the high degree of interdependence we have reached, and which will only increase in the years ahead, lends a powerful weight to the idea that we need a new approach – a new vision of global governance which not only embraces more nations at the highest level of decision-making, but more issues and more concerns. A vision which addresses not only capital movements and trade liberalization, but also all the other subjects which must be embraced in an improved concept of global management.

# Chapter 3

# Part I.  Trade and the environment

## Introduction

*Sir Leon Brittan\**

My suggestion for a high level meeting on trade and environment came from the assumption that, underlying all the genuine complexities, there were a limited number of issues which could be resolved by elevating the level of the debate and opening it out to a wider public.

I had the impression that, while there were extremists on both sides of the argument, a broad consensus could be achieved between traditional free-traders who, nonetheless, saw the importance in today's world of accommodating environmental concerns in trade policy, and environmentalists who saw that their objectives could best be achieved by incorporating them in that system in a reasonable way, rather than pursuing policies which would, however unfairly, be interpreted as protectionist in effect, if not in intention.

Let me begin by setting out a personal and ambitious vision of how trade, environment and development can better interact.

## THE NEED FOR AN INTEGRATED APPROACH

The cornerstone of the European Commission's approach to the environment is our commitment to the concept of sustainable development. That objective was highlighted by the Earth Summit in Rio in 1992, where 178 states committed themselves to sustainable development, and for global measures to be adopted in the fields of environment, development, social and economic policies.

The key to a successful policy on trade and environment seems to me to pursue in a coordinated way that concept of sustainable development. This, in turn, means that in every area of WTO activity, and not simply the deliberations of the Committee on Trade and the Environment, we need to apply Rio Earth Summit principles. In particular, we need to reconcile the competing demands of economic growth, environmental protection and social development. Pursuing any one of these three at the expense of the other two will inevitably lead to an unbalanced approach.

There is already a need to reconcile trade policy with other public policy objectives, such as consumer protection. There needs to be a balance between a liberal, forward-looking trade policy and the need for effective regulatory measures, for

---

* Vice-President, European Commission.

example on product safety. If we get the balance wrong, in one direction or another, we will end up either with inadequate recognition in trade policy terms of legitimate environmental concerns, or with "green protectionism". We need a balance, and an integrated approach to policy making.

## SUSTAINABILITY IMPACT STUDY

For its part, the Commission has launched a sustainability impact study – the first phase of which will produce results before the Seattle Ministerial – on the likely impact on sustainable development of a Round based on our proposed Millennium agenda. I believe that this will be a valuable contribution to the trade and environment debate. When an agenda for a new Round is, as we very much hope, set out at Seattle, the study can be further refined. This is a very difficult exercise but one of immense importance. I hope others will pursue a similar path and that we can cooperate to quickly develop international best practice.

Let me turn to some key areas of the trade and environment debate where I believe that the approach I have outlined, one firmly based on sustainable development principles, can point the way forward. In all these, I should stress that the WTO cannot, on its own, provide all the answers, and that much work will also be needed in national capitals to coordinate trade and environmental policy.

## MULTILATERAL ENVIRONMENTAL AGREEMENTS

It is important, in my view, to foster effective multilateral agreements (MEAs) so as to have a common base, agreed to among as many states as is feasible, for tackling particular environmental problems, including both national and international ones such as the protection of global resources, and animal welfare. Such MEAs are clearly preferable to unilateral action, which will often rightly fall foul of WTO rules. The problem is that even multilateral agreements are not necessarily proof against a WTO challenge of such agreements by non-members.

I strongly believe that what we need is a framework to help ensure compatibility between MEAs and WTO rules. Where an MEA commands wide support among WTO Members, we need to be more confident than at present that WTO trade rules accommodate the aims of the parties to the MEA, and would allow the necessary trade measures to be taken under such an MEA. If we need a new interpretation of, or even a textual amendment to, WTO rules, to achieve that confidence, I believe we should go down that route.

We must be cautious about the scope for the use of trade measures against non-members of MEAs. I believe there should be a series of agreed principles for such cases. Before taking trade measures against non-members, MEA members should exercise all possible efforts to persuade non-members to cooperate with the environmental objectives of that MEA, and should offer non-members the possibility of joining the MEA. Trade measures should only be considered as a last resort, and should be no more restrictive to trade than is necessary to ensure the effectiveness of the goals agreed by MEA members.

I believe it is important that WTO members should resolve this conundrum as soon as possible. Early agreement – which meets the kind of criteria I have outlined, whether formal or informal – that they will not take dispute settlement against action taken under MEAs would seem a highly desirable course of action.

## PROCESS AND PRODUCTION METHODS

There has also been discussion of the extent to which process and production methods can legitimately be taken into account in framing trade rules.

It is undesirable for each WTO member to take whatever trade measures it sees fit, based on its view of the acceptability of the way in which products are made in third countries. Such an approach is subjective and therefore arbitrary. It risks damaging one of the great virtues of the GATT system, namely its transparency and predictability. It is one thing for there to be an agreed international standard on a particular production method or use of a particular substance, such as CFCs. It is quite another for each WTO member to decide, purely unilaterally, that it disapproves of some practice elsewhere in the world, and for it to ban imports on that basis.

## LABELLING

It is clear that a multilaterally agreed ban is justified in a few cases. In many more cases a labelling solution may be the best way to tackle the problem.

It seems to me perfectly legitimate to inform the consumer that particular goods have been produced in third countries in a way which meets certain defined standards or is, at least, more environmentally friendly than other methods. The consumer is then in a strong position to make an informed choice based on the importance they attach to the overall environmental impact of production methods, even among apparently identical products.

Process and production methods are, therefore, closely linked to the very important area of eco-labelling. In that context I think it is important to agree on, and adopt, a clear and workable approach to the compatibility of labelling schemes with WTO rules.

I do not see a need to make an artificial distinction between the product itself and the way it is made. It seems to me legitimate for the label to describe the environmental impact of production methods as well as the content of the product, provided the criteria for granting that label are objective.

I think that we should seek a clear understanding that voluntary labelling schemes are compatible with GATT rules provided they conform to certain agreed requirements. Such schemes must be transparent in that producers need to know how to apply for recognition, and consumers need to have proper information about what the label actually indicates. Based on these understandings, such schemes should be facilitated and encouraged.

Compulsory labelling schemes obviously raise further questions since they force producers to create separate production arrangements for those markets which require labelling. They, therefore, need to meet tighter requirements for WTO approval. Further work is urgently needed on what those requirements should be. They should be no more trade-restrictive than is necessary. There should also be some basis for claiming that the environmental objective is a substantial one that cannot be achieved by less restrictive means. Provided that we can create a clear set of principles which avoids the abuse of such schemes for protectionism purposes, they too should be available as part of the environmental policy tool kit.

## PRECAUTIONARY PRINCIPLE

There is a dilemma for policy makers when partial, but not complete, evidence becomes available that products may be harmful to the consumer, or damaging to the environment, or both. I accept the legitimacy of the concept of precaution in the field of environment and health. However, there are dangers in allowing a general, open-ended precautionary principle without defining what it means, and in what circumstances it might be used.

Using such a principle as the basis for action designed to reduce risks to zero would be unjustified. Indeed, it is difficult to think of any aspect of life where risk can be eliminated altogether. In a sense, we need to ensure that the costs and benefits of precautionary action are looked at in a coordinated way, taking into account sustainable development principles, so as to have reassurance that such action is not excessive in relation to the objective.

The best way forward, in my opinion, is to ensure the right balance between prompt action where justified and the avoidance of overkill. The precautionary principle has already been recognised in international agreements but not explicitly in the WTO, although several key provisions explicitly allow for precautionary action.

We should, together, reflect on how to give the precautionary principle greater definition, while also preventing it from being invoked in an abusive way.

## COHERENCE OF POLICY MAKING

I have focused on these areas as concrete ones in which a coordinated approach to trade and the environment will, in my view, yield considerable benefits. They suggest that the WTO and its member governments need to cooperate effectively together, not only within the WTO but also in the various UN and other international bodies pursuing issues such as environment and development. Governments should pursue a coordinated approach, ensuring that action in one forum is, to the greatest extent possible, consistent with action in another.

## DEVELOPING COUNTRIES AND THE ENVIRONMENT

Within the context of coherence, it is important for all WTO members, including developing countries, to pursue integrated trade and environmental policies based on sustainability, and to seek agreement on what that should be.

If successful, the prize is huge: clarity in the rules to be met; fairer competition between developing and developed countries (since multilateral rules and agreements imply operating to a common set of agreed international disciplines); and firmer guarantees against unilateral action. It is infinitely better to have an internationally agreed approach on the way to accommodate legitimate environmental concerns in the multilateral trading system, than to allow these concerns to be reflected in inconsistent, unilateral measures.

However, it is not simply in a negative way – through preventing unilateral action – that an environmental trade policy, based on sustainability, can be of benefit to developing countries. Environmental best practice can positively help the process of creating jobs and welfare in all states, including developing ones.

The trade system can help promote that process in a variety of ways. Tariff policy is one example. If tariffs in developed countries are structured in a way which encourages the import of raw materials through low tariffs, and penalises manufactured goods through high tariffs, this sends a distorted and environmentally unhelpful signal. It suggests that the way to maintain income is to continue to trade in those raw materials, at whatever environmental costs – for example to forests – rather than to move up the production chain and add value to those raw materials. If, on the other hand, tariffs on manufactured goods are lowered in the new Millennium Round, that will be good for trade and good for growth, but also it will form part of a policy for the environment which specifically helps developing countries.

## TRANSPARENCY AND CIVIL SOCIETY

To achieve such an outcome I strongly believe that here, as in other areas of trade policy, a high degree of transparency will help us enormously. There may have been a time when trade was a technical subject discussed only among experts in private meetings, but that time has now passed. To have legitimacy, the trade system must also have the support and understanding of all of us, experts and non-experts. The EU is already active within the WTO in putting forward ideas to improve transparency, including ideas relating to the circulation of documents and more general openness in WTO processes. We are also working hard to gather the views of civil society and have, for example, organised a series of "outreach" meetings with NGO's to discuss the New Round.

## SEATTLE MINISTERIAL

I believe that Seattle should set an overall guideline that the objective of the New Round is to produce a sustainable outcome. I also believe that ministers should, in the jargon, "mainstream" sustainability so that negotiators in each individual group should have particular regard to promoting that outcome.

In addition, WTO members should commit themselves to coherent decision-making between the WTO and other international organisations, and to make sure that the process launched at Seattle promotes a genuine coherence of approach between the various areas of public policy at stake.

It is also important to continue the process of capacity-building among WTO members to ensure the ability to negotiate and implement WTO deals effectively. Negotiators need to know about sustainability, and to have the right help on hand, for example environmental regulatory capacity, in order to do justice to the implementation of new agreements affecting trade and environment.

Finally, I should pay tribute to the work of the Committee on Trade and the Environment. It would be counter-productive for the committee to be the only place in which environmental considerations are addressed. Nevertheless, it should remain as a key partner in a coordinated approach.

## CONCLUSION

We have an ambitious agenda ahead of us. The European Union is committed to doing its part to achieve both economic growth and prosperity, and an environment which we can, in all conscience, bequeath to the next generation.

# Chapter 4

# Part I.  Trade and the environment

## Introduction

*Klaus Topfer\**


Economic liberalization has produced economic growth in many countries around the world, helped to create job and investment opportunities, and increased the incomes of many people. However, we are also experiencing ever-accelerating planetary environmental degradation and the associated economic costs.

The problems range from an alarming loss of productive lands, because of desertification and soil degradation, to the highest rates of species extinction in recorded history. 1998 was the record year for losses, at least $89 billion worth, due to storms, floods, droughts, fires and other weather-related disasters.

These enormous losses, when added to the global economic instability in parts of Asia and Latin America, are sending clear signals that governments must be even more vigilant to ensure that economic liberalization is strictly designed to serve the ultimate goal of sustainable development.

Trade, environment and development policies are all inextricably linked. The challenge that lies ahead is in realizing the benefits of a strong rules-based multilateral trading system while addressing the environmental degradation of this century. This challenge must be taken up jointly by trade, environment and development ministries. We cannot isolate trade or environmental policy from the impacts of international debt, the need to alleviate poverty, the equitable imperative to transfer technology and the need to enhance the capacity of developing countries to face the challenges of sustainable development.

Over the last few years, solid progress has been made in building greater understanding among environment and trade officials. Nevertheless, the trade and environment debate continues to be a work-in-progress. The recent problems encountered by the parties negotiating the Biosafety Protocol to the Biodiversity Convention demonstrates unequivocally that it is time to build rational, balanced policies and guidelines for making sustainable development and trade policies fully complementary.

After almost a decade, we have failed to articulate clear, acceptable trade and environment policies because too much has been demanded of the WTO and too little has been done in other fora, both at the national and international levels. Despite the need for a broader discussion about trade and environmental issues, environmental policy makers have not yet fully engaged in trade and environment

---

* Executive Director, United Nations Environment Programme.

policy deliberations. We must begin, at once, to work together in earnest to build sustainable global economies.

The United Nations Environmental Programme (UNEP) is ready to play its role and to work in coordination with other international institutions, such as the WTO and UNCTAD, as well as with civil society. The Governing Council has given UNEP a strong mandate to assume a key role on environment and trade. UNEP is working closely with governments, international institutions and civil society to develop and implement a trade and environment work-plan that is consistent with the concerns and development priorities of countries. Close cooperation already exists between UNEP and the WTO, and we propose to strengthen and deepen this collaboration.

Specifically, UNEP is exploring possible modalities for enhanced institutional cooperation. For example, our institutions could strengthen cooperation with respect to the sharing of documents, as well as access to, and sharing of, experience. UNEP welcomes an opportunity to consult with WTO member states and the secretariat on elements of enhanced future cooperation. UNEP also will continue to confer a high level of importance on full and effective participation by all affected parties – governments, scientists, industries, NGOs and the public – in shaping environmental policy.

Building mutually supportive environment and trade policies requires more than just bringing together the right partners. We must integrate sustainable development principles into macroeconomic policy at the national and international levels.

Ecological limits must be set by science and embodied in law. Within these constraints the market can operate as a coordinating mechanism to determine prices, outputs and methods of production through the interplay of supply and demand. While market-based instruments can be effective tools for achieving environmental goals, it is governments that must harness the power of the markets toward fruitful ends. The role of government intervention and regulation must therefore be protected.

The "deregulatory" approach of international trade liberalization will, in some cases, run counter to the "regulatory" approach needed in many instances to internalize environmental costs, and to otherwise ensure that economic activity remains within the limits of the biosphere.

## FIRST STEP

### Identify the environmental strengths and weaknesses of existing and proposed rules

Governments are already discussing the possibility of expanding the rules of international trade, of further integrating them into policies that, ten years ago, were not even associated with trade policy, such as intellectual property standards, competition policy, investment policy and government procurement. This integration will have implications that reverberate far deeper than simple commercial transactions. These are not simply rules governing tariffs and trade.

But we lack empirical data as to how this deeper integration will affect other aspects of public policy. Despite almost a decade of analysis of trade and environment issues, we still lack a solid, analytical comprehension of these basic linkages. In particular, we must increase efforts to enhance the capacity of developing countries to actively participate in the development and implementation of sustainable trade policies.

UNEP will make it a priority in the coming years to collect empirical data as to the environmental consequences of international economic policies. If negative causal relations exist, now is the time to identify the necessary adjustments. Positive synergies must be exploited.

## SECOND STEP

### Exploit the environmental strengths and benefits of economic liberalization

Both trade and environment officials are committed to sustainable development so it is not surprising that there are many fruitful areas for common endeavor. Many countries have identified, for example, the environmental and trade benefits of removing price-distorting subsidies. Of course, such work must be undertaken in the light of the potential impacts that the removal of such subsidies might have on the social and economic fabric of all the countries concerned.

The environmental costs of these distortions are now known to be staggering. Experts estimate that these inefficient policies cost society over $50 billion in fishing subsidies; over $300 billion in energy subsidies and over $350 billion in agricultural subsidies.

Tackling subsidies is only the first step toward creating more environmentally and economically efficient markets. Markets will not achieve true efficiency if prices do not reflect the full cost of goods and services.

Full cost internalization is good environmental policy, and it is also good economic and trade policy. For example, without the Montreal Protocol's success in protecting our ozone layer, monetary damages in the fisheries, agricultural and other economic sectors would have amounted to several hundreds of billions of dollars. These costs arise from reduced plant photosynthesis and a disruption of aquatic food chains, quite apart from damage to human health.

UNEP is assisting developing countries to identify and employ policies for internalizing the full environmental costs of production in a manner that takes into account social considerations, as well as institutional, financial and human capacities and concerns related to market access and competitiveness. Developed countries must enable developing countries to reduce the potential for negative environmental impacts from trade liberalization.

Despite the obvious long-term benefits, cost internalization and other policies to ensure the environmental sustainability of development can impose short-term costs. UNEP, therefore, also calls on the international system to support the development and implementation of sustainable trade policies in developing countries, in accordance with the principle of common but differentiated responsibilities. Success in deflecting some of the environmental impacts of trade liberalization will benefit the entire planet, so it is natural that the costs be shared.

As Nelson Mandela noted during the last WTO Ministerial:

"There can be no refusal to discuss matters such as ... the environment, but equally all must be prepared to listen carefully before judgments are made. If developing countries feel that there is nothing to gain except further burdens, then it will prove difficult to deal with these crucial matters."

## THIRD STEP

### Articulate and clarify the fundamental principles of international environmental policy that must be accommodated by the rules

International environmental laws represent a delicate balance between what science tells us the physical environment demands, and what actions will command the consent of scores of governments with different interests and concerns. These laws are contained in highly complex agreements. Despite the different types of environmental problems, and the different solutions applied, international environmental policies are unified by a core set of environmental principles based on stronger science, cost-effective policies and a commitment to international equity. Together these foundation principles constitute a sort of environmental constitution and policy framework for the future.

This framework is effective. But it must be articulated more clearly, and the compatibility between these framework principles and the rules of international trade must be made explicit. UNEP's work in the coming year will be to elucidate how core environmental principles actually function, and how they reflect a consistency and predictability in the policy choices in multilateral environmental agreements.

## FINAL STEP

### Determine how the multilateral trading system can accommodate fundamental environmental principles within sustainable development

Environmental policy develops from the "bottom up", by responding to complex, and sometimes incomplete, scientific and technical information on a wide range of environmental problems. It reflects the complexity of the world it is attempting to preserve, and is based on a consensus derived from scientific evidence and the best judgment of scientists, engineers, and technical and legal experts from developed and developing countries, all working together.

So too, must trade policy be developed with a holistic understanding of the complex systems it impacts, and with a firm commitment to sustainable development. Economic liberalization has vastly different effects depending on the underlying social, economic and environmental conditions.

Standing, as we are, on the precipice of a new millennium, in which environmental protection and economic development together hold the key to our very survival, we must demand more of ourselves and of our institutions. Heeding the echoes of our own voices, we must ensure that "environmental protection constitutes an integral part of the development process". We must fashion new policies to reflect our knowledge that "peace, development and environmental protection are interdependent and indivisible".

# Chapter 5

## Part I.  Trade and the environment

### Introduction

*Ian Johnson**

## A VIEW FROM THE WORLD BANK

I am most grateful to Director-General Renato Ruggiero for the invitation to participate in this important meeting. Jim Wolfensohn wanted to be here himself and he has asked me to report back to him on the proceedings. It is an honor to represent my institution at such an important meeting. The breadth of experience gathered here testifies to the complex nature of the issues that we must tackle.

The challenge we face is to take advantage of the trade and investment flows that have helped lift millions out of poverty while doing a better job of protecting the environment. If we are to make some headway in meeting this challenge, we need to try and answer three questions.

- Does trade liberalization help or hurt the environment?
- Are trade restrictions appropriate for achieving environmental goals?
- How can the World Bank and other multilateral development banks promote sensible trade and environment policies?

First, does trade liberalization help or hurt the environment? The answer, of course, is that it may go either way. It depends which sectors of the economy expand or contract as a result of liberalization. Equally crucial are the effectiveness of the liberalizing country's environmental policies and how much of its trade-generated wealth is used to improve the environment. In the long run, trade liberalization leads to an increase in income that is vitally important both for reducing poverty and for improving environmental quality.

There are significant differences from one country to another. But trade liberalization tends to expand the export sector while forcing the contraction of the protected, import-competing sector. There is no rule as to whether industries that damage the environment or their more benign counterparts will benefit most.

Historically, a good deal of attention has been paid to cases where environmentally-damaging industries have expanded. But a number of recent studies have highlighted cases where trade liberalization has promoted better environmental practices. For example, in countries as far apart as Côte d'Ivoire and the Philippines, recent World Bank studies have shown that soil erosion and water

---

* Vice-President of Environmentally and Socially Sustainable Development at the World Bank.

pollution can be reduced by shifting resources away from import-competing annual crops, like upland rice, to export-oriented tree crops where soil erosion rates are five to ten times less (Repetto, 1989; Coxhead and Jayasuriya, 1995). The economic gains from reduced soil erosion are often enormous, sometimes as great as 10 per cent of agricultural GDP (Dixon *et al.*, 1997). The shift from subsistence agriculture to labor-intensive manufactures characteristic of rapid development can also be environmentally benign, as can the later shift from manufactures into services.

Global agricultural liberalization is likely to be very environmentally beneficial since much of the agriculture that has grown up behind high protective barriers in developed countries is very intensive in its use of chemicals and pesticides. This has been a particular problem here in Europe, where rivers and groundwater are frequently polluted by runoff from intensive agricultural operations. Agricultural liberalization of the type begun under the Uruguay Round will reduce worldwide pollution by reducing the artificial stimulus to agricultural production in developed countries and increasing output in developing countries where fertilizer use per hectare is frequently one twentieth the level in the highly protected countries (Anderson, 1992).

But a liberal trading regime is not enough. Indeed it can create severe environmental pressures when environmental policies are inadequate. Unregulated logging and fishing are cases in point. On the other hand, sound policies can help in reducing pollution. For example, cutting subsidies to the energy sector in Eastern Europe and the former Soviet Union has led to substantial reductions in emissions.

A lot has already been done to put in place the environmental policy frameworks needed for sustainable development in developing countries that are liberalizing their trading systems. However, the environmental consequences of trade reform are difficult to gauge in advance and serious environmental problems may emerge. When this happens it is tempting to backtrack on the trade reforms and return to a path of poor economic performance and low growth. This is almost invariably the wrong course to take. The best way forward is usually through the implementation of appropriate and strengthened environmental policies.

While trade liberalization may increase the income available for improvements in environmental quality, a great deal depends on how developing countries use their increased wealth. World Bank research estimated that real incomes in the developing countries grew by $60 to $100 billion as a result of the Uruguay Round (Martin and Winters, 1996).

If only part of these gains are spent on the environment, developing countries will be able to make a start at tackling some of their most pressing environmental problems such as increasing access to safe water and sanitation and reducing airborne particulates and sulfur dioxide. Domestic development policies and priorities will, in the final analysis, be the primary determinant of environmental outcomes.[1]

In most instances, trade policies are not the best way to attain environmental objectives. Even if they can sometimes bring about environmental improvements, they are

---

[1]  Bank research and other research on the relationship between income and a range of environmental indicators reveals very strong links. Access to safe water and to sanitation increase very rapidly with income. Pollutants such as airborne particulate matter and sulfur dioxide, which blight the local environment in many cities in the developing world, increase at low incomes but fall rapidly thereafter as pollution policies are implemented more effectively, and the economy shifts increasingly from manufactures to services. Municipal wastes per capita increase with incomes, but the resulting pollution problems are typically more readily managed in higher income cities. Only carbon dioxide emissions, for which environmental concerns are global rather than national, have continued to rise rapidly with increasing incomes.

usually less effective than policies targeted directly at the environmental problem. Since virtually all environmental damage is related to production or consumption, trade measures can only be justified if more direct types of action do not work or are not feasible. Caution, however, must be exercised because these trade measures may cause both economic and environmental damage. I repeat, the best remedy is usually to use instruments that deal directly with the environmental distortion.

Incidentally, a worrying feature of using trade restrictions for environmental ends is the "cover" they may provide to special interests seeking protection from more efficient foreign producers.

It should also be borne in mind that allowing unilateral trade sanctions against pollution or environmental degradation in another country would fundamentally shift the trading system towards one based on power rather than rules. Unilateral sanctions are only likely to be effective when imposed by large countries on small countries. As a consequence, only the concerns and preferences of large countries would have much chance of redress. Issues of equity need to be addressed.

Countries that disagree with the internal environmental policies of another country have many policy options other than trade sanctions. These include simple exchange of information as well as the development of international policy guidelines. Where the citizens of one country feel strongly enough, private consumer boycotts may be effective in changing policies. Labeling options, such as the dolphin-safe labeling scheme used for tuna in the United States, may also create pressure for improved environmental policies.

In addition, many co-operative policy approaches are available when actions in one country affect the environment in another. They range from multilateral environmental agreements (MEAs) to catchment-based water and air quality management systems. There are now at least 20 multilateral environmental agreements with trade provisions in effect to deal with global environmental problems.[2] Clearly, however, this plethora of agreements raises a serious need for co-ordination to ensure consistency.

This brings me to the question: How can the World Bank and other multilateral financial institutions respond to these challenges?

One thing is clear, none of us can do it alone. We need to think more broadly, more strategically, and over a longer time frame. We must find a better balance between financial, institutional, human and trade-related issues; and we need to strike more effective partnerships with governments, international organizations, the private sector, and civil society. (These are the kinds of issues dealt with in Jim Wolfensohn's *Comprehensive Development Framework*.) We need strengthened strategic partnerships not only with the World Trade Organization, but also with the United Nations Environment Program.

For their part, the World Bank and other MDBs are already supporting developing countries to implement trade and environmental reforms which a growing number of countries recognize as complementary.

---

[2]   These agreements include the Convention on International Trade in Endangered Species (CITES), the Montreal Protocol on Substances that Deplete the Ozone Layer, and the Basle Convention on Transboundary Movements of Hazardous Wastes. These agreements rely on the General Exceptions provided under Article XX of the GATT, which provides only limited exceptions to GATT disciplines for environmental purposes. There is a potential problem of inconsistency between the GATT and MEAs since the general exceptions principle of GATT (Article XX) provides for exceptions only under a very restricted set of conditions. As Eglin (1995) argues, it is unlikely that problems of inconsistency between a multilateral environment agreement and the GATT would arise between parties to the environmental agreement. But problems could arise if trade measures justified by the environmental agreement were applied to non-members of that agreement.

The World Bank's support for trade policy reform is familiar to many of you – since 1980, we have lent to over 80 countries in support of their programs of trade liberalization and economic reform. Less well-known is our rapidly growing support for *environmental* reform. We are currently assisting 65 countries improve their environmental performance through 130 loans totaling over $10 billion. These loans support the strengthening of institutions for environmental management and enforcement, as well as the introduction of policies and incentives which penalize environmental degradation and encourage its protection and enhancement.

These programs are part of a "new environmentalism", geared towards long term sustainable development that emphasizes land tenure reform, market-based instruments, public involvement through education and empowerment of the civil society, partnerships with the private sector and NGOs, and capacity building. (See World Bank 1995, for a detailed discussion of the nature of these reforms.) A feature of this approach is the use of efficient, market-based solutions, as distinct from command and control, wherever possible. Clearly, there remain many difficulties in pricing important environmental values such as ecosystem and cultural values.

Co-ordination of environment and trade policy is vital. The fact that trade liberalization may put pressure on some environment resources strengthens the case for better environmental management and must be used to build broad support for environmental policy reform. A case in point is East Asia where the economic crisis may have a significant impact on the environment as logging, mining and fishing activities accelerate to generate export earnings.

There are some encouraging signs that some countries are seeking to integrate their trade and environmental reforms. A growing number of countries undergoing macroeconomic reforms, for example, are also requesting assistance for strengthening environmental policies. Since 1988, some 60 per cent of countries receiving adjustment loans to improve macroeconomic and trade policies, have requested complementary support from the World Bank for environmental reforms. Some interesting cases include The Philippines, Jamaica, Peru and Sierra Leone.[3]

---

[3]    The Philippines received two structural adjustment loans in the 1980s, as well as an economic recovery loan after the election of the Aquino government in 1986. Policies with environmental ramifications included energy pricing, agricultural input pricing and the pricing of irrigation water. In 1991 an explicit environmental adjustment loan was aimed at environmental policy reforms, institutional strengthening, fostering community-based resource management, and establishment of a protected areas system.

Jamaica received three structural adjustment loans in the 1980s, in addition to sectoral adjustment loans on trade, the financial sector, and the agricultural sector. Resource and environmental policy initiatives linked to these loans, including land tenure assessment capacity, is being upgraded, and environmental regulations, reforms and the promotion of low-cost soil conservation measures are being prepared. As part of the 1993 private sector adjustment loan, the Natural Resources Conservation Authority is being strengthened for the environmental impacts of expected growth in the forestry, mineral and coastal resources sectors.

Peru embarked upon an important process of economic liberalization three years ago, and requested assistance from the World Bank. When it became clear that this would make Peru's (export) fishing industry more competitive and would place extra pressure on scarce fish stocks, the government promulgated a substantially stronger fishing law, which became a key element in the World Bank's support for the adjustment program.

As part of the 1994 sectoral adjustment credit in Sierra Leone, the Bank assisted the government in the preparation of a national environmental action plan. This plan is targeted at reducing the environmental impacts of expected growth in the forestry, mineral and coastal resources sectors.

# CONCLUSIONS

Finally I should like to draw some conclusions.

First, open trade and good environmental policies are naturally complementary. Neither alone will be sufficient to promote development, but the two together are a powerful force for clean and broad-based development.

Secondly, good environmental policies will typically target the source of the environmental problem – which usually lies either in production or in consumption. For this reason, trade policies generally play a minor role in good environmental policy regimes.

Thirdly, we now have a great deal of experience in designing and implementing environmental policies that are effective for developing countries. My group at the World Bank has very active programs with over 60 developing countries. Formulating these policies involves a great deal of consultation with governments, with NGOs, and with civil society, and I look forward to working with them in this process.

# ATTACHMENT I

## Choice of environmental policies

What policies are feasible and appropriate to deal with environmental problems will depend upon the source of the problem and on the policy making regime. A wide range of economic policy tools is available to address the distortions in both the trade and the environmental policy arenas. A fundamental principle of economic policy is that policy instruments should be targeted to affect the distortion concerned as directly as possible. Since virtually all environmental damage is related to levels of production or consumption, rather than to levels of trade, this suggests that environmental policies should be targeted directly to production or consumption.

The widely accepted "polluter pays principle" meets this criterion by focusing on the costs created by pollution. However, it will not always be easy to implement, particularly where sources of pollution are widely dispersed or political resistance is strong. In such cases there are other approaches, such as the use of tradable emission permits, that are also efficiently targeted. Only if none of the efficient policies are feasible might it become necessary to fall back on indirect, and less efficient measures of which trade policies are only one example. Caution must be used as bad policy packages may cause both economic and environmental damage.

In those cases where trade liberalization does exacerbate environmental distortions, the choice is between dealing directly with the environmental distortions, and backtracking on liberalization. The best remedy in this situation is typically the introduction of policies that deal directly with the environmental distortion. This use of complementary policy adjustments is central to the World Bank's approach to dealing with the interlinkages between trade and environmental concerns.

## Trade and environmental problems – and solutions

Most environmental problems can be traced back to externalities – situations where polluters do not have to take into account the costs they impose on others. By contrast, the central problem for trade policy arises from the actions of special interests, who press for policies which benefit them at the expense of the community at large. The special interest problem also bedevils policy making on the environment, with special interests seeking policies which mini- mize the costs they pay, even at the expense of policy effectiveness. Esty (1994) highlights the importance of pressure groups in the setting of US fuel economy standards for automobiles – he argues that the regulations were, in fact, designed in part to protect US manufacturers, particularly at the expense of European producers.

The challenge, in both the environmental and trade arenas, is to design a policy framework that will yield policies that are economically beneficial and politically acceptable. The GATT system of international co-operation has been enormously successful in improving trade policies over the past 50 years; the formulation of environmental policies is a newer and, in many respects, more challenging endeavor. However, as Esty (1995) has observed, many of the fundamental approaches used by the GATT in overcoming resistance from special interests, such as regular negotiations, reciprocity and compensation may be helpful in securing international co-operation on environmental issues.

## ATTACHMENT II

### Trade restrictions and WTO rules

The relationship between WTO rules and environmental policies has received a great deal of attention in recent years. When considering the use of trade restrictions to deal with environmental policies, I think it is useful to distinguish three types of interactions between countries:

- where use of an import causes environmental damage in the importing country;
- where there is environmental damage in the exporting country; and
- where there are environmental spillovers between countries.

In the first case, current WTO rules allow the problem to be dealt with as long as the policies do not discriminate, other than through tariffs, between domestic and imported goods (the national treatment principle of the WTO) or between different suppliers (the most-favored-nation principle). Important examples of this type of policy are provided by taxes on motor vehicle fuels levied on both domestic and imported fuels, and by environmental requirements like the use of catalytic converters on both domestic and imported motor vehicles.

In the second case, where there is environmental damage in the exporting country, current trade rules do not allow a country to impose trade sanctions on a country for environmental damage occurring within the exporting country without offering compensation for the resulting loss of market access. The *tuna-dolphin* case between the United States and Mexico and the *shrimp-turtle* case between the

United States and Mexico involved environmental spillovers of this type. The United States sought to ban the import of tuna caught by means that caused environmental damage outside US jurisdiction that the United States was unwilling to accept. There would seem to be large risks involved in changing the rules to allow countries to unilaterally impose – without political cost to themselves – sanctions on exports from countries whenever they disagreed with the domestic environmental policies of another government. Such a right would be irresistibly attractive to special-interest groups seeking protection and could easily destroy the integrity of the liberal trading system built up over the past 50 years.

Allowing unilateral trade sanctions against local pollution in another country would fundamentally shift the trading system towards one based on power, rather than rules. Unilateral sanctions are only be likely to be effective when imposed by large countries against small countries. As a consequence, only the concerns and preferences of large countries would have any chance of redress, and this redress would be achieved at the expense of the sovereignty of the small countries forced to submit. No wonder that many developing countries view such policies as a move toward "eco-imperialism" and that such policies frequently are strenuously opposed both by developing country governments and by environmental groups in developing countries. Remember that unilateral trade sanctions are seriously incomplete as environmental policies; they are likely to address only environmental concerns about the export sector, ignoring damage occurring in the majority of the economy.

Countries that disagree with the internal environmental policies of another country typically have many links other than trade for approaching the disagreement. Some such differences arise from differences in the information available about environmental impacts – and can be resolved through discussion and information exchange. The development of international policy guidelines on environmental best practices may help in achieving a degree of harmonization where this is appropriate. But policy harmonization will never be complete because of differences between countries in their ability to absorb particular pollutants, in their income levels and in preferences. Where the citizens of one country feel strongly enough, private consumer boycotts may be effective in changing policies found to be offensive. Labeling options, such as the dolphin-safe labeling scheme used for tuna in the United States, may also create pressure for the desired change in policy. In the final analysis, countries that feel strongly about an environmental policy issue are able to negotiate the withdrawal of a trade right *as long as* they compensate the other country through trade concessions on other products.

In the third case, where there are environmental spillovers between countries, the situation is more complex since sovereign countries cannot implement policies, such as the "polluter pays principle", to deal with damage that extends beyond their jurisdiction. Typically, the best approach to dealing with these problems will be a co-operative solution where countries work to ensure that the international spillovers are taken into account by their producers and consumers. There are likely to be many efficient co-operative solutions of varying degrees of political acceptability and, if one of these approaches is implemented, all countries can be made better off. Non-co-operative approaches such as the use of unilateral trade sanctions are likely to be very poor alternatives to co-operative solutions, especially, as is usually the case, when the trade flow has no direct bearing on the environmental problem. Only after better policy options have all been reviewed and rejected as infeasible should the use of trade policies be considered.

**Appendix**

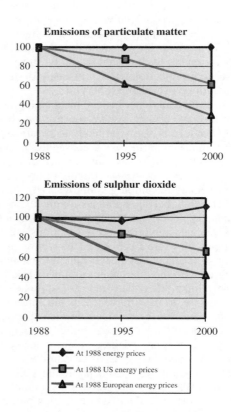

Figure 1. Effects of energy prices on air pollution in Poland.

## REFERENCES

Anderson, K. (1992), "Effects on the Environment and Welfare of Liberalizing World Trade: The Cases of Coal and Food" in Anderson, K. and Blackhurst, R. eds., *The Greening of World Trade Issues*, London: Harvester Wheatsheaf.

Coxhead, I. and Jayasuriya, S. (1995), "Trade and Tax Policy Reform and the Environment: The Economics of Soil Erosion in Developing Countries", *American Journal of Agricultural Economics* 77(3): 631–44.

Dixon, J. *et al.* (1997), *Expanding the Measure of Wealth: Indicators of Environmentally Sustainable Development*, Environmentally Sustainable Development Studies and Monographs, Series No. 17, World Bank, Washington DC.

Eglin, R. (1995), "Trade and the Environment in the World Trade Organization", *World Economy* 18(6): 769–79.

Esty, D. (1994), *Greening the GATT: Trade, Environment, and the Future*, Institute for International Economics, Washington DC.

Martin, W. and Winters, L. A. (forthcoming), "The Uruguay Round and the Developing Countries", Chapter 1 in Martin, W. and Winters, L. A. eds., *The Uruguay Round and the Developing Countries*, Cambridge University Press, Cambridge.

Munasinghe, M. and Cruz, W. (1995), *Economywide Policies and the Environment: Lessons from Experience*, World Bank Environment Paper Number 10, World Bank, Washington DC.

Repetto, R. (1989), "Economic Incentives for Sustainable Production" in Schramm, G. and Warford, J. eds., *Environmental Management and Economic Development*, Johns Hopkins University Press, Baltimore.

Steer, A. (1995), "Trade and the Environment: Friends or Foes?" *Leaders*, September.

World Bank (1995), *Economywide Policies and the Environment*, Policy Paper for the Board of Executive Directors.

World Bank (1995), *Mainstreaming the Environment, The World Bank Group and the Environment since the Rio Earth Summit*.

# Chapter 6

# Part I.  Trade and the environment

## Introduction

*Maritta R. Von Bieberstein Koch-Weser**

IUCN is the world's largest union working for the environment. It is comprised of 74 governments, more than 180 state and government agencies, and 650 NGO members. We have a global secretariat and a network of more than 12,000 scientists and lawyers working as volunteers. Our members and volunteers operate in 138 countries. We have 42 offices world-wide.

Our mission is to influence, encourage and assist societies throughout the world to conserve the integrity and diversity of nature, and to ensure that any use of natural resources is equitable and ecologically sustainable. We therefore take a deep interest in trade and environment issues.

We wish to see global and regional trade regimes that place a premium on conservation as well as the rights and responsibilities of communities, countries and corporations to establish sustained use, and equitable sharing of the benefits of natural resources.

We are prepared to play our part. While the subject of trade and environment is relatively young, IUCN has a comparatively long history of work in this field.

- We have worked extensively on trade and the threats it poses to species. Trade Record Analysis in Flora and Fauna in Commerce (TRAFFIC), established jointly with the World Wildlife Fund (WWF) works closely with the Convention in the International Trade in Endangered Species (CITES).
- We are working on the impacts of trade on biodiversity. This includes specific work on: the impact of Trade Related Intellectual Property Rights (TRIPs); rules on biodiversity conservation; sustainable use; and distributional equity. This also includes detailed recommendations to the scientific bodies of the Convention on Biological Diversity (CBD) at its meetings this year.
- We are building capacity in our members and others (particularly governments and civil society in the South) on the relationships between trade rules and the mandates of the multilateral environmental agreements.
- We are developing international law and policy analysis and co-ordination through the work of our Environmental Law Centre. Their analysis of the development of trade rules between the conclusion of the Uruguay Round and the Singapore Ministerial Conference (from Marrakesh to Singapore), and the

---

* Director-General, IUCN – The World Conservation Union.

implications for the multilateral environmental agreements (MEA's), is essential reading.
- We are working towards better understanding of sustainable use and equity in conservation and natural resource management, so as to gauge the impacts of trade liberalization on communities' capacity to manage resources.

Here the issue is that even where liberalization has promoted growth, the benefits of that growth are often poorly distributed and repatriated with devastating consequences for natural resources, communities and human and environmental security.

- We focus on the role of incentives and subsidies within trade rules in supporting sustainable use of natural resources, from fish, to freshwater, to plant biodiversity, to entire ecosystems.
- We had a role in the creation and the work of the International Centre for Trade and Sustainable Development, and can play a role in nurturing multi-stakeholder dialogue on these issues.

But what of the future? There is an increasing desire in IUCN to focus on the *positive* role that trade might play in promoting conservation, sustainable use and social equity. However, to enable the WTO and others to promote this role we need to send strong messages on both substance and process.

- *Capacity building.* We must build stronger capacity within countries to understand the linkages between environment and trade, probably most efficiently on specific issues as they arise. For example, we are working in three regions to identify the linkages between the CBD and WTO rules, in the fields of agriculture, fisheries and forests.
- *Intellectual property rights.* The trade and environment communities must make a concerted effort to address the specific public concern related to intellectual property rights, the sharing of benefits from the international use of genetic resources, and biosecurity.

Our law centre and biodiversity unit, together with our regional programmes, are working to make specific recommendations to the CBD and the WTO. We stand ready to bring different parties together to forge a way forward in this critical post-Cartagena period.

- *The need for a forum.* We need to create a forum for regular high level dialogue and action, such as a standing committee on trade and environment, the development of which has been promoted by IUCN since before the Singapore Ministerial Conference of the WTO.
- *Civil society.* We must continue to recognize the role that civil society (environment, development, unions) can play in looking at the necessary synergies between environment, development and trade policy.

We welcome the increased recognition by WTO that greater transparency is not only an important element in its dealings with civil society, but an essential element of an open and efficient trade regime. However, we hope that lessons can continue to be learned from the UN and environment conventions which, in the last 10 years, have become more open and responsive institutions.

IUCN has a wealth of experience in and a strong mandate to promote the engagement of civil society and will play a fuller role in developing procedures for greater access and participation. We welcome calls for evaluation of the Uruguay Round on sustainable development but ask that the evaluation be extended to the rules that are applied today, and that conclusions be drawn to inform the 2000 Round. IUCN also gives importance to the agriculture negotiations which will have significant direct and indirect impact on biodiversity and sustainable livelihoods.

All of the above will require, at both the international and regional levels, the highest degree of co-operation and input from academia, the legal profession, trade experts, the conservation community, the development community and other organizations of civil society. Issues which are highly technical and complex should be distilled and made more accessible to broader communities – that is our collective responsibility.

IUCN will be proactive in responding to these challenges. One contribution we hope to make will be to convene small, technically focused trade and environment fora – both globally and regionally. These fora will bring together different expertise, experiences and perspectives. They will be places where we can roll up our sleeves and find common ground. They will be designed to add momentum to the trade and environment dialogue in the face of a daunting negotiation timetable, and what might become increasing hostility. IUCN will bring to bear its special convening ability as well as its sound science and technical, legal and political analysis.

We owe it to our members, governmental as well as non-governmental, to play this role as the pace of regionalization, globalization and harmonization accelerates.

# Chapter 7

# Part I. Trade and the environment

## 1. Linkages between trade and environment policies

*Durwood Zaelke**

## INTRODUCTION

These symposia are an acknowledgement of the importance of trade and environment, and of trade and development, and the urgent need for the multilateral trading system to integrate these concerns more closely into its day-to-day work.

They touch on two aspects of a single, indivisible and overarching goal – sustainable development. This goal is enshrined in the preamble of the WTO agreements, which exhorts WTO members to promote trade:

"while allowing for the optimal use of the world's resources in accordance with the objective of sustainable development, seeking both to protect and preserve the environment and to enhance the means for doing so in a manner consistent with their respective needs and concerns at different levels of economic development."

Before we can make real progress towards this goal, discussions about environment and development – including those in these two WTO symposia – must be combined and considered together. Development and environment are partners in a common endeavor: one that was defined by the nations of the world in the Rio Declaration and Agenda 21, which articulated a detailed plan for achieving sustainability. The liberalization of trade in goods, investment, services, government procurement and the creation of rules on intellectual property as well as every other aspect of the WTO's work program must promote this goal.

I hope it is with a sense of urgency that our governments address these interlinked issues of trade, development and environment, both at the WTO as they prepare for the 1999 Ministerial, and in other international institutions, so as to strengthen the rules-based multilateral trading system and create a fair and sustainable international economic system.

Let us return to an exploration of the main linkages between trade and environment policies. The linkages are extensive. They cover the relationship between WTO rules and other international law such as the MEAs; WTO and national environmental laws; government procurement policies; eco-labeling; biodiversity protection and so on. I am not going to repeat almost a decade of discussion on these topics. Instead, I want to step back and observe that these linkages between trade,

---

* President, Center for International Environmental Law, Washington D.C. and Geneva.

other economic activity and the environment is what sustainable development is all about.

As the WTO is now required to pursue the goal of sustainable development, it must understand and embrace three key principles that are the heart of sustainable development: full cost pricing and market efficiency; equitable wealth distribution; and sustainable scale. In the context of these three key principles, I will discuss the linkages between trade and environment, focusing mainly on where trade liberalization moves us away from sustainability. Three main issues arise.

- First is the relationship between trade liberalization and *efficiency*. To what extent does international trade promote efficiency, and thereby allow us to produce more from less and minimize our impacts on the natural environment?
- Second is the relationship between trade liberalization, *equitable wealth distribution and the demand for environmental protection*. To what extent does economic liberalization encourage a fair distribution of wealth and how does this distribution, in turn, encourage greater demand and capacity for environmental protection?
- Third is the relationship between trade liberalization, growth and what I will call a *"sustainable scale of economic activity"*. In other words, to what extent does international trade allow us to create an economic system that operates within the boundaries of our ecological systems – the various source and sink capacities – of the planet?

These three issues are almost unimaginably complex. Nevertheless, I will attempt to outline some of the main considerations and some issues that deserve further consideration.


## TRADE AND EFFICIENCY

It is often argued that international trade promotes sustainable development by improving efficiency. Efficiency is important because it allows us to produce more with less, and thereby reduce our use of the world's scarce resources. Efficiency, in turn, is promoted by trade liberalization in at least three ways:

- it encourages national specialization according to comparative advantage;
- it promotes economies of scale; and
- it promotes competition, which acts as a catalyst to innovation and productivity growth.

These arguments are correct but, unfortunately for the environment, they are only part of the story.

The other part is that for trade to promote efficiency, we need to use law to get the price right. Economic liberalization is not enough – we need regulation to ensure that market failures are addressed; that costs are fully internalized; that resources such as forests, fisheries, and minerals are valued correctly; and that property rights are assigned. These are basic economic truths that every first year economic student understands.

Yet, accurate pricing is overwhelmingly the exception rather than the rule, and thus market failures are exacerbated by trade liberalization, which, by extending these national market failures into an international market, may promote inefficiency rather than efficiency, and environmental damage rather than environmental protection.

The extent of this inefficiency and environmental damage is unknown. But it is potentially massive. By consuming our natural capital in this way, we are borrowing from the future. This is a debt that must ultimately be repaid.

Over the last decade, hundreds of theoretical articles and papers have been published that acknowledge this fact. What is missing, however, are detailed, grounded studies of how past liberalization has affected the environment and what policies are required to address these affects. The UNEP/UNCTAD cases studies are therefore a welcome step in the right direction.

In some cases, technical analysis will show that better national environmental law and enforcement will be required. This will often be the case in countries that do not have, or cannot afford, effective enforcement. By failing to implement national measures, these countries are impoverishing themselves by selling off their natural heritage at far less than its true value. The real beneficiaries of these policies are consumers in the North, whose consumption is effectively subsidized by current and future generations in the developing country – something that is repugnant to both distributional equity and sustainable development.

However, the answer to these problems is not to impose unilateral trade sanctions. Nor is it to turn the WTO into an environmental organization. Rather, the WTO should work more closely with other intergovernmental organizations to examine how economic liberalization affects social and environmental systems, and what responses will be both efficient and equitable. How can a system be established to internalize costs and, at the same time, ensure, as required by the WTO Preamble, that developing countries still receive a "share in the growth in international trade commensurate with the needs of their economic development"?[1]

A couple of considerations are relevant here. Where the price of environmental improvement can be passed on to the consumer, then developing countries will benefit from both higher prices and greater environmental protection. In these cases the "polluter pays principle" should be implemented to ensure that costs are fully internalized.

Conversely, where the price cannot be passed on additional measures will be necessary to ensure that developing countries maintain the same, or improved, market access, and receive a fair share of their product's value. In these cases, industrialized countries must actively assist by granting favorable access to new technology and offering technical and financial assistance as promised at Rio.

## TRADE, WEALTH AND ENVIRONMENTAL PROTECTION

A second linkage between trade and environment is the question of whether trade promotes environmental protection by increasing and equitably sharing wealth. Once again, the link is not so clear. It is true that studies have shown that as wealth

---

[1] WTO Agreement, Preamble.

increases, so too does the demand and capacity for environmental protection. However, two questions may be raised about this conceptually pleasing win-win hypothesis.

First, wealth and environmental damage may, in reality, be positively linked. OECD over-consumers, for example, undoubtedly do far more damage to the environment than do people in developing countries. According to one estimate – one person in the United States represents twice the impact of a Swede, three times that of an Italian, 35 times that of an Indian, 140 times that of a person born in Bangladesh or Kenya and 280 times the impact of someone born in Chad, Haiti or Nepal.[2]

Second, even if there is a positive relationship between wealth creation and environmental protection, liberal trade may not promote an equitable distribution of wealth that promotes environmental protection. According to the United Nations Development Programme incomes are diverging – the ratio of the income of the world's wealthiest 20% to that of the poorest 20% rose from 30 to 1 in 1960, to 60 to 1 in 1991, to a startling new high of 78 to 1 in 1994.[3] This should come as no surprise to anyone versed in the basics of economic theory: while markets may produce wealth, they are not very good at distributing it.

In our national systems, governments have the role of redistributing wealth to create a just and equitable society. By contrast, at the international level, in the absence of a global government – something that is neither desirable nor possible – there is no guarantee that global markets will ensure a distribution of wealth that creates a just world society. Indeed the present system, despite the cooperative institutional arrangements that govern it, resembles more a form of "international economic Darwinism".

Why then, in practical terms, is this unjust distribution of wealth occurring? One reason is that WTO rules in new areas of economic liberalization may prevent countries from regulating to ensure that wealth produced in their national market stays at home.

For example, rules at the WTO apparently consider the inappropriate application of the "national treatment" principle to new areas of the national economy. While under Ricardo's theory of comparative advantage, "national treatment" makes sense in the context of trade in goods, it is less clear how it should apply to new areas such as foreign investment, services and government procurement.

In these cases, foreign firms – often large, transnational firms with industrialized country shareholders and management – exploit the comparative advantage and take the profits home. While the host country certainly benefits from trickle-down advantages, such as technology transfer and more sophisticated managerial practices, these benefits must be weighed carefully against the resources and income transferred out of the country both now and in the future.

Clearly more work is required to examine how trade liberalization is affecting the distribution of income, and how in turn this affects the capacity and demand for environmental protection.

More work also needs to be done to implement the principles of "common but differentiated responsibility" and "special and differential treatment" that are

---

[2]   Erlich P. and A. Erlich, "How the Rich Can Save the Poor and Themselves", *Pacific and Asian Journal of Energy*, 3.
[3]   UNDP, *Human Development Report* (1997).

necessary to ensure that the transition to a sustainable economy is a just and equitable transition for developing countries and labour.

More work needs to be done on the principle of "technology transfer". To be meaningful, promises of technology transfer must be backed up with new amounts of money. The TRIPS Agreement would be a good place to start – to make sure developing countries get the technology they need.

Given the extent of income divergence, and the impact of this divergence on developing countries, WTO Members may wish to explore the use and limits of the national treatment obligation, and whether other approaches could be adopted to ensure a more just distribution of wealth from trade liberalization.

## TRADE AND SCALE

I would like to move to a third linkage – that of "sustainable scale". This is the big one – the first principle – yet it is the one most often overlooked.

Does economic liberalization promote a scale of global economic activity that will remain within the ecological boundaries set by the planet? According to the ecological economist Herman Daly:

"Further economic growth beyond the present scale is overwhelmingly likely to increase costs more rapidly than it increases benefits, thus ushering in a new era of 'uneconomic growth' that impoverishes rather than enriches".[4]

The concept of sustainable scale is finally entering into the mainstream literature, albeit in more mildly phrased language. According to the OECD:

"the negative scale effects of globalization may turn out to be very large, effectively swamping any positive technological and/or structural effects".[5]

The OECD also notes that:

"There is considerable uncertainty about the long-term ability of the environment to withstand the pressures of even the current scale of economic activity, let alone the scale that might exist after the world economy has become more globalized".[6]

Given these uncertainties, governments must take precautionary measures to prevent environmental harm. Waiting until science is certain, or technological developments or structural shifts mitigate these pressures, is not enough to ensure our survival.

A powerful example of the limits on the scale of economic activity is global climate change. Climate change shows that the scale of economic activity has already exceeded the sink capacities of the earth's environment. The Inter-governmental Panel on Climate Change estimates that we must cut greenhouse gas emissions by

---

[4]  Daly H. and J. Cobb (1998), in *International Environmental Law and Policy*, Hunter, Salzman and Zaelke.

[5]  OECD (1997), *Economic Globalization and the Environment*, 26.

[6]  *Ibid.*

half to stabilize the planetary climate system. Yet we all know how far we are from achieving this goal.

How can questions of scale be better addressed? Government action through MEAs offers the best tools. WTO rules must ensure that governments, collectively, can adopt precautionary measures to ensure that the economy respects the limits of ecology. Ultimately, we will need stronger MEAs, with stronger sanctions and other positive measures.


## CONCLUSION

These three principles of ecological economics – economic efficiency, just distribution and sustainable scale – are the heart of sustainable development, and the WTO and WTO Member governments must embrace them and their related legal principles in order to promote the real welfare gains the world needs in the coming century.

To conclude, I would like to offer four ideas about next steps for the trade, environment and development communities, working in conjunction with the WTO.

First, the WTO should promote policy integration. Trade policy cannot be considered in isolation from other environment and development policies. Environment and development are what are often referred to as "horizontal issues"; they affect and are affected by each aspect of the WTO's work program. All WTO committees should therefore have the mandate to examine these issues explicitly as part of their ordinary work. This would require greater cooperation among environment, development and trade officials in national governments. It would require organizational restructuring of the Secretariat, and it may slow the WTO's work down – but it is critical nonetheless.

Secondly, the WTO should expand its recent efforts to work with other institutions to ensure global policy coherence. We welcome the statements by governments, UNEP and others in favor of greater cooperation between the WTO and UNEP. Greater cooperation with other UN agencies would allow the WTO to help countries determine what kinds of national and international policy frameworks are necessary to address the market failures I mentioned earlier, and to ensure trade promotes efficiency.

Thirdly, environmental rules and institutions, including the MEAs, should be strengthened to help countries mitigate the environmental impacts of economic liberalization in a manner that respects their development priorities and rights of market access. For example, environmental agreements must include dispute settlement mechanisms that are as effective as the WTO's.

Finally, WTO Members should pause and evaluate before proceeding with further liberalization. The WTO must assess the role of the national treatment principle in new areas of economic liberalization. As the institution moves from liberalization of trade in goods into new areas – government procurement, investment, services – its work is no longer legitimized by the theory of comparative advantage and the risk grows that new rules will be designed to enable economic exploitation by multinational actors.

In addition, the WTO Members must evaluate the impact of the economic liberalization on their social and environmental systems. This assessment must be both forward looking (it must examine the impacts on sustainability of proposed liberalization) and it must be backward looking (it must consider the impacts of the Uruguay Round).

If we are really committed to creating the best trading system possible, then we must learn from the past and plan carefully for the future. A sustainability assessment is an essential part in this process. Civil society is unlikely to accept proposals for further trade liberalization in Seattle or beyond until we all fully understand the impacts of the Uruguay Round. This is our best guide to the future.

# Chapter 8

# Part I.  Trade and the environment

## 1.  Linkages between trade and environment policies

*Dr Sylvia Ostry**

In the Uruguay Round, the main debate, apart from agriculture, was over the inclusion of the so-called new issues: services, intellectual property, and investment. The focus was on economic regulation and domestic policy – indeed it was on the economic regulatory state.

Meanwhile the forces of technology and globalization, with a little help from the IMF and the World Bank, made the regulatory form too powerful to resist. While there are clearly costs to economic regulatory reform it is fairly easy to prove that benefits outweigh the costs. However, while the economic regulatory state was withering away – at least in the OECD countries and in the middle-income developing countries, the so-called emerging markets – the social regulatory state was hardly thriving.

The social regulatory state – which began in the late 1960s, picked up speed in the 1970s and 1980s, and continued through the 1990s – deals with a range of regulations concerning the environment, food safety, occupational health and safety, industrial relations, etc. It is quite true that in the Uruguay Round we did deal with social regulation, technical barriers to trade (TBT) which were amended from the Tokyo Round and sanitary and phytosanitary measures (SPS), but they were a low profile issue.

My view is that – unlike economic regulation where there is, for a variety of reasons, a consensus on how to measure costs and benefits, and on who will be winners and losers – there is no consensus within the OECD countries, and certainly not between the OECD countries and most developing countries, on social regulation – how you would measure it and how you would allocate costs and benefits.

I can't make up my mind whether, or not, there exists a fundamental conflict between paradigms: between the economic paradigm and the ecological paradigm. Even if that fundamental conflict doesn't exist, I would really like to operationalize the notion of sustainable development and I would like it in operational terms, i.e. I would like to be able to measure costs and benefits, etc.

Even if there isn't a fundamental conflict between these two models, there are clearly enormous difficulties in reaching operational approaches to dealing with the three issues of trade, environment and development.

Let me give you one example. The trading system really operates, and couldn't operate any other way, but through the notion of what is called diffused reciprocity: "I'll do

* Senior Research Fellow, Centre for International Studies, University of Toronto.

my thing, you do your thing and we will balance it out". But that is an alien notion in the environmental area because these are clearly global common issues.

What I see emerging as reciprocity is a totally different notion: "We'll do our thing and, in exchange, the developing countries want technology, finance and capacity building". That is a very different deal from: "I'll lower my barriers, you lower your barriers". I don't know whether you can get that deal or not.

What I am really saying is that the engine that drove the trading system was based on an offspring of the enlightenment. The new engine, the mental engine, the model of sustained development, while it may not be in fundamental conflict, will not be so easily reconciled.

The stakes are really high. I think the legitimacy and credibility of the WTO is in the balance so let me give you some suggestions. I think there are two routes to dealing with this. One is the litigious route. But you cannot change this system by doing it in a litigious mode. We do not want to move from laissez faire to laissez reglé to laissez legité, although that would be one route. The other is the political route, and it has got to be the preferred choice.

There should be an executive committee of trade ministers and they must meet with the environment ministers. The development issue involves the World Bank and UNCTAD, and there is a technology issue. You are not going to deal with the technology issue without having an institution to bring it together. The environmental issue demands a new environmental institution.

# Chapter 9

# Part I. Trade and the environment

## 1. Linkages between trade and environment policies

*Hanns R. Glatz**

The International Chamber of Commerce (ICC) firmly believes that there is no inherent conflict between preserving the earth's environment and fostering economic growth. Indeed, the technological innovation and financial resources generated by global economic growth must be increasingly harnessed to bring about environmental improvements. Economic growth is necessary in order to generate the resources needed to develop and invest in clean technologies.

Business can contribute to sustainable development through wealth creation in an environmentally sound manner by the use of innovative technologies and management systems. While business remains indispensable to building a cleaner and healthier world, a much wider sense of partnership between all environmental stakeholders is essential if the right balance is to be struck between environmental protection and economic development.

ICC is of the view that the WTO's Third Ministerial Conference, drawing on the work carried out so far by the WTO Committee on Trade and Environment (CTE), should agree to undertake more formal negotiations with a view to clarifying WTO rules in relation to trade and environment issues.

ICC considers that, among these issues, WTO ministers should give priority attention to the relationship between WTO rules and the use of trade measures in multilateral environmental agreements (MEAs). Business is particularly concerned with the uncertainty and potential threat to trade flows created by discrepancies and inconsistencies between WTO rules and the provisions contained in MEAs on the use of trade measures to achieve environmental objectives.

There is a growing realization of the need to address the relationship between trade measures contained in several existing MEAs and WTO rules, in terms of their consistency with basic WTO disciplines, and of their potential misuse for protectionist purposes. These MEAs include the Convention on International Trade in Endangered Species of Wild Fauna and Flora (CITES), the Basel Convention on the Transboundary Movement of Hazardous Wastes and their Disposal, the Montreal Protocol, the United Nations Framework Convention on Climate Change and the forthcoming Bio-Safety Protocol, as well as others.

This issue has been extensively discussed by the CTE since its establishment. In this context, ICC welcomes the information exchange and constructive dialogue

*Member, Commission on International Trade and Investment Policy, International Chamber of Commerce (Daimlerchrysler).

that has been initiated between the CTE and the secretariats of several MEAs in order to enhance domestic coordination on issues relevant to both the WTO and environmental negotiations and agreements. As most WTO members are also parties to key MEAs, a coherent approach should be taken by national officials in these fora.

However, unless concrete measures are taken by the WTO, and those bodies governing MEAs, to ensure consistency between WTO rules and trade measures contained in existing and future MEAs, and to prevent the use of otherwise legitimate MEA instruments to disrupt trade, then the scope for trade restricting conflicts will grow.

While there has not yet been a WTO dispute specifically related to trade measures contained in MEAs, the possibility of such a case in the future should not be discounted. The increasing attention paid to trade measures in existing MEAs, and in those agreements still under negotiation, highlights the need for the CTE to continue work to develop a more coordinated approach in order to avoid potential conflicts.

In a policy statement entitled "Trade Measures for Environmental Purposes" issued in November 1996, in advance of the First Ministerial Conference of the WTO held in Singapore in December 1996, ICC put forward some concrete proposals towards this goal.

ICC considers that international co-operation among countries in the form of MEAs is the preferred means of addressing transboundary or global environmental problems. ICC also recognizes that such initiatives may involve the use of specifically agreed upon provisions for trade measures in MEAs to achieve the environmental objectives of the agreements. However, the ICC subscribes to the widely accepted view that trade policy measures should not be the first-choice options for enforcing MEAs.

As a matter of principle, the use of trade measures in MEAs to achieve environmental objectives should only be contemplated as a last resort, following the proper consideration of all alternative policy options. Trade measures should only be used when alternative measures would be ineffective in achieving the environmental objective without the complementary use of trade measures.

## BASIC DISCIPLINES FOR TRADE MEASURES IN MEAS

ICC believes that the use of trade measures in MEAs to achieve environmental objectives should be subject to a number of basic disciplines. When considering the inclusion of trade measures, states negotiating an MEA should:

- demonstrate that the proposed trade measures are directly related, necessary, and proportional to the achievement of the environmental objective they are addressing;
- resort only to trade measures that are no more trade restrictive than required to achieve the environmental objective, and which do not discriminate arbitrarily or unjustifiably;
- ensure that the MEA specifies as precisely as possible what trade measures it calls for;
- base any trade measure adopted for the purpose of meeting environmental objectives in MEAs on sound science, and also take into account public health objectives;

- ensure that trade measures are permitted only in MEAs on which there is a genuine multilateral consensus, and which address broad transboundary and global environmental concerns;
- allow for truly global participation, defined as "participation by countries which account for a substantial proportion of the activity giving rise to the agreement";
- consult representatives of business in the process by which trade measures to be included in MEAs are considered, designed and negotiated; and
- conduct this process in an open and transparent manner.

Private sector participation would allow negotiators of the MEA the benefit of the insights and expertise of those enterprises and industries that engage in the activity affected by the proposed trade measures. This private sector input would also help to secure the necessary level of business support for the proposed MEA.

## PROCESS FOR DEVELOPING WTO-CONSISTENT TRADE MEASURES IN MEAs

ICC strongly believes there is a need to develop further internationally agreed criteria for the use of trade measures within the context of MEAs, in order to minimize opportunities for protectionist and trade-disruptive measures. This may be achieved by applying clearly defined presumptions of WTO consistency to specific trade measures considered for inclusion in MEAs. Such criteria would provide an effective guide for the development and design of trade measures in MEAs, and ensure mutual consistency between international environmental and trade law. ICC is of the view that the WTO is the best-suited negotiating forum for developing such criteria.

The process for developing such criteria should be transparent and open to all stakeholders – and in particular to the international business community – so that the stakeholders may be informed and involved in an effective manner. These criteria should be brought up for periodic review within the WTO, so that they reflect both new developments and experience.

There is a strong need for closer coordination in the negotiation of MEAs between departments of national governments responsible, respectively, for environmental policy and international trade policy.

## FORM AND APPLICABILITY OF CRITERIA FOR THE USE OF TRADE MEASURES

ICC favors an "ex-ante" approach to determine the WTO consistency of trade measures pursuant to MEAs. MEAs and the trade measures they contain which meet the criteria (including those outlined previously), or are amended to do so, should benefit from a presumption that such MEAs serve a legitimate environmental purpose, and that these measures are necessary to achieve it. The "ex-ante" approach should be complemented by periodic and limited "ex-post" reviews to verify that the criteria continue to be adhered to.

It would also be desirable for the WTO members to develop further criteria to assist panels convened to hear disputes about the measures – including disputes in which one of the parties is a WTO member but not a signatory of the MEA in question. Also to determine whether such measures are arbitrarily or unjustifiably discriminatory, or constitute a disguised restriction on trade.

As a first step towards the development of legally binding WTO criteria governing the use of trade measures in MEAs, discussions on this issue currently underway within the WTO Trade and Environment Committee should lead to the formulation of a set of guidelines, prepared and issued by the CTE. These guidelines could then form the basis of an "Understanding", or interpretative statement, which would need to be formally adopted by the Council of the WTO. ICC considers that this process is the most likely at this time to allow rapid and substantial progress in the development of WTO criteria on the use of trade measures in MEAs.

Some have recommended that trade measures pursuant to MEAs be accommodated by the WTO through an outright amendment of Article XX of the original GATT. ICC feels that further consideration should be given to the potential unforeseen consequences of amending the basic text of existing trade law. Furthermore, such an amendment may not be necessary or achievable at this time. The development of guidelines, and the experience gained from their application in the form of an "Understanding", could prove extremely valuable in considering the most effective and efficient way in which the GATT might be amended in due course.

# Chapter 10

# Part I.  Trade and the environment

## 1.  Linkages between trade and environment policies

*Dr J. D. A. Cuddy**

From UNCTAD's perspective, the issue that needs to be discussed is how to promote the integration of trade, environment and development. This is the mandate we received from Agenda 21 and UNCTAD IX. Four clusters of problems can be identified for which solutions have to be found.

- There is a certain lack of balance in the trade and environment debate as it provides insufficient attention to issues of concern to the developing countries.
- The debate provides too little attention to the fact that the major constraint facing many developing countries in responding to environmental challenges is the lack of technical, institutional and supply capacities, and that many environmental problems in developing countries are of a very different nature.
- There is insufficient understanding of the economic and social implications of certain trade measures for environmental purposes for countries at different levels of development.
- There is not sufficient political will to take account of the previous points in building a broad-based agenda on trade and sustainable development.

## PROBLEMS

### Lack of balance in the trade and environment debate

It is sometimes mentioned that in order to make progress on trade and environment, there is a need to get the developing countries on board. Our experience at UNCTAD, in particular the work we are doing in the field, is that the developing countries are already on board to the extent that they are fully committed to both trade liberalization and the multilateral trading system, as well as to enhanced environmental protection and sustainable development.

Indeed, starting from a position where several developing countries had argued that there was essentially no linkage between trade and environment issues, developing countries have not only acknowledged such linkages, they are also proposing

---

* Officer-in-Charge, Division on International Trade and Commodities, UNCTAD.

a constructive agenda in dealing with them. The great interest in technical assistance for capacity building demonstrates developing countries' interest in further shaping such agenda.

There is, however, considerable dissatisfaction that, for the most part, the trade and environment debate has explored only some aspects of the linkages. The CTE discussions, for example, have focused largely on issues such as the relationship between trade measures in multilateral environmental agreements (MEAs), the provisions of the multilateral trading system and eco-labelling. While these are important issues, it should be noted that "developing country issues", such as market access and technology issues, appear to have received far less attention not only here at the CTE but also in other multilateral fora.

While there is a continuous move to legitimize the use of trade restrictions (including unilateral and extra-territorial restrictions) based on non-product related process and production methods (PPMs), much less attention is given to encouraging the dissemination of environmentally sound technologies (ESTs), which would help developing countries in moving towards more environmentally friendly PPMs.

Similarly, while some would like an explicit recognition to extend the coverage of the TBT Agreement to include eco-labelling schemes (including non product related PPMs), there seems to be much less effort to examine how developing countries can benefit from trade in environmentally preferable products which use traditional and indigenous knowledge. There is also a need to prevent the erosion of market access of developing countries arising from the obligation to comply with environmental requirements of developed countries. This could be achieved through systems of mutual recognition based on the concept of "equivalent environmental standards" between developing and developed countries.

Recent negotiations on the Bio-safety Protocol, the PIC Convention and also on the Basel Ban Amendment have shown a specific interest of developing countries in trade measures which avoid transfrontier movement of pollution and environmentally damaging products from developed countries. However, while some want to accommodate eco-labelling using life cycle analysis in the TBT Agreement, it has not been possible to make progress on guidelines for some kind of labelling concerning trade in genetically modified organisms (GMOs), whose environmental and health effects would become known only after several years.

## Lack of economic capacities to respond to environmental challenges

While there has been a lot of attention regarding the environmental effectiveness of trade and other measures, the capacity building needs in developing countries to enable them to meet stricter environmental norms and enhance environmental performance has been underestimated. It is not lack of interest which hinders faster progress, but the inability of many developing countries to bear the related adjustment costs.

Most developing countries lack implementation and enforcement capacities and have little experience with the use of economic instruments for environmental policy making. There is a lack of funding for strengthening such capacities, in particular under MEAs such as CITES and the Basel Convention. In addition, developing countries may have difficulties in responding to national environmental standards and regulations in developed countries (e.g. with regard to bans on the use of azo dyes or penthachlorophenol (PCP)) and there may be insufficient funding under bilateral and multilateral aid programmes to facilitate capacity building and access to technology to resolve these problems. UNCTAD's 1998 Least Developed Countries report provides some examples of LDCs having suffered significant losses in export revenues because of their inability to respond to environment and health related requirements in export markets.

## Lack of full understanding of the economic and developmental implications of the use of some instruments for environmental purposes

Expectations of some may have been geared too much towards blunt policy solutions, such as trade measures, whereas the complexity of the issues seems to suggest a gradual approach and a priority for enabling measures which create conducive economic conditions for dissemination and effective use of ESTs. Particularly, environmental problems created by the informal sector receive insufficient attention. This is the case although the informal sector often accounts for 50 per cent or more of the management of environmentally problematic natural resources, such as heavy metals or hazardous chemicals, and is a key source of pollution.

Although the "precautionary principle" plays an important role in environmental policy making, it should not prevent the devising of comprehensive and balanced packages of policy instruments to address all aspects of an environmental problem. There has often not been the time to study the underlying economics of environmentally motivated trade measures, or other environmental measures which affect trade. In fact, there is a general lack of information on analyzing the economic and social adjustment costs in developing countries. Experience with the implementation of the Montreal Protocol, for instance, indicates that in order to meet their commitments, developing countries would need to change their entire structure from small to large scale production, acquire more land, and develop different labour and operational skills to phase out CFCs from the foam sector.

## Lack of political will

These imbalances in the agenda become especially important as there has been little progress in implementing enabling mechanisms at the multilateral level. The recent assessment of progress in the implementation of Agenda 21 by the United Nations General Assembly was frustrating because so little progress has been made on what Agenda 21 calls "implementation issues" such as finance, access to environmentally sound technologies and, perhaps to a lesser extent, capacity building.

Imbalances in the trade and environment agenda can only be addressed if sufficient attention is placed on the "sandwiching" of trade measures with other supportive or enabling measures. Finance and technology constitute important areas where there has been little progress. If the ultimate objective of trade measures is to fulfil environmental objectives, then such objectives cannot be met by the trade measure alone, unless trade is the cause or way of dissemination of the environmental problem. In fact, trade measures without enabling measures may cause more environmental damage and further hamper the capacity of developing countries to move towards sustainable development. The argument that enabling measures lie outside the purview of the WTO is no longer sustainable because the purview of WTO has been made very broad by the Uruguay Round Agreements.

## SOLUTIONS

### Greater balance in the trade and environment debate

Finding a certain balance in the terms of reference of the CTE has been a difficult task. Such balance could be lost if issues of concern to developing countries were to receive less attention than others. Also, greater attention must be given to measures which take account of the difficulties of developing countries in integrating trade and environment: such as S&D provisions; measures which provide better access to information, such as transparency and notification provisions; and measures which may assist small and medium sized enterprises in responding to environmental challenges. Furthermore, it is important to ensure that all aspects of the issues on the agenda receive adequate attention. For example, attempts to clarify possible inconsistencies between MEAs and the rules of the multilateral trading system should also include some consideration of the concerns of many developing countries, and NGOs in these countries, for example, with respect to differences in the IPR concepts and regimes in the Convention on Biodiversity on the one hand and the WTO TRIPS Agreement on the other.

### Building capacities to respond to environmental challenges

Strengthening capacities for policy analysis, and better co-ordination between trade and environmental policies could help to reduce some of the obstacles to the achievement of sustainable development in developing countries.

UNCTAD is working together with UNDP in capacity building in trade and environment, with a view to strengthening research capacities, promoting dialogue between trade, environment and development communities and trade and environment policy co-ordination as well as the effective participation of developing countries in international deliberations. We also work closely with UNEP, the WTO and civil society.

Similarly, UNCTAD is about to launch a UK-funded project on enhancing domestic policy co-ordination and policy analysis in 10 developing countries, including a number of least developed countries. The project aims to promote a process for building and strengthening human and technical resources in developing countries – within relevant government departments, overseas missions, NGOs and research institutes – through workshops, roundtable discussions and studies. The project will also promote research in developing countries as well as facilitate networking between developing country research institutes.

The use of multi-stakeholder approaches, and the facilitation of business partnerships, are another important step in building capacity and promoting policy co-ordination. Multi-stakeholder fora are of particular relevance when interests of different groups have to be reconciled. UNCTAD's joint work with UNEP in this regard shows that multi-stakeholder approaches may also help in finding packages of measures to anticipate economic and social implications of globalization and trade liberalization.

## Improving understanding of the economic and developmental implications of the use of some instruments for environmental purposes

Information on the specific environmental, economic and social implications of environmentally motivated trade measures, and environmental standards on trade, is extremely scant. Therefore, much required market signals conducive to innovation and cost-efficient ways of meeting certain environmental targets are poorly understood. Only recently, the secretariats of UNCTAD and OECD have launched more systematic research in this respect and a synthesis report by OECD on experience gathered with the use of trade measures in three MEAs highlights directions of further analytical and empirical work in this regard. Preliminary analysis by UNCTAD of specific material and country cases for the Basel Convention, for instance, reveals that the economic and social adjustment costs are significantly underestimated, and that even the environmental objectives might be compromised. Only a pro-active government role, using regulatory and economic instruments, and the collaboration of all concerned stakeholders, can correct the undesirable effects. Lessons from such work are not only interesting for the governments of these concerned developing countries, they also offer valuable advice to MEA negotiators.

To improve the assessment and understanding of the potential environmental, economic and social ramifications of trade measures – particularly those that are highly restrictive such as bans – UNCTAD sees much merit in giving more consideration to a proposal which was made at the Information Session of the CTE with selected MEA secretariats on 23 July last year. Referring to recent practice in the final negotiations of the Convention on Prior Informed Consent, the conclusions of the information session recommended that working groups of trade experts reviewing the multi-faceted effects of trade measures in MEAs may be set up. Such working groups could also be useful at bilateral level when considering the introduction or modification of trade measures or environmental standards with trade effects. UNCTAD would be prepared to support the work of such groups with its analytical and empirical knowledge and carry out specific analysis, if desired. We feel that it is important to promote such working groups and multi-stakeholder fora at national level; to address information gaps; and to consider packages of measures for achieving the objectives of MEAs in a cost-efficient and socially equitable way; as well as to build consensus on policy choices to be made.

In the WTO context there is also the need to stress the importance of sound science versus the use of precautionary principle in the case of environmentally related trade restrictions. It can also be debated whether to go beyond the concept of least trade restrictiveness to the concept of proportionality, which implies a trade off between trade losses and environmental gains. In this context, the concept of the risk of non-fulfilment could be reinterpreted to include such a trade-off.

## Showing greater political will

Progress in constructing a more balanced agenda and strengthening the development dimension, can be made only to the extent that countries, in particular developed countries, show greater political will. This includes, for example, the full and timely implementation of the developed countries' Uruguay Round commitments in areas such as textiles. But such political will also has to be shown outside the WTO context, for example through greater progress in providing finance, facilitating access to and diffusion of ESTs and capacity building, supported by multilateral and bilateral aid programmes.

## UNCTAD'S CONTRIBUTION

UNCTAD of course stands ready to contribute to these efforts in accordance with our mandate. For example, we have developed a very comprehensive programme of technical cooperation for capacity building which counts on the generous support of several member States, UNDP and UNEP. Activities consist of policy-oriented studies, workshops and seminars, the compilation and analysis of information, and training through global, regional and country projects. As far as possible our programme uses local research and NGO capacity. It pays special attention to the least developed countries (LDCs).

This programme contributes to strengthening capacities for policy-oriented research in developing countries and helps to develop a "positive agenda" on trade and environment for developing countries. In particular, it aims at strengthening capacities for policy co-ordination at the national and regional levels as well as for the effective participation of developing countries in multilateral deliberations on trade, environment and development.

# Chapter 11

# Part I. Trade and the environment

## 2. Synergies between trade liberalization, environmental protection, sustained economic growth and sustainable development

*Martin Khor**

I will try to answer whether there usually, and necessarily, are such synergies, especially between liberalization, environment and development. Then I will try to suggest some areas where liberalization could help environment and sustainable development; and also some areas where careful management of the liberalization process is required to aid sustainable development. Finally, I will cover some systemic issues about the WTO and its link to the trade, environment and development debate.

The framework used here is that of the relation between trade and sustainable development, thus placing "environmental concerns" in the context of development, or the need to fulfil human needs for all in the present and future generations.

Since natural resources and carrying capacity are limited, sustainable development requires equitable solutions in which the rich bear the greater share of the burden of adjustment to a more environmental system. The rich nations, and the elite of the South, should bear the costs for changes to production and consumption patterns and levels, and lifestyles, whilst poor people everywhere, and developing countries, should be given the economic and environmental space to fulfil their right to development.

Some members of the environmental community call this the principle of "fair shares in environmental space" and have mapped out in detail the cuts and changes in consumption and output that can be done in the North, in order to free up resources for the South to develop. Assistance to the South should be through aid and technology transfer, but also through fair rules in trade and finance that fully take into account the needs of developing countries, as well as the equity principle.

## LIBERALIZATION AND SUSTAINABLE DEVELOPMENT

There is often an assumption in the trade community that trade and trade liberalization usually leads to a better environment and also to growth and development. This assumption is correctly challenged by many civil society organizations, especially

---

* Director, Third World Network, Malaysia.

environmental, consumer and health groups. They point out that in many cases international trade has facilitated the transfer of technologies, products and consumption patterns that are harmful to the environment, to long-term development prospects and to human health.

The spread of toxic wastes and hazardous chemicals, the unsustainability of modern chemical-based agriculture, the environmental damage due to extraction of minerals and timber, the threats posed by nuclear materials, the epidemic of deaths due to the trade in tobacco products, and the replacement of breast-feeding with cow-milk powder are just a few examples of how trade facilitates unsustainable patterns of production and consumption.

Trade can bring economic benefits, but not in all cases or for all countries or communities. Factors determining benefits, costs and the net outcome include the nature and prices of, the demand for, and the capacity to supply the products exported by a country; as well as the nature and prices of products it imports.

It is not necessarily so that the balance of these factors results in a positive net outcome for any country or all countries. For example, many developing countries still mainly export raw materials. The continuous decline of their commodity prices, especially when contrasted with rising prices of industrial products they import, has depressed their export earnings, and has contributed significantly to their long-standing debt crisis and to stagnation and continued poverty.

Moreover, when these poor countries reduce import duties, the cheaper imports often take over the markets of local products of small and medium sized local firms that are unable to compete, causing the phenomenon of "de-industrialization". This point should be re-emphasized as commodity prices are presently once again falling rapidly, causing great distress to many exporting countries.

Trade and trade liberalization can thus have positive and negative effects. It follows thus that liberalization cannot be the ultimate goal of a process, even (or especially) in the WTO. The ultimate objective of trade and the trade system should be sustainable development, and liberalization should be pursued only when it contributes to that objective.

A deep understanding of the conditions, and of the stages and levels of development, required for liberalization to have positive effects on sustainable development is urgently required. Correspondingly, when those conditions are not present, liberalization should not be pursued. In cases (products, sectors, conditions) where there are negative effects, "synergy" cannot be claimed between liberalization, environment and development. In such cases, liberalization should not be pursued (at least not yet), and in fact a reversal to some degree may be needed if the goal of sustainable development is to be achieved.

A deep and honest review of the Uruguay Round agreements is thus required, and sections of these should be amended where it is found that they impede or undermine sustainable development. In particular, the WTO system (in fact, the major or dominant members) must not shy away from allowing developing countries much more leeway and flexibility in implementing the agreements, including exemptions from liberalization obligations in selected areas where such flexibility is necessary to their development needs.

For example, many developing countries could face social, economic and environmental dislocation if they take liberalization measures under the Agriculture Agreement and later find that their small farmers are unable to compete with cheaper imports. Thus, WTO Members should consider exempting food produced for domestic consumption, and the products of subsistence farmers and small farmers, from the Agriculture Agreement's obligations on import liberalization and domestic subsidies. This would enable the developing countries to pursue the goal of food security, the protection of small farmers' livelihoods and the promotion of sustainable agriculture.

This would be an example of "synergy" between the proper treatment of liberalization (in this case, recognizing its limitations and negative aspects) and the pursuit of sustainable development (in this case, food security, sustainable livelihoods and sustainable agriculture). There are other examples where state intervention and international cooperation are required to channel trade towards sustainable development goals.

The commodity trade is damaging to both the environment and to development prospects, especially in the light of further depression of commodity prices. A new round of international commodity agreements could help to at least reduce the problems. Producing countries could, according to an agreed plan, produce less quantities (which would reduce the glut of supply, and also reduce pressures on natural resources and the environment). At the same time consumers would agree to pay higher prices for commodities to reflect their ecological and social values.

Developing countries that are exporters would produce less volume but receive attractive prices and levels of export earnings and developed countries that import would pay more, and thus to some extent offset the long-term trend decline in the commodities–manufactures terms of trade. This would be in the spirit of implementing the "common but differentiated responsibility" principle.

The trade community should re-orientate the trading system to be more responsible in promoting safe products and to discourage or bar the trade in harmful products. For example, domestically prohibited products should not be exported; at the least such exports should be conditional on a "prior informed consent" (PIC) basis. This procedure (which can also be upgraded to a ban) should then be applied to hazardous products (as it has in the Basel Convention on toxic wastes).

At the very least, the WTO should not stand in the way of efforts by other international organizations and by governments to discourage the use of products harmful to health and the environment. For example, the US government is taking legal action on the tobacco industry (including obtaining large compensations for harmful effects of smoking) to curb cigarette sales and advertising. Yet it aids American tobacco companies to spread their products to developing countries by pressurising these countries (by threatening to apply unilateral Super 301 action or to use free-trade rules in the WTO) to open up their markets to foreign firms. After several Asian countries succumbed to these threats, the rate of smoking increased as consumers were influenced by the high-pressured marketing efforts of the tobacco multinationals.

The commercial interests of major trading countries cynically over-rode the health interests of trading partner countries, seriously damaging the trading system's credibility. In another topical case, negotiations for a biosafety protocol under the Biodiversity Convention reached a near-consensus in February 1999 but were undermined by the US (which is not even a member of the Convention) and a handful of countries that put their commercial interests before global ecological and safety concerns.

Negative actions, like these two examples that so blatantly make use (or abuse) the slogan of "free trade" to sabotage vital health, safety and environmental concerns are precisely the reasons for the rapid erosion of public confidence in the "free trade" and, by association, the WTO system. They make the attainment of "synergy" between trade and environment so difficult. Fallacious claims should not be made by WTO members that "free trade principles" disallow countries (even acting in concert in a multilateral Convention) from agreeing on actions towards responsible regulation of harmful products with potentially devastating effects.

## SOME AREAS OF SYNERGY BETWEEN LIBERALIZATION AND SUSTAINABLE DEVELOPMENT

Developing countries face protectionist measures in the North on several of their exports. This is well known in the trade community. These measures should be removed in the interest of the goal of sustainable development. Among these are tariff escalation, in which raw materials are imported at very low (or no) duties, but the tariffs are progressively increased if the materials are processed. This discourages developing countries from processing their raw materials due to the obstacles placed in the developed countries on importing processed materials.

Developing countries can obtain significantly greater value-added and gross revenue if they are able to process their raw materials and export them, and even more so if they produce manufactured products out of them. For example, processed wood fetches a higher price than saw logs, and furniture earns much more than processed wood. The exporting country can thus earn many times more from the same volume or quantity of raw material should the material be converted to a processed or manufactured form before export.

The country could be encouraged to reduce the rate of extraction or exploitation of raw materials (thus reducing the pressures on the environment) and instead put more efforts into exporting processed and manufactured products. However this requires increased market access, particularly in the developed countries which should thus remove the practice of tariff escalation. It also requires that developing countries are permitted to restrict the export of their raw materials in raw form so that the domestic processing and manufacturing sectors can have adequate supply. In the past, some developing countries have come under pressure because they took such measures.

The misuse of anti-dumping measures, as a protectionist and anti-competitive action, also hinders sustainable development in developing countries as it discourages or depresses their exports of the items subjected to these measures. The misuse of such measures should thus be stopped.

Developing countries find another major protectionist obstacle in the TRIPS agreement which is a protectionist device that enables technology owners to reap extra profits from monopoly pricing, whilst hindering, or altogether preventing, the transfer of technology. There can be "synergy" between liberalization and environmental protection, as well as development, if exemptions or flexibility in implementing provisions of the TRIPS agreement are permitted for environmentally-sound technologies and products, in order that developing countries can have greater and cheaper access to them. Also, flexibility is needed in order to discourage the viability and spread of products that are harmful to the environment and human health. This has been suggested by India in the Committee on Trade and Environment and should be seriously considered.

An example of how IPRs hinder technology transfer is the case of some Indian companies that manufacture products that use CFCs, which are to be phased out under the Montreal Protocol for causing harm to the ozone layer. The protocol includes articles on technology transfer to the South on fair and favourable terms. Three of the companies successfully commissioned a local institute to produce a substitute for CFCs. However the patent rights to the substitute substance, HFC 134A, are held by a few multinationals. Some of the Indian companies were willing to pay the market price or more for the use of the technology but a multinational holding the patent refused to license it unless it could take a majority share in the companies' equity. This shows the predicament of developing countries that are promised technology transfer on favourable terms but, instead, face obstacles to accessing technology even if they are willing to pay commercial terms.

In order to have "synergy" between liberalization, environment and development, the TRIPS agreement should be amended to exempt environmentally sound technology from patentability.

An area of even greater concern to civil society is the TRIPS Article 27.3b relating to biological materials. It obliges countries to patent micro-organisms and to accord protection to plant varieties. This opens the road to patenting of life forms and biological materials, especially those that have been subjected to genetic engineering. The adverse effects include the facilitation of the appropriation of traditional and indigenous knowledge by local communities about the use of biological resources by corporations that are able to (or claim to) meet the patent test; the promotion of environmentally harmful technologies; and the promotion of technologies that are against the interests of small farmers (such as the "terminator technology" or "suicide seeds", i.e. seeds which are engineered not to reproduce themselves so as to deprive farmers from saving them for the next harvest).

Again, the relevant clauses of the TRIPS agreement should be amended or "liberalised" so that the protectionist and unethical barriers it facilitates can be removed. This is an important area where "synergy" between liberalization and sustainable development can be attained.

# SYSTEMIC ISSUES

One reason civil society views the WTO with scepticism is its non-transparent and non-participatory nature where the majority of developing countries (and the majority of WTO members) are unable to adequately have their views represented and reflected in the decisions and policies. Most decisions are really made by a few major countries, and groups of countries, particularly the US and the EU. The most important meetings are held in small informal groups to which most developing countries are not invited. Even when there is no consensus on some important issues advocated by the major countries, due to opposition from several developing countries, these issues are invariably put through the WTO system until agreements are produced. This was evident at the Singapore Ministerial Conference in relation to new issues, and again at the Geneva Conference of 1998 where a decision on electronic commerce was pushed through.

For several years now, following the Uruguay Round's conclusion, there is a growing and widespread view that the WTO rules are stacked against the developing countries. Not only are the benefits shared inequitably, but some countries (and developing countries as a whole) are likely to suffer net losses.

Developing countries now find themselves in the midst of serious problems arising from their having to domestically implement what they agreed to multilaterally. A review of these problems arising from the WTO agreements, and a process of amending these agreements in order to improve them and make them more suitable for developing countries, are urgent and will require enormous efforts.

Yet ever more "new issues" are being advocated, mainly by the major countries, even a new comprehensive Round. Such a demand, if it succeeds, would deprive developing countries and civil society the opportunity to contribute properly to reviewing and revising the existing agreements. The energies and very limited resources would be devoted to the "new issues" which have very serious implications, especially for the environment and sustainable development.

The lopsided nature of the WTO system and its trade rules is what makes developing countries and many civil society organizations around the world so suspicious of the WTO. It is also a major reason why the WTO is not seen as an appropriate forum in which to discuss the complex and important issues relating to trade, environment and sustainable development. The WTO is seen as an organization dominated by a few major powers, which are usually able to provide their interpretation of issues, and to make this interpretation formally acceptable to all.

The systemic issues of transparency and participation in the WTO should be resolved as soon as possible, otherwise the atmosphere of suspicion, and the tense relations between civil society and the trade system, are bound to continue.

# Chapter 12

# Part I.  Trade and the environment

## 2.  Synergies between trade liberalization, environmental protection, sustained economic growth and sustainable development

*Dan Esty\**

## ECONOMIC INTEGRATION AND ENVIRONMENTAL PROTECTION: SYNERGIES, OPPORTUNITIES AND CHALLENGE

Trade and investment liberalization promise to bring great benefits to the people of the world. In recent decades, the opening of markets in many regions have resulted in the lifting of hundreds of millions of people out of the abyss of poverty. The gains from trade-driven economic growth offer a promise of improved environmental conditions as well. But there is no guarantee that this link will be made; or, to be more precise, carefully considered policy will be required to ensure that trade gains also yield environmental benefits. Finding ways to achieve these mutual returns and to maximize the synergy between freer trade and better environmental quality is an issue of great urgency.

It is now clear that poverty often leads to environmental degradation. People who are very poor, and who are not certain where their next meal is coming from or how they will heat their home or cook food for their children tend to make short term choices that frequently disregard the dictates of sound resource management. Whether it is people cutting down trees for fuel wood that are otherwise needed to prevent soil erosion and facilitate the purification of ground water, or governments that subsidize oil on the assumption that their people are too poor to pay the market price, the impact is harmful both as a matter of sound economics and good environmental policy.

Increasing wealth offers an opportunity for some share of the financial gains obtained to be invested in improved pollution control and resource management. It is perhaps axiomatic that wealthier people will spend more money on environmental quality than poor people. But even more dramatically, wealth is often an indicator of the capacity to invest in technological change that so often appears to be the critical factor in moving towards improved ecological and public health.[1] Across

---

\* Yale Law School, Yale University, USA.
[1]    See Esty, D. and M. Chertow (1997), "Introduction", in *Thinking Ecologically: The Next Generation of Environmental Policy*, New Haven: Yale University Press.

the developing world, investments in environmental infrastructure – wastewater treatment facilities, efficient power plants, drinking water supply systems, waste disposal facilities – can increasingly be found in countries where economic growth has a firm foothold. Deeper and broader economic expansion, pushed forward by free and open markets, offers the promise of bringing environmental as well as material gains to untold hundreds of millions of citizens of this planet.

But alongside the opportunities that economic growth provides lie substantial challenges. First, in too many places, economic progress has occurred in a manner that has led to serious and unnecessary environmental degradation. Too little attention has been paid to the byproducts of growth and to the dictates of *sustainable* development. Sustainability requires ongoing and careful consideration of the downsides of both economic growth and trade and investment liberalization. In many places, the headlong pursuit of material gain has blinded both the public and policymakers to the significant offsets against social welfare that will accompany economic growth if policy goals are defined too narrowly. In this regard, no nation should forget the lessons of Eastern Europe and Russia. Today, the legacy of the mindless industrialization under communism can be seen across this region in the form of devastated communities, water that is not only unfit to drink but so corrosive that it cannot be used in industrial processes, abandoned toxic waste dumps seething with harmful chemicals, and air that is thick with smoke and laced with toxic materials. Simply put, economic expansion can lead to advances in social welfare, but there is no guarantee that it will.

The upside of globalization and the potential for improved quality of life from sustained economic growth has another risk that must be managed. Specifically, economic change creates both losers as well as winners. The rise of vibrant new industries and the jobs that come with them are matched in many places with the collapse of older economic structures and the jobs that go with those. Too often we look at aggregate or average data and see the gains without realizing that buried within these growth figures are individuals and communities that are not seeing better days. If the momentum for continued trade and investment liberalization is to be sustained, attention must be paid to those who have, to date, only seen the negative face of globalization.

In addition to creating the potential for economic losers, the evolution towards integrated worldwide markets poses a threat to more localized communities and the values the citizens of these communities cherish. Indeed, the greatest risk of backlash against globalization arises from a coalescing of those who perceive themselves to be giving up too much in return for the economic gains made possible by the elimination of trade barriers. Whether it is French farmers who see their way of life threatened; American consumer groups who fear that the high regulatory standards they have fought for in the US context are threatened by GATT; Indian villagers who believe that the WTO's protection of intellectual property rights will deprive them of their traditional agricultural practices; or rain forest dwellers in South America who witness the pressure for expanded timber imports as a dire threat to their traditional lives, there is a sense that important community values may be undermined by global forces that exceed the scope of any government to control.

The social impacts of liberalized trade and the prospect of a backlash against globalization has been raised by both academics, such as Dani Rodrik and this author, as well as politicians from Bill Clinton to Tony Blair to Nelson Mandela and Sir Leon Brittan. Even among those who are the winners from globalization, there is a growing recognition that economic integration must be undertaken in a kinder and gentler fashion. In fact, the theme of this year's mega-capitalist gathering, the World Economic Forum in Davos, was "responsible globality".

Ensuring that the upsides of globalization can be achieved without suffering the potential downsides is, I believe, one of the central public policy challenges of our era. The transition to fully integrated worldwide economy does not have to leave tens of millions of people out in the cold. Providing those who suffer transitional losses with some support and the training necessary to achieve success in the new economy of the future is essential. Similarly, designing institutions and rules for international economic interaction that protect important public values, including a desire for environmental protection, is also important.

Meeting this challenge will require actions from national governments, non-governmental organizations, and other institutions in society. There is also an important role for the emerging institutions of global governance including, most prominently, the World Trade Organization (WTO). Indeed, given our emphasis here today on the work of the international economic system and the WTO, I would like to focus on the role that the WTO can and should play to mitigate these strains and to maximize the potential gains from trade and investment liberalization.

The centerpiece of this effort for a kinder and gentler globalization must be an initiative to improve the institutional workings of the WTO and the substantive rules of the GATT to strengthen the performance and legitimacy of the international trading system. The WTO should be viewed as both authoritative and fair in making judgments about economic integration and how international economic interactions connect with other important values such as the environment.

This question goes to the heart of the WTO's future. Absent sufficient legitimacy, decisions that emanate from the WTO will not be accepted as part of the process of global governance. The legitimacy challenge has a number of dimensions. First, in both its rulemaking and its adjudicatory roles, the WTO needs to be recognized for its authoritativeness. The success of international organizations in general, and of the trade regime in particular, depend on a capacity to produce "correct" answers to the issues that must be addressed. The trade regime, over the past fifty years, has been quite successful in developing a core underlying theory and a set of well established rules that can be applied in a context of disputes. But increasingly the tensions over trade stray beyond the boundaries of economics into other policy arenas including the environmental domain. If the WTO is to be perceived as legitimate in dealing with conflicts that arise beyond the periphery of trade law, it must draw on those with relevant expertise, including technical and scientific environmental knowledge.

In addition to a capacity to produce substantively correct answers, the WTO faces a further challenge of being perceived as fair. Fairness has both procedural and substantive dimensions. From a process point of view, all those who have an interest in the outcome of a decision must be given an opportunity to be part of the decision process. Substantively, the rules of international trade, as embodied in the GATT, must be applied in an even handed way over time and across issues. The results that emerge must not appear to advantage systematically any particular group or nation or to advance trade values over other important concerns including environmental protection.

Legitimacy is also a function of the responsiveness and representativeness of those making decisions. Whenever political choices are made at highly centralized levels, such as the WTO, there exists a very real risk that the distant localized citizenry will feel that its voice has not been heard. To overcome this "democratic deficit" the WTO must establish procedures to ensure that it both gathers views from the world's grassroots and also openly and clearly communicates the results of its decision processes to the public. The thought that member states will, as a matter of governmental function, perform this opinion gathering and information dissemination role is misplaced.

First, governments often do not communicate well. Non-governmental organizations (NGOs) frequently do a better job. Second, and more importantly for some issues, the debate will be more refined and the result more representative if the discussion occurs at the global scale rather than through a series of national debates that are only linked at the WTO. Third, more international and public debate, indeed, more robust politics at the global level will facilitate creation of a sense of community at the international scale which will make deeper trade and investment liberalization possible. Moreover, political give-and-take at a worldwide scale is essential to successful global governance in general and a thriving WTO in particular.

## OPPORTUNITIES

The WTO needs to work to mitigate the tension between trade and investment liberalization on the one hand and environmental protection on the other. There are a number of elements that might be folded into such a strategy.

## SUBSTANTIVE CHANGES TO THE GATT

If possible synergies between trade liberalization and environmental protection are to be realized, the rules of the GATT must not be slanted, nor even appear to be slanted, toward the promotion of trade interests at the expense of other values, including environmental protection. The sense of balance that would be necessary is not now present. In particular, Article XX is perceived, at least as it is currently applied, to elevate trade goals over environmental ones. In particular, the reading of the "necessary clause" as requiring that environmental policies be "least trade restrictive" appears to put a very high, and many would say unreasonable, hurdle in front of environmental policymakers. The problem, from an environmental point of view, is that there is almost always some less trade restrictive policy option available. If trade restrictions are employed, there is always an option of using an environmental label. If an environmental label is used, there was always the option of providing environmental education. The edge of this slippery slope can never be reached.

Thus, the search for a substantively neutral set of GATT rules to guide the clash between trade and environmental goals should begin with an administratively-agreed-upon redefinition of "necessary" as employed in Article XX, to mean "not disproportionate". Under this test, an environmental policy that appeared to be in tension with trade goals would be accepted as legitimate if it were found to have a basis in science and to have trade impacts that were not disproportionate to the environmental gains being sought.

Such a standard would help to ensure that legitimate environmental policies "including the use of ecolabels, recycling mandates, and packaging limitations" would be deemed appropriate and GATT-consistent so long as they were not recklessly constructed in ways that had unnecessary trade impacts.

Another substantive amendment to the current GATT structure that would facilitate peace between the trade and environment camps would involve the recognition by the GATT that, in an ecologically interdependent world, *how* things are produced is often as important as *what* is produced. In particular, environmental standards that relate to production processes and methods (PPMs) cannot always be rejected and judged indiscriminately to be violations of the GATT. In particular, where PPMs are aimed at transboundary environmental harms that spill across the borders of the producing country, there should be no doubt but that such standards are, at least theoretically, legitimate. It would be appropriate, again, to spell out limitations on the use of PPM standards. Such disciplines might, as above, be focused on the scientific foundations for the standards as well as the proportionality between the environmental gain to be obtained and the trade impact suffered.

More broadly, anywhere that international environmental agreements have been achieved, including ones that have trade mechanisms embodied in them, there should be a presumption that parties acting in accordance with an international environmental agreement are not in violation of their GATT obligations. Protecting multilaterally determined environmental policies is absolutely essential if unilaterally determined standards are to be avoided. By administrative determination, the WTO should therefore declare that any international environmental agreement that attracts a substantial degree of support from the affected nations shall be viewed as necessary and appropriate under Article XX. Such a ruling would definitively put to rest the fears of environmentalists that, in the future, when trade and environmental principles clash, the trade rules will automatically trump.

The WTO would also benefit from clarifying that, under the TBT and SPS Agreements, legitimate environmental policies will be protected from GATT attack. Environmental policies that are challenged should be presumed to be legitimate unless the party bringing the challenge can demonstrate that the standards employed do not have a scientific foundation or that the trade impacts are disproportionate to the environmental benefits.

## PROCEDURAL ADVANCES

As important to the future legitimacy of the WTO – and the possibility of making trade and environmental policy more mutually reinforcing – as substantive updating of the GATT rules is, procedural advances are equally important. The GATT is still perceived by far too many people across the world as a mysterious "black box" decision-making mechanism. Important commitments have been made in recent years to increase transparency. These initiatives must be shifted into higher gear.

First, all WTO documents should be presumed to be in the public domain, unless a significant reason can be advanced for keeping them confidential. Secondly, meetings of the GATT Council should be made open to NGOs. The gains to be had by having these organizations attend and be able to report back to their memberships across the world "facilitating understanding of the WTO decision-making" far exceeds any risk that might come from having the debates take place in public. Indeed, given the large number of officials who are already in the room, there is very little that is secret about these discussions. The possibility that NGOs might take advantage of their presence to somehow manipulate the outcomes of the council is far fetched.

The real risk of special interest manipulation of WTO outcomes lies not in what occurs in formal meetings but rather the influence that is exerted behind the scenes and through informal channels. The response, moreover, to the risk of special interest distortions should be a much more vigorous set of lobbying restrictions. All contacts between WTO staff (and perhaps national representatives of the WTO as well) and business or other non-governmental interests should be disclosed. Strict limits should be put in place on the sorts of meals, trips, or gifts that any of these officials can receive from those who have business before the WTO.

To further the commitment to transparency, WTO dispute resolution proceedings should be conducted in the open. These proceedings have increasingly become quasi-judicial and the myth that what is provided is some sort of negotiating forum should be exploded. Indeed, it is important that the trend, already launched in the Uruguay Round, to move these proceedings towards a more formal judicial model be continued. The value of having definitive rulings that can be cited as precedent is significant. The appellate body has already demonstrated its value by sharpening considerably the opinions that have been rendered in a number of recent cases. Moreover, one of the tenets of a sound judicial process is that the proceedings that lead to decisions be open for all to see and understand.

Another procedural advance that the WTO should consider is expanding participation in the Committee on Trade and Environment (CTE). Too often, the CTE debate is dominated by a narrow set of trade perspectives. If this group is to be taken seriously and its work is to contribute to resolutions of trade and environment conflicts, the environmental voice must be much more clearly represented.

The WTO might also consider undertaking environmental assessments of the potential impacts of future rounds of trade liberalization. The parties to the North American Free Trade Agreement undertook environmental reviews during the course of their negotiation and the results were quite helpful in identifying potential pollution and natural resource sensitivities that could be addressed in the course of the negotiations. Such a review need not go into every detail of every tariff reduction nor should it attempt to model the environmental implications of every commitment that is under consideration, but the broad scale effects of major initiatives could be analyzed for potentially beneficial results.

Perhaps the most important procedural advance that the WTO should undertake centers on understanding NGOs as having a salutary impact on the international trading regime. In particular, NGOs, representing both business and other interests, are often able to serve as "competitors" to governments in the policymaking process. In dealing with issues such as the environment, which have high degrees of uncertainty, it is extremely valuable to have multiple perspectives on any issue in question. Too often, past WTO debates have been constrained by the fact that almost everyone involved comes out of a trade-oriented culture. By bringing to bear additional perspectives from environmentalists and others, the decision process will be enriched. More importantly, the likelihood that the WTO will achieve "right answers" will be significantly advanced.

NGOs offer, moreover, the promise of providing a proxy for public participation in WTO decision-making. Given the highly centralized nature of the international trading regime, it is unrealistic to think that everyday citizens will have much opportunity to contribute to or hear about the decisions that are being made in Geneva.

But NGO representatives can ensure that the voices of the public are heard and that the decentralized citizenry across the world feel better connected to the WTO in its global governance role.

## SYNERGISTIC ISSUE AGENDA

There are a number of issues that might be pursued as central elements of the upcoming Millennium Round of GATT negotiations that would provide both trade and environmental benefits. These issues deserve special consideration because they offer the prospect of bridging, at least to some degree, the gap between the trade and environmental communities.

## SUBSIDIES

The elimination of environmentally harmful and trade disruptive subsidies offers potential for significant benefits both ecologically and economically. A number of areas appear ripe for the picking.

Recent studies suggested that almost all of the worlds fisheries are depleted and at a risk of overexploitation. One reason for this resource strain is government subsidy of fishing fleets. One important step toward a world of sustainable fisheries would be the elimination of government inducements to support expanded fishing.

Government support for agriculture also creates economic incentives that are environmentally damaging. Farm price supports, in particular, induce farmers to occupy marginal lands. Rather, for example, than leaving riparian zones untilled as a way of protecting the adjacent river or stream, government subsidies often push the farmer to plant right up to the edge of the water body. Subsidies provided on a quantity basis lead farmers to undertake much more chemical-intensive agricultural practices in order to attempt to push up their yields. Again, these subsidies are disruptive to trade and result in serious environmental problems.

Perhaps the greatest area of environmental threat caused by government subsidies lies in the energy realm. Government practices that reduce energy prices blunt the incentive for efficiency in conservation, thereby causing more fuel to be burned and more pollutants to be admitted. Energy subsidies are particularly egregious in the current policy context where there is a great struggle underway to find effective global solutions to the problem of greenhouse gas emissions.

## STRENGTHENING THE INTERNATIONAL
## ENVIRONMENTAL REGIME

While substantial elements of synergy between trade and environmental goals can be achieved by sharpening the trade policy agenda, there are important additional elements of reinforcement that will require better international environmental policy-making. Indeed, nothing would advance "trade and environment" harmony more than the creation of a global environmental organization (GEO) to work alongside the WTO. The existence of a GEO would relieve the WTO of the responsibility for sorting out environmental issues that arise in the international policy context. Just as the WTO looks to the IMF for guidance on how to handle issues of exchange rates, if an effective GEO were in existence, trade officials could adopt by reference the substantive and technical judgment of this body as the underpinning for trade policy decisions.

The economic logic for having a mechanism to ensure that global scale externalities are internalized and thus that the international economic regime is able to achieve optimal allocative efficiency, maximum social welfare, and minimum environmental degradation is significant. Support from the trade community for creation of a GEO might well give such an initiative important momentum. Change in the international policy domain is always slow, particularly in light of the current low esteem with which much of the UN is viewed. But signals from world economic leaders that they perceive value in restructuring the international environmental regime might well be an important force for making change happen.

## CONCLUSION

The world's trade and environmental policies promise to continue to intersect in the years ahead. Managing the challenge of interdependence between these policy fields presents real challenges. But important opportunities to achieve synergies between the goals of trade and investment liberalization and environmental protection are also available. Whether the international trading system will step up to these challenges and opportunities remains in doubt.

I believe that the success of the WTO in responding to the trade and environment issue is not peripheral but rather central to the organization's own future. Failure to attend to environmental issues and other social values concerns that arise in the context of efforts to open global markets threatens to detract from the proper functioning of the international economic system and perhaps even generate a serious backlash against globalization, with all its attendant negative potential. The logic of cooperation in pursuit of synergies is great, but moving from talk to action will require real leadership.

# Chapter 13

# Part I. Trade and the environment

## 2. Synergies between trade liberalization, environmental protection, sustained economic growth and sustainable development

*Dr Vandana Shiva**

## CREATING AN ENVIRONMENT AND DEVELOPMENT APARTHEID

This session is supposed to be on synergies between trade, environmental protection and sustainable development. However, there can be no synergies between systems that have been deliberately set apart as is the case with two separately organized symposia, one on trade and environment and the other on trade and development.

Environment and development are intimately connected, especially in the lives of the third world poor whose livelihoods depend directly on ecological capital, not on finance. This two thirds of humanity has often been described as "eco-system people" who depend on their local ecosystems for their economic well being, in contrast to the planetary nomads whose lives depend on predation of the earth's resources.

Since it is the poor whose right to development needs protection and, since for the poor the right to development is based on a right to environment, the synergy between trade, environmental protection and sustainable development is best worked out through the lives of the two thirds majority. This synergy was also recognized in the right to development resolution of the UN.

The Declaration on Right to Development as contained in UN General Assembly Resolution 41/128 of 4 December 1986, declares:

"i.  Right to development is an inalienable human right by virtue of which every human person and all peoples are entitled to participate in, contribute to, and enjoy economic, social, cultural and political development, in which all human rights and fundamental freedoms can be fully realized.
ii. Human right to development also implies the full realization of the right of peoples to self-determination, which includes the exercise of their inalienable right to full sovereignty over all their natural wealth and resources."

The right to development was thus primarily articulated as an inalienable right to full sovereignty over natural resources. These, in the perspective of Third World communities, are the pre-conditions for environmental protection and conservation of resources.

* Director, Research Foundation for Science, Technology and Ecology, New Delhi, India.

The separation of the environment and development agenda in the separately organized meetings on trade and environment, and trade and development, will undo both environment and development in the south.

It will also unnecessarily orchestrate a north/south split since it will be northern governments who will call for use of trade related environmental measures and southern governments who will resist on the grounds of market access. It also pushes southern governments into equating market access and exports with "development", even though export-oriented policies are pushing the poor in their countries deeper into poverty, and threatening their very options for survival by diverting scarce land, water and biodiversity to meet the luxurious needs of rich northern consumers at the cost of their basic needs of food, water and livelihoods.

Separating "trade and environment" and "trade and development" in this artificial way shuts out third world people's development concerns. The trade-related environment measures that northern governments talk about are restricted to exports to northern markets. Thus, through a schizophrenic definition of the problem, the third world poor are excluded from the impact of trade liberalization on their lives, and solutions to their poverty are ignored. The environment and development apartheid also creates a north/south and rich/poor apartheid. Conflict rather than synergy is the legacy of apartheid.

# IMPACT OF TRADE LIBERALIZATION OF AGRICULTURE ON THE ENVIRONMENT AND THIRD WORLD POVERTY

Trade liberalization of agriculture through the Agreement on Agriculture of the Uruguay Round, and similar policies implemented through structural adjustment programmes of the World Bank and IMF, shifts agriculture from small scale biodiversity-based family farms to large scale monocultures for exports. On the one hand, this leads to non-sustainable use of land and water and destruction of biodiversity, on the other it leads to destruction of rural livelihoods and, hence, a decline in food entitlements and food rights.

Trade liberalization of agriculture has worsened third world poverty and aggravated environmental destruction.

Food and agriculture policies of third world countries are shifting from "food first" to "export first" policies. They are diverting scarce resources from food production and livelihood generation to luxury production for exports. Shrimps, flowers and vegetables are being produced for rich consumers in the north, while the poor in the south have their ecosystems and livelihoods destroyed. Both the environment and development rights of local communities are being undermined, as is evident in the case of shrimp exports and flower exports.[1]

"Export first" policies are also changing cropping patterns and input patterns, and threatening the environment through biodiversity erosion and chemical pollution.

---

[1]   Shiva, V. (1998), "Globalisation of Agriculture, Food Security and Sustainability", RFSTE, New Delhi.
    Shiva, V., A. H. Jafri and G. Bedi (1997), "Ecological Cost of Economic Globalization: Indian Experience", RFSTE, New Delhi.
    Shiva, V. and G. Karir (1997), "Chemmeenkettu: Towards Sustainable Aquaculture", RFSTE, New Delhi.

In addition, they are leading to severe underdevelopment and poverty by pushing poor peasants into debt and suicides.[2]

The central level of trade liberalization of agriculture is that countries do not need to grow their own food. They can export agricultural commodities and import food. As Timothy Josling, a free trade economist, states:

"A country's best guarantee of food security is a diversified export sector that provides the funds for needed imports, along with a sound macro economic policy to keep those exports competitive."

See Josling, T. (1998), *Agricultural Trade Policy: Completing the Reform*, Institute for International Economics.

One of the instruments of macroeconomic policy is devaluation. This increases the volume of exports while leading to a decline in the value. It also increases the costs of imports of basic commodities. Food security is therefore undermined because countries get trapped in the "trademill" of increasing exports, thus undermining domestic production of food, while they also have to bear a higher foreign exchange burden to import food.

The interests of global trade are clearly antithetical to the environmental interests and development interests of local communities who bear the ecological and socio-economic costs of environmentally destructive and anti-poor trade regimes. This impact needs to be fully assessed before a new round is initiated.

# BIODIVERSITY AND BIOTECHNOLOGY: AN EXAMPLE OF TRADE CONFLICT WITH BOTH ENVIRONMENT AND DEVELOPMENT

WTO-led trade policies are also threatening to undermine the Multilateral Environment Agreements such as the Convention on Biological Diversity (CBD). In the CTE, the conflicts between CBD and TRIPs has already been raised by India. Another serious conflict has emerged between the WTO agenda and the CBD agenda in the context of the Biosafety Protocol.

Biodiversity is the basis of all biological production in agriculture, forestry and fisheries. The right to biodiversity is both an environmental right and a development right.

The CBD creates an international economic discipline which ensures the conservation and sustainable use of biodiversity, and which recognizes the sovereign right to third world communities and countries to their biodiversity wealth. On the other hand, free trade rules create an environmental non-discipline which destroys biodiversity and encourages non-sustainable use.[3]

---

[2]    Shiva, V. and A. H. Jafri (1998), "Seeds of Suicide: Ecological and Human Costs of Globalization of Agriculture", RFSTE, New Delhi.
      Shiva, V. (1998), "Globalization of Agriculture, Food Security and Sustainability", RFSTE, New Delhi.
[3]    Shiva, V., A. H. Jafri and G. Bedi (1997), "Ecological Cost of Economic Globalization: Indian Experience", RFSTE, New Delhi.

Further, since biodiversity is the basis of 70 to 90 per cent of livelihoods in the Third World, destruction of biodiversity translates into destruction of development options for the poor.

The access to biodiversity for people's development is also undermined by the TRIPs agreement. TRIPs allows and encourages the piracy of indigenous knowledge, on the basis of which the majority of the third world meet their economic needs and protect their right to development.

The granting of Exclusive Marketing Rights (EMRs) to pharmaceutical and agrichemical corporations in India under WTO pressure is an example of trade-triggering processes of underdevelopment and de-development in the Third World.

Intellectual property rights (IPRs) on seeds will also increase the costs of agricultural production, pushing poor peasants into debt, and as in the case of India, into suicides.[4]

This is why third world communities, and environment and development groups in the north and south are calling for a removal of biodiversity and life-forms from the TRIPs agreement (see Action Aid, Patents and Food Security and Resolution of Global Citizens Meeting on Genetic Engineering and IPRs, 9 and 10 March 1999).

Biotechnology is an aspect of biodiversity utilization which has both environmental and development implications. Trade interests have introduced the unscientific assumption of "substantial equivalence" of GMOs and natural organisms. However, all scientific research is indicating that GMOs have unique ecological impacts which are different from the naturally occurring counterparts. Independent research is being censured as in the case of Dr. Arpad Pusztai's work which showed that genetically engineered potatoes had serious impacts on organs and immune systems of rats.

Article 19.3 of the CBD required parties to investigate the need for a biosafety protocol. Such a protocol was being negotiated over a six-year period and was to have been finalized in Cartegena, Columbia, in February 1999. An international environmental regulation was, however, subverted in the interests of trade. As the US representative stated, they could not accept environmental safety regulations of GMOs since this would undermine the trade rules of the WTO. There is clearly an absence of synergy between trade and environment in the important area of biosafety. The collapse of the biosafety negotiations is an example of the discordant relationship between safety objectives and profit objectives.

Further, the ecological impacts of GMOs affect the livelihoods of poor peasants through risks of creation of superweeds with herbicide-tolerant genes moving to related species, or creation of super pests as pests develop resistance to pesticides produced by genetically engineered plants. These ecological risks translate into a development cost for poor peasants. A trade and environment conflict is therefore also a trade and development conflict in the case of biosafety.

These are the reasons why calls for a five-year moratorium are emerging worldwide for a ban on commercialization while biosafety regulatory systems are put in place nationally and internationally, and while public sector research on the ecological and health risks, and ecological impact of GMOs is strengthened and promoted.

The fact that citizens both in the north and south, along with governments of the south are calling for biosafety regulations also establishes that this issue cannot be

---

[4]    Shiva, V. (1998), "Globalization of Agriculture, Food Security and Sustainability", RFSTE, New Delhi.

interpreted on the basis of north/south polarization or environment/development polarization.

## SUSTAINABLE AGRICULTURE: HARMONIZING TRADE, ENVIRONMENT AND DEVELOPMENT

Sustainable agriculture is a positive example of an activity which maximizes both environment and development objectives. However, current trade rules in the Agreement on Agriculture fail to build a synergy between development and environment by failing to provide incentives to sustainable agriculture.

Sustainable agriculture changes systems of agricultural production on the basis of environmental sustainability. This should have impact on trade, since trade measures need to reflect the positive externalities of sustainable agriculture and the negative externalities of non-sustainable industrial agriculture. However, environmental policies in the agricultural agreement have been put into a "green box" which excludes policies that are not deemed to have a major effect on production and trade. Green box policies include "produce retirement" programmes, "resource (land) retirement programmes", environmental programmes, marketing information, and infrastructure.

Governments are encouraged to offer financial support to farmers who wish to change their occupation, on the condition that they do not return to farming and will also have no say in what happens to the land they leave. Such "resource retirement" exemptions are also linked to re-privatization of agricultural land. Since only the affluent countries can pay their farmers to stop producing food and stop using land, the "green box" exemptions only apply to the developed countries.[5]

By this, sustainability has been blunted, and non-sustainable commodity production has been protected and promoted through the rules of the Agreement on Agriculture.

In the Third World, sustainable agriculture requires the protection of small peasant farms, the recognition of the multi-functional nature of agriculture and the exclusion of biodiversity and seeds from TRIPs monopolies.

Trade liberalization is, in fact, doing the reverse. It is promoting the extinction of small farms by undoing land reforms, and it is equating agriculture with manufacturing and, hence, undermining the ecological and cultural dimensions of agriculture. It is imposing monopolies on seeds through TRIPs.

The Uruguay Round Agreement calls for reviews of the Agreement on Agriculture and the TRIPs Agreement. Both these reviews should be based on criteria of sustainability and food rights. The reviews should also take seriously the civil society call for removal of biodiversity and seeds from TRIPs and staple foods from the Agreement on Agriculture.

If trade rules are to protect sustainable activities, rather than undermine them, sustainable agriculture needs to be at the core of an international regime governing trade in agriculture. Such a regime would be both pro-nature and pro-poor. It would

---

[5]   Shiva, V. and A. H. Jafri (1998), "Seeds of Suicide: Ecological and Human Costs of Globalization of Agriculture", RFSTE, New Delhi.

allow trade to operate within environmental and development limits and criteria, instead of undermining both environment and development objectives.

The Agreement on Agriculture needs to be reviewed on grounds of sustainability and justice. Environmental objectives require that non-sustainable and sustainable production are kept distinct throughout the life of a product, and the environment costs of production are internalized.

Development objectives require that livelihoods and food security are protected and a "bread box" created to allow countries to make policies for protection of livelihoods and food security.

Sustainable agriculture will be the test of the environment and development content of the WTO. If the WTO can change to mainstream sustainable agriculture, both environment and development objectives will be met. If the WTO continues to undermine sustainable agriculture, "environment" and "development" will remain "fig-leaves" to cover a non-sustainable and unjust trade regime.

# Chapter 14

# Part I.  Trade and the environment

## 2.  Synergies between trade liberalization, environmental protection, sustained economic growth and sustainable development

*David Spencer**

The chapters by Dan Esty and Martin Khor remind us that we need to take a balanced view of the relationship between trade liberalization and the environment. We must recognize the importance of appropriate environmental and social policies. These are needed to address market failure through promoting better valuation of environmental costs and benefits, and to deal with the complex interaction between poverty and environmental degradation.

The focus should be on identifying ways to capture the benefits of both trade liberalization and environmental protection. Dan Esty makes a very important point when he says that one of the central public policy challenges of our time is to ensure that the upsides of globalization can be achieved without suffering the potential downsides.

The economic growth associated with trade liberalization clearly imposes significant environmental and social challenges. Trade liberalization also holds out the promise of a more efficient allocation of resources, higher incomes that could be spent on promoting environmental and social objectives, and access to a wider range of goods, services and technologies.

It has become common to talk about the scope for "win-win" outcomes – the scope for trade reforms which will enhance the contribution of trade to promoting economic growth while also facilitating better environmental outcomes.

However, the big challenge is to also search for "win-win-win" (i.e. win-cubed not win-squared) outcomes – trade reforms that also take account of social equity concerns. Martin Khor's chapter highlights this point forcefully.

The WTO can make a vital contribution to enhancing the role of the multilateral trading system in promoting sustainable development. In particular, it can promote reform to a range of policy interventions which have too often exacerbated environmental problems while proving inefficient in achieving their intended objectives.

The wastage of resources through these policy failures is staggering. Estimates suggest that between US$500 billion and US$1,000 billion are provided in subsidies each year to the energy, transportation, water, agriculture and fisheries sectors. Some US$300 billion of this goes to agriculture alone.

---

* Deputy Secretary, Department of Foreign Affairs and Trade, Australia.

Some subsidies may be justified to address market failures, reward positive externalities or meet social objectives. But many studies have identified major inefficiencies with existing subsidy policies, so that often they are ineffective in achieving their objectives, accelerate depletion of natural resources and degradation of the environment, and accentuate rather than reduce inequities in income distribution.

The agriculture sector has seen some important reforms in recent years, but most of the continuing high levels of support in OECD countries takes the form of production-linked assistance that encourages overproduction and environmentally-harmful farm practices.

However, environmental concerns have increasingly been cited as one of the factors contributing to the "multifunctionality" of agriculture in OECD countries, and used as an argument to slow down the pressure for reform in these countries.

If it is considered that environmental or other social objectives require maintenance of some agricultural practices, this would be achieved most effectively by policies targeted at these practices and the desired environmental or social benefits.

Most importantly, the interests of other countries, and particularly of developing countries need to be fully taken into account. The multilateral trading system has been distorted for too long because of the absence of adequate discipline on agricultural policies. It would be a sad day if environmental concerns – which provide a strong argument in support of the urgency of greater agricultural policy reform – were used to slow down the pace of needed reforms.

Debates in the Committee on Trade and Environment have laid the basis for identifying a set of issues which should receive priority in future trade negotiations. Australia recently submitted a paper to the committee which tried to elaborate on this core set of reforms. Australia has joined with other Cairns Group countries and the United States in tabling an additional paper in the committee specifically addressing the issue of export subsidies.

In addition to the elimination of export subsidies there must be substantial reductions in agricultural domestic support and significant market access improvements.

Studies have also identified significant subsidies in the fisheries sector which have contributed to the serious problem of overcapacity in the world fishing fleets. There is increasing recognition of the need for urgent action to address the current unsustainable use of fishery resources. This will clearly require improvements in fishery management regimes, but there is also a need for urgent action in relation to fisheries subsidies and this should be another priority in future trade negotiations.

Improved transparency and greater monitoring and assessment of the size and forms of fisheries subsidies is a vital first step and we need to build on the efforts already underway to gather this information in several international fora.

We need to ensure an assessment of whether existing WTO disciplines can be used effectively in limiting the impacts on production and trade of fisheries subsidies or whether additional disciplines are necessary, particularly to eliminate subsidies that contribute to fisheries overcapacity. Australia has joined Iceland, New Zealand, the Philippines and the United States in issuing a joint statement on 12 March on this important issue.

Another priority for the WTO must be the elimination or reduction of tariff peaks and tariff escalation for a range of sectors where these remain significant. In particular, tariff escalation may hamper the ability of countries that export unprocessed resource-based commodities to innovate and diversify their export structures through moving into greater value-added activities.

The WTO Ministerial Conference in Seattle at the end of 1999 offered an opportunity for the international community to make a firm commitment to address major trade distortions. This must include tariff peaks and tariff escalation in sectors like agriculture, textiles and clothing and leather goods, and agricultural and fisheries subsidies.

On trade grounds alone WTO Members should recognize the importance of delivering substantial reforms in these areas. But the severity of many environmental and social problems provides an additional imperative for early, substantial reforms in these areas.

These reforms will only be achieved if there is the political will to accept the need for reform despite domestic sensitivities. The WTO by itself cannot ensure the engagement of this needed political will. This is where public opinion and public debate amongst WTO Members will have a crucial role.

Clearly, we need to keep the contribution which trade reform can make to sustainable development in perspective. Many other actions are also needed. These include the adoption of appropriate environmental and social policies and responding to the development aspirations of developing countries. But trade reform can make a vital contribution to sustainable development.

Given the urgency and seriousness of many economic, social and environmental problems, we must initiate significant reforms to a range of distorting policy interventions. What is needed now is a vigorous public debate. We must be able to seize the opportunity presented by the Seattle Ministerial Conference to agree on a forward-looking agenda for trade negotiations that genuinely responds to the needs of the new millennium.

# Chapter 15

## Part I.  Trade and the environment

### 2.  Synergies between trade liberalization, environmental protection, sustained economic growth and sustainable development

*David Schorr**

This chapter concerns fishery subsidies, an issue to which the WWF is devoting substantial resources. However, it also makes some remarks putting this discussion of synergies into a broader context. The topic of fishery subsidies is becoming increasingly familiar. This chapter will simply review a few basic facts.

First, fishery subsidies amount to tens of billions of dollars annually, and take a wide variety of forms. While much smaller in absolute amount than subsidies in the agriculture or energy sectors, they amount to an estimated 20–25% of the total value of the landed catch of commercial fish annually. This is equivalent to the heaviest subsidies in other sectors.

Secondly, subsidies at this level have inevitable trade distorting effects, as has been repeatedly recognized in this chamber by delegations and the WTO Secretariat alike.

Thirdly, some of these subsidies have clear negative impacts on development. Many subsidies support the operation of distant water fleets fishing off the coasts of developing countries, where they offer what amounts to unfair – and economically inefficient – competition with local fishermen. Moreover, much of this fishing takes place under access agreements that are negotiated in the context of a power dynamic that does not always return benefits to the developing country partners. These facts have consequences both for the growth of developing countries and for their food security.

Fourthly, the environmental impacts of these subsidies is undeniable. It is now broadly acknowledged that many of these subsidies contribute directly or indirectly to the over-capacity of the world's fishing fleets that today helps drive over-fishing. Some experts estimate that the world's fleets are up to 250% larger than can be sustainably utilized. The UN Food and Agriculture Organization has concluded last month a voluntary plan of action for managing fishing capacity, including the reduction of harmful subsidies. Beyond over-capacity, the link between fishery subsidies and the depletion of fish stocks is increasingly clear. While the data is still too scarce, preliminary analyses suggest that the direct link between subsidies and depletion is real. The most depleted fisheries are often those in which the most

---

* Director, Sustainable Commerce Program, World Wildlife Fund, USA.

heavily subsidized fleets are active. Conversely, the most heavily subsidized fleets appear to be over-represented in depleted fisheries.

In essence, we – governments and taxpayers – are paying for the plunder of our ocean resources, and we are doing so while impeding development and distorting trade. Not bad for one day's work.

I do not mean to suggest that the problem is simple. Let me start by stating the clear premise that not all fishery subsidies are bad. Some may contribute to the transition to sustainability by helping reduce capacity or by encouraging the adoption of cleaner technologies. Others may play a legitimate and vital role in the development strategies of some developing countries. We must recognize that even as we seek to reduce the capacity of the world's fleets in aggregate, some developing country fleets may need to grow in order to meet the legitimate development goals of their countries.

What will be needed will be careful work to agree on how to distinguish good subsidies from bad, along with new international disciplines to eliminate the bad while monitoring the good to make sure that they remain so.

Another important problem that complicates efforts to reduce harmful subsidies is the continuing lack of good data about the specific nature of existing subsidies. We actually don't know very well where the money goes. I will return to this theme later.

The FAO process now getting underway may help address both the need for better definitions and more data. Yet the FAO process is a voluntary effort, carried out essentially at the national level, with few mechanisms for well-coordinated international work. We need to go further, towards new, binding, international disciplines on fishery subsidies.

The WTO has a clear role to play, in three ways.

First, we need much better enforcement of current WTO rules – particularly Article 25 of the Subsidies and Countervailing Measures, which requires notification to the WTO of all subsidies, as defined by the Subsidies Code. It is a scandal – an absolute scandal – to observe the wholesale disregard for this rule in most cases. Last September, WWF published a paper in which we concluded, after a careful review of WTO notification submissions, that 90% of all fishery subsidies – nine out of ten subsidy dollars – are administered in violation of Article 25's notification requirement. These subsidies are either not notified, or notified with such inadequate information that the notices are essentially useless. Given the "lose-lose-lose" nature of fishery subsidies, it is no wonder most WTO members prefer to hide their subsidies than comply with WTO's rules. This lack of compliance must end. I note that the EU has shown leadership in improving the quality of its notifications, and that the United States is making efforts to do the same. We must complete this process.

Secondly, it is important to maintain some aspects of the current SCM Agreement that are scheduled to sunset this year. In particular, I am referring to the "serious prejudice" clause of Article 6.1 of the agreement, which could play a vital role in allowing challenges to fishery subsidies that are actionable under today's rules.

Thirdly, we need to go beyond the current rules, to negotiate new, binding international disciplines on fishery subsidies. Current WTO rules cannot do the job alone, neither can the voluntary FAO process. The WTO should join FAO, UNEP, and other relevant bodies to launch negotiations of new disciplines as soon as possible.

# SYNERGIES

Let me now turn to several comments about the context in which we are discussing "win-win-win" synergies.

We have been hearing about "win-wins" since the birth of the WTO. In fact, it used to be fashionable among some members of the trade elite to assume that all you needed to do to accomplish synergies is to liberalize trade, and that the other "wins" would follow automatically. Fortunately, this rhetoric has now grown rather stale. There is a broader recognition, evident in many of the interventions here, that achieving "win-win-wins" will require real political will and hard work – work to negotiate the necessary outcomes.

In this regard, I would like to note the importance of the statement by the governments of Australia, Iceland, New Zealand, the Philippines, and the United States calling for the WTO to pursue work on fishery subsidies. To my knowledge, this is the first time any serious effort has been made to give priority to a topic for negotiation here based largely on a concern with sustainability, rather than a concern with the kind of traditional commercial interests that otherwise drive the WTO agenda. These five governments deserve real commendation for their leadership in this regard. They have shown the first evidence of the necessary political will, and I look forward to the hard work yet to come. I urge other WTO members to join their initiative without delay.

It bears noting that the willingness to engage in "win-win-win" synergies by WWF and others amounts to something of a leap of faith – some might say a misguided leap of faith – for those of us who have had very little reason to believe the WTO will produce results for sustainable development other than by accident. This willingness to consider engagement is a result both of changes in the political context, and of the substantive posture of the issues.

It represents a significant opportunity for a more productive dialogue, for a dialogue quite different from the non-dialogue over using trade standards to impose environmental standards which environmentalists are mistakenly supposed to desire. This comment leads me to close by turning to five essential points in which "win-win-wins", as well as broader reforms of the WTO, should be viewed. These are pre-requisites for success in both endeavors.

# PRE-REQUISITES FOR SUCCESS

First is to recognize the need to limit the WTO's role on the environment. The polarized rhetoric of the trade and environment debate has convinced some governments that environmentalists seek to use the WTO to advance a broad agenda that would inappropriately burden the WTO. The real environmental objective, however, is just the opposite. Current and emerging conflicts between WTO rules and environmental policies begin with the failure of the WTO to recognize that its operations already bring the WTO into direct contact with environmental laws and values. An explicit recognition of these trade and environment relationships would be the first step toward limiting the WTO's responsibility for managing them, in favor of an enhanced role for other governmental organizations and authorities.

I would like to stress that some of the best opportunities to realize "win-win-win" synergies lie outside the mandate and scope of the WTO, and can be much better pursued through "parallel" arrangements within regional trade agreements. We have examples already of such parallel arrangements that focus on convergence, i.e., *convergence*, not harmonization, of environmental standards, and that are contributing to the kind of international cooperation that must underlie the "win-win-win" agenda.

Secondly, the role of sustainability assessments is fundamental. A first and indispensable step towards rationalizing debate over the relationship between the WTO and sustainable development will be for the WTO and its members to conduct thorough assessments of the environmental and social impacts of WTO rules. To be meaningful, these assessments must be both retrospective (looking at the impacts of the Uruguay Round) and prospective. Impact assessments should begin now, and continue in stages until the conclusion of any new negotiating round. The process for such assessments should be fully participatory, and they should aim to identify areas in which existing WTO agreements and new negotiations have or will have significant positive or negative social and environmental effects. WWF is committed, with other NGOs, to working on such assessments.

Thirdly, achieving sustainable development will ultimately require an integrated approach to economic, social and environmental policies. If the WTO is to live up to its mandate to support sustainable development, that integration will have to be reflected in both the WTO's internal operations and in its relations with external organizations. Internally, the time has come to "mainstream" environmental concerns into the work of all relevant WTO bodies and agreements, rather than leaving the topic to the debate of a single, disconnected committee. Externally, the WTO must forge serious working relationships with international bodies expert in environmental and developmental concerns.

Formalizing such relationships could allow the WTO to "outsource" policy judgments that are beyond its competence and abilities (e.g., judging the environmental efficacy of disputed national measures and of hypothetical alternatives to them), while opening avenues for developing innovative packages of integrated policies (e.g., in the course of efforts to discipline subsidies that harm both trade and the environment).

Fourthly, the issue of market access. Market access is not only a developing country concern – it can also be an environmental concern, both to address tariff escalations that increase pressure on the natural resource base, and to address the poverty that does often drive environmental degradation in the developing world. I call on the United States, Europe, and others to give serious consideration to recent calls for zeroing out all tariffs in products from least developed countries, and I reject the hollow excuses offered by policymakers who argue that since average tariffs on LLDC products are already very low, this objective has already been met. We must frankly confront concerns about the potential of environmental reforms of the WTO to reduce market access, particularly of developing countries. Environmental reforms must include a commitment to ensure adequate safeguards against green protectionism.

Fifthly, and finally, I would like to make a comment on the role of multilateralism. The path towards sustainable development must be essentially a multilateral one. Unilateral environmental trade measures should only be an instrument of last resort, and do not constitute a lasting solution to the problems that trigger their use.

Situations where they are used generally signal a failure of the existing multilateral rules, and the need for urgent adjustment of those rules. In the trade and environment context increasing the effectiveness of multilateral environmental agreements and ensuring that the WTO does not usurp their jurisdiction, or undermine them in any other way, will be a vital step towards rules that more effectively promote multilateralism in place of unilateralism. WTO Members must act responsibly to support multilateral action on all the major challenges facing the international community, and not just those pertaining to trade relations.

We can achieve synergies for trade, development, and the environment. But these synergies will require a broad and deep commitment to working for real change in the approach of the WTO to the management of globalization. The three priorities we seek in "win-win-win" are inherently and inextricably linked. We need each other, as surely as we can each block progress on the others' agendas. The next six months will be a crucial test of the WTO and its member governments to respond to this challenge. It is a test we cannot afford to fail.

# Chapter 16

## Part I. Trade and the environment

### 3. Interaction between the trade and environmental communities

*Prince Sadruddin Aga Khan*

I would like to offer a few brief comments on the interaction between trade and environment communities.

To begin with, I would like to express my hope that the two high-level symposia on the relationships between trade and environment, and trade and development will yield real progress towards the common goal of sustainable development.

This high-level symposium on trade and environment had its genesis in a proposal made by Sir Leon Brittan at the Policing the Global Economy Conference convened by the Bellerive Foundation and Globe International in Geneva last March. The concept of a high-level meeting was later supported at the 50th anniversary celebrations of the multilateral trading system, where President Clinton and others made reference to the need for such a meeting to "break the log-jam" on trade and environment issues.

An essential step towards breaking this "log-jam" is improving interaction between trade, environment and other affected communities. It is my fervent hope that this process will not end here, but that we can take it through the next Ministerial and continue building on this foundation.

# Chapter 17

# Part I.  Trade and the environment

## 3.  Interaction between the trade and environmental communities

*David Runnalls* *

The International Institute for Sustainable Development has been one of the few from the environment and sustainable development community which has consistently held that trade liberalization, with proper safeguards, can contribute to the achievement of sustainable development.

Indeed, I would argue, in some cases, that the income generated by increased market access and trade could be critical to finding the large sums of money which developing countries will require to make the transition to sustainable development. But we are very rapidly becoming a threatened if not an endangered species. The trade community is in danger of losing its constituency for liberalization with both the environment and the development communities, north and south.

A few years ago this might not have mattered, but the experience of the Multilateral Agreement on Investment, and I may add the experience of the fast-track negotiations in the United States, should have taught us all by now, that civil society feels that it should and can have a real influence on the debate over trade liberalization.

I do not think it is at all far fetched to assume that any millennium round agreements could face real problems in national parliaments and legislatures without further progress made in the incorporation of sustainable development and environmental considerations into the work of the WTO. As Sylvia Ostry has said, if the trade system does not find a way to accommodate the legitimate aspirations and demands of civil society for sustainable development, it faces a crisis of its own legitimacy. For those of you who make a living in the trade business, you will know that is not a statement that she makes lightly.

I would suggest that very real efforts must be made well before the beginnings of the millennium round, in fact well before the beginnings of the Seattle meeting, to demonstrate to ordinary citizens of the world that liberalization can bring positive sustainable development benefits. And I deliberately say sustainable development. I was one of the few speakers at the very first GATT trade and environment NGO meeting to make the connection between "trade and sustainable development" rather than the rather simple-minded connection between "trade and environment".

Perhaps the most unfortunate aspect of these symposia is the physical separation of the issues of trade and environment from trade and development. Those of us who believe that sustainable development, unlike trade, is an end in itself (as the

---

* Interim President, International Institute for Sustainable Development, Canada.

OECD said), believe that it is not possible to separate the environmental issues from the sustainable development issues.

What then can be done over the next few months to restore some confidence in the trading system on the part of civil society, and I would suggest on the part of many southern countries? I should preface my remarks by saying that much has been made of the failure of the Rio bargain. I was in Rio; I realized the bargain; I now realize that it has failed. I think it has failed for reasons that we have not quite appreciated, and this I think will be of interest to our colleagues in the south. I think the real bargain failed principally because the countries of the north failed to take the northern agenda particularly seriously.

The northern agenda of climate change, deforestation and biodiversity has not been a high priority for most northern governments since the time of Rio. As a result, the other part of the bargain, which is trade, access to markets, technology transfer and finance has also fallen off the table.

I would suggest to our colleagues from the south that we may well see in the millennium round the real possibility of the south making gains on its part of its agenda in exchange for some progress from the north on issues of sustainability. If we are right that trade liberalization is not on its last legs, but on shaky ground in many northern countries, northern governments will be pressured to include sustainable development considerations in the next round. I would suggest to our southern colleagues that offers a real possibility for a new bargain.

What can we do immediately? First I would support the call, made by Sir Leon Brittan, for a sustainability assessment, not an environment assessment, but a sustainability assessment of the next round. It is much more difficult to do than an environmental assessment, but we have many of the necessary tools. I would suggest, as well, that it is possible that one could begin to test the methodology for this sort of assessment by doing a post-hoc assessment of the sustainability impacts of the Uruguay Round. Here I would urge all of us not to make the perfect the enemy of the good – these things will be difficult to do and it will take us time to work out the methodology.

As a second step, I would suggest to the WTO that the OECD offers a very useful example when it comes to "mainstreaming sustainable development". On taking office, the Secretary General of the OECD appointed a group of 14 wise men and women to advise him on how to integrate sustainable development into the work of the organization. I would suggest similar action at the WTO well before the beginning of serious negotiations on the millennium round. Sustainable development is not just environmental protection – sustainable development touches on all the work of the WTO and needs to be built into the work of all of the organs of the WTO.

Thirdly, the WTO must become far more serious about sustainable development in the south.

Fourthly, is the idea we have been promoting of a standing conference on trade and environment, to bring together civil society, governments and the private sector as well as trade and people involved in the multilateral, environmental agreements to provide a forum for discussion about the relationship between trade and the MEAs.

Fifthly, at some stage we will have to take seriously the whole question of PPMs. I would argue that rules for PPMs, and rules for the use of the PPMs, are better than the current system. But I would suggest that when the climate change convention comes into force, with its multiple targets and multiple requirements, this whole question of when it is proper to apply PPMs to particular products will come under discussion in major way.

Sixthly is the wish, which has been raised a number of times, for much greater transparency in the work of the WTO.

Finally, we would strongly suggest that the WTO does not attempt to deal with the issue of investment in the next millennium round. The kinds of regime necessary to deal with investment and investment rules are very different from the kinds of regime needed to apply rules to one time only trade transactions.

# Chapter 18

# Part I. Trade and the environment

## 3. Interaction between the trade and environmental communities

*Michael Windfuhr**

## INTRODUCTION

Talking about the interaction between the trade and environment communities means, first and foremost, talking about improving the existing interaction between these communities. It also involves taking into account several different types of actors and organizational levels of both the communities, as well as other communities whose interests are subject to the relationship between trade and environment.

I will attempt to discuss this issue of interaction in five steps. This chapter will start with some general remarks on the need for a better integration of trade and environment concerns in the development of future trade policies, as well as at the organizational level. It will include benchmarks for building up an effective – or improving the existing – interaction between the trade and environment communities. Then, elements for improved interaction between trade and environment communities will be examined at different levels:

- firstly, at the national level;
- secondly, at the intergovernmental level; and
- thirdly, at the level of civil society focusing on public interest actors.

The chapter will conclude with some ideas for instruments to improve the interaction between the trade and environment communities and with recommendations for first steps.

The German NGO Forum on Trade and Environment was established in the follow-up process to the Rio Conference on Environment and Development. It represents most of the important development and environment national governmental organizations (NGOs) of the country. The trade working group started in 1993 during the Uruguay Round of the GATT and has become an important contact point for information dissemination, as well as for keeping regular contacts with government and parliamentarians. The ideas presented in this chapter have been discussed in the German NGO community in our common work on trade issues during the last five years. Nevertheless, the selection of arguments and proposals remains the

---

*Coordinator of the Working Group on Trade of the German NGO-Forum on Environment and Development, and Vice President of Germanwatch, e.V.

responsibility of the author. Therefore, the chapter cannot be read as a position paper, but it draws on ideas discussed in the NGO community.

The arguments below are formulated in a short, direct and concrete manner, bearing in mind that much more supportive arguments could well be added to them. The beginning arguments deal with the question of why an improved interaction of trade and environment communities will be useful, and will create synergies. The following four sections present concrete proposals for improving the interaction. Not all the proposals may be easy to incorporate into the WTO framework of rules and procedures. It is also obvious that some of them may find a lot of resistance from WTO Members. Nevertheless the Trade and Environment Symposium offers an important chance to raise concerns stemming from the ongoing debate of NGOs and other civil society groups.

Many of these ideas are not only valid for improving the interaction of the trade and environment communities, but also for the interaction with other communities. Even if NGOs, by their nature, are often single issue organizations, it is the challenge of sustainable development, which requires an integrated approach to many problems, that has widened the analyses and often the work of NGOs considerably.

## THE NEED TO BETTER INTEGRATE THE TRADE AND ENVIRONMENT COMMUNITIES

The central aims of international cooperation set forth by the international community are contained in the Charter of the United Nations. Kofi Annan, the Secretary General of the United Nations, has pointed out on several occasions during the last two years that the overarching obligations for states under international law come from the Charter, especially on implementing human rights. Moreover, in the series of world summits at the beginning of this decade, most states have committed themselves to a comprehensive policy framework, spelled out in different declarations and plans of actions. The central objective of these commitments is the realization of sustainable development – which means the right of every individual to a full implementation of all human rights, including economic, social and cultural human rights, and the right to a safe environment and to development.

Even if the understanding of sustainable development, and which policy means are best to implement it, still allows some debate, an increasing common understanding has emerged in the last few years which realizes the need for a coherent policy approach in different policy arenas. As mentioned in the Agenda 21, trade policy is an important way to foster sustainable development. Yet full implementation of sustainable development requires parallel endeavors in many policy fields. Therefore, it requires a great amount of policy coordination and policy coherence to find synergies, and to avoid conflicts between different instruments.

The objective of better interaction between different policy areas calls for an identification of synergies, but also for an identification of possible conflicting obligations and possible controversies about the use of means and instruments. It is, therefore, of utmost importance to debate about a better interaction between different policy areas. An improved coordination, and the development of a coherent policy approach, is especially needed on trade policy, and other objectives like environment and development, due to the increasing role international economic policies play at national levels. In both directions (synergies and conflicts) a better interaction can help to find the right measures, and can avoid the use of conflicting instruments or the pursuit of contradictory aims.

The implementation of a comprehensive concept of sustainable development – as mentioned in the Rio Principles, the Agenda 21 and many additional policy documents – requires that environment and development policy objectives should not be seen as separate issues or considered as side events of international economic policy making (which can only be dealt with in side agreements or under exemption clauses, or according to special and differential treatment provisions). Coherence in policy development requires a mainstreaming of these concerns in all international economic policy making. They should not even be separated under different items. They need to be seen as policy areas whose progressive realization also depends on successes in all other policy areas.

Both issues have been separated in the organization of these two symposia. On the one hand, the idea of combining them in the same time period demonstrates that both issues are equally important and interrelated. On the other, it misses the chance to link the two differing policy areas together, thus showing an understanding of their interconnection. This could make it more difficult to integrate the unique challenges both areas face regarding trade policy instruments. Moreover, it decreases the chance to view synergies between implementing trade, environment and development policies. It also makes it more difficult to mark possible trade-offs between the two topics, and thus it becomes even harder to limit or decrease concerns which certain country groups will have when they tackle either of the two issues.

Without taking adequate development concerns into consideration, it could be difficult to provide more space for environmental protection. Moreover, without taking care of environmental limitations, development policy could become self-destructive. It will be of great importance for the future agenda of the WTO to mainstream both issues at the same time when considering their implications, or challenges, to trade policy.

The importance of the international trade regime has grown considerably with the Uruguay Round and the establishment of the WTO. Trade rules are setting standards for more and more areas of national policy making. The dispute settlement provides, at the same time, one of the few powerful enforcement mechanisms in international law. It is this far-reaching scope of the multilateral trade rules and disciplines which makes it essential to study and discuss linkages to other policy areas.

A greater and improved interaction can help to raise public concerns about the actual or potential impact of certain trade rules on the environment, or other policy areas. An early detection of possible impacts can help to design policies which then can be more adequately oriented towards mitigating, or minimizing, negative impacts on the environment, or other policy areas. This can lead to deeper policy integration, a wider acceptance of, and broad compliance with, trade rules, and an improved overall effectiveness of the trade policy regime in the light of sustainable development. Integrating concerns and needs, as well as respecting limitations coming from other policy areas, will be one of the biggest challenges for the WTO system in the next millennium.

The implementation of sustainable development should be carried out through the WTO. The international community needs different fora, rule-based implementation systems and specialized organizations to fully guarantee and implement sustainable development. What is needed is to increase the overall effectiveness of the system, and the mutual recognition and respect of policy regimes.

Therefore the WTO has to respect and consider other concerns in developing their own rules. Specific mechanisms for conciliation or solution at the international level are needed for possible cleavages, or conflicts, between the challenges of differing policy areas, between possibly conflicting obligations under different international treaties or conventions. These cleavages or conflicts cannot be overcome in the dispute settlement of one policy area alone. The intergovernmental organizations or fora dealing with development, environment and human rights issues need to be taken as seriously as those dealing with economic matters. The current bias towards strengthening only parts of the institution at the international level, while other areas suffer from shortages in money and influence, will not foster long term sustainable development.

Discussing the interaction between the trade and environment communities should bring forward new ideas, instruments and institutional mechanisms to enhance the policy effectiveness at the international and national level towards sustainable development. This means that concerns about development must have an integral influence on the interaction between the environment and trade communities. The interaction has to be more than just a friendly exchange from both sides – environmental purists and trade liberalization advocates. Taking on board at an early stage concerns from other policy areas can help to establish a rule-based trading system favouring sustainable development.

The forms of interaction have to be innovative and rule-based, giving both sides equal access. They should also follow the principles of democracy, participation and transparency. Participatory activities without an honest, open dialogue with clear rules will neither strengthen policy effectiveness nor obtain public acceptance for multilateral disciplines.

## INTERACTION OF TRADE AND ENVIRONMENT COMMUNITIES AT THE NATIONAL LEVEL

Problems of policy coherence between trade and environment policies are not only, or not even especially, a problem at the international level. They start at the national level, where inter-ministerial arrangements, like regular consultations, common hearings, etc., are still not the rule. The importance of economic or trade ministries is much higher than those ministries dealing with environmental issues in most countries, as well as in the Commission of the EU.

Interactions of trade and environment communities must start at the national level in order to achieve greater policy coherence at the international level. The impact of trade policies on the environment (as well as in other policy fields) are felt most keenly at the national level, or even regional or local levels. An assessment of policy outcome, and the identification of possible conflicts, must therefore start at the national level, which, in turn, would make international politics more sensitive and responsive to these problems.

The interaction should best involve actors at different levels within national politics – from the government, the administration, the legislative bodies, the judicial system and also the broader public. All these levels should be sensitized and should raise concerns if necessary. European NGOs observed during the Uruguay Round, and afterwards, that parliaments at the national level were very often badly informed about developments in the new trade negotiations at the international levels. Almost all national assessments were lacking an estimation about possible outcomes and consequences which the new international disciplines would have.

An expanding body of international disciplines – which limits the capacities of states to govern their own policies – requires a careful judgment about possible consequences. This is not to discourage international solutions to global problems. On the contrary, it is to encourage a better and more informed assessment of policy outcomes, especially focussing on cross-sector outcomes.

The WTO should, therefore, encourage and support activities of governments to assess existing and future trade policy outcomes. Governments should hold regular consultations with parliamentarians and with other groups concerned, or directly affected, by trade policies. Assistance from the international level would be very valuable, especially for all those countries who are already facing problems in adapting their national legislative and administrative procedures to WTO disciplines.

Moreover, WTO Members should consult at the national level with non-state actors, and especially with NGOs, before a position is taken with regard to WTO matters and negotiations. Regular consultations between governments and NGOs should be encouraged, especially concerning new negotiations.

These groups should also take part in pursuing a transparent and public assessment, as mentioned above. An assessment at the national level should not be limited to economic consequences alone. A sustainable development assessment, for instance, could be of great help in identifying relevant problems linked to existing international trade policy obligations, or to possible new trade rules or disciplines. The DG 1 together with DG 11 of the Commission of the EU have recently decided to pursue such an assessment. A first study of a possible methodology has been undertaken by the Commission. An international NGO has also presented a paper with first ideas for such a sustainable development assessment of trade policies.

## INTERACTION OF TRADE AND ENVIRONMENT COMMITTEES AT THE INTERGOVERNMENTAL LEVEL

An improved interaction faces several problems due to the current structure of work inside the WTO.

- The many meetings makes it difficult for countries, even those with large delegations to the WTO, to follow ongoing business. Not every country has interest in all fields of WTO negotiations but only eight countries have accredited more than ten diplomats with the WTO, while 24 of the WTO Members do not have a mission in Geneva and six do not even have a mission in Europe. This enlarges the problem for governments regarding their daily work at the WTO, because it is already difficult enough to follow all regular issues, not to mention other policy areas like environment or development.
- The problem is aggravated due to the fact that many meetings are held informally, which makes it very difficult for those not present to know what has been discussed, even if the chairperson summarizes the results at the beginning of the

next formal session. Probably both trends are difficult to stop because the WTO is dealing with many issues and informal meetings can contribute to better negotiations. Nevertheless, an urgent need exists to reconsider the working structure, because it is becoming difficult for developing countries to fully follow all the negotiations. Also the "informalization" is reportedly increasing, making it even more difficult for other observers (UN agencies and the like) to follow the debate. For example, the Committee on Trade and Environment (CTE) often meets on an informal basis, making it difficult for observers to follow the work.

- Another sensitive area is the de-restriction of documents. Even if NGOs can see the need to have restricted papers in all international negotiations to facilitate compromises, they can also see a considerable difference between the release of documents in other international areas, as in the UN system. Even in very sensitive areas like human rights, countries want to have much more open and transparent access to documents and agendas for future meetings.

So long as agendas, or certain drafts of important papers, are not made public in advance, interaction between the trade and environment communities (and also others, like the development community) will be weak. Making WTO documents available to the public, both in draft as well as in final form, remains an important task. The agenda of important meetings should also be made available early enough to facilitate NGOs, inter-governmental organizations (IGOs) or other communities having input, especially at the national level before WTO Members have fixed their own positions. Dissemination of documents should also mean more than just putting documents on the world wide web. It would be important to develop mechanisms for a timely and broad dissemination of documents, such as mailing lists and information points.

Part of a strategy to improve the interaction between the trade and environment communities at the intergovernmental level would be to strengthen the cooperation between the WTO and other relevant IGOs. Formally, the WTO has cooperation agreements with other agencies working in the field of international economic policies. This should be widened to other relevant IGOs (including FAO, WHO, the human rights system, etc.). A broader cooperation has already started relative to LLDCs. Some observers have also been invited to the formal meetings of the CTE. Nevertheless, more cooperation agreements should help to improve capacity building inside the trade community.

The same is true for improved cooperation with the Multilateral Environmental Agreements (MEAs). They should have regular consultative status with the WTO because it would help to identify possible conflicts, but also synergies. It can increase policy coherence. Despite the still unclear relationship between obligations under MEAs and under the WTO, it is important to consider independent institutions which could handle disputes or cleavages between them.

An important part of developing an understanding of the linkages between trade and environment is done through dispute settlements in the WTO. Improving the interaction between the trade and environment communities must also include dispute settlement, especially because awareness by the public and Member states in the WTO dispute settlement process is growing rapidly with respect to the importance of the process. Review of the dispute settlement understanding (DSU) will increase transparency, and also confidence in the dispute settlement process.

Without changing the government-to-government character of the dispute settlement, transparency and participation in the process can be increased considerably, allowing a much better integration of concerns from other policy areas.

Two steps seem to be of first importance to increase the interaction at that level:

- the early release of documents and files, including not only the submissions but also any analyses like background information provided by the WTO Secretariat or panel reports; and
- offers to parties other than the participating states (non-participating Members as well as the general public) to submit written or even oral statements.

Again a comparison with other international arenas, especially the UN system shows that release of important documents, and also the right to submit written or even oral contributions, is often possible not only for other IGOs, but also for NGOs. This is also true in other highly sensitive areas where duties or obligations of governments are negotiated and fixed.

# INTERACTION AT THE INTERNATIONAL LEVEL WITH CIVIL SOCIETY GROUPS

At several points in this paper the role of civil society groups, such as NGOs and social movements, have been mentioned as important partners in improving the interaction between the trade and environment communities. NGOs have some crucial knowledge and valuable information, because they often represent groups which are directly affected. This will help any assessment of the effects of trade policies on other policy areas. This broader participation can help to identify concerns of the general public early on, and to increase policy effectiveness by avoiding negative results. Article V of the Marrakesh Agreement establishing the WTO allows the General Council to "make appropriate arrangements for consultation and cooperation with non-governmental organizations with matters related to those of the WTO". The current procedure by the WTO of inviting NGOs to certain fora is based on the simple fact that they are known to the WTO because of their activities in the field of trade policy. It has been a very informal arrangement.

To improve the interaction and cooperation, probably the best option would be to make an arrangement for consultation and cooperation similar to that which has developed in the UN system under the Economic and Social Council. In that procedure, NGOs can apply for consultative status. An intergovernmental commission grants the status which then gives NGOs, depending on their status, certain rights to make oral and written submissions, or even at the highest level to add issues to the agenda. The ECOSOC procedure was, for a long time, only accessible to international NGOs but has also been recently opened to national NGOs.

Such a formal procedure is a much better way to deal with many concerns governments do have towards the huge number of NGOs and the question of legitimacy and representation of NGOs. Again, the experience with ECOSOC procedure shows that it should only grant such status if certain criteria are fulfilled. Furthermore, the experience with NGOs in other fora shows that, in almost all issues, there are only a limited number of NGOs involved and eager to contribute to policy developments at the international level. In those fora where a huge number of NGOs are interested to contribute or observe, the NGOs have developed their own way of dealing with the representative issue by creating special subgroups (caucuses), which prepare common statements, etc.

Establishing a consultative status system inside the WTO for civil society groups may take some time because it may also be controversial. Therefore some immediate steps could be taken to improve the participation of civil society groups. Most of them have already been mentioned. For example, increased openness and transparency in the access to papers and the agenda, allowing for more participation at the national level but also in the WTO itself, including accepting inputs from relevant groups to the dispute settlement procedure.

## SPECIAL ISSUES IMPORTANT FOR IMPROVING THE INTERACTION

Members report regularly to the WTO about national implementation of the trade policy review mechanism. This procedure could also be used for giving the results of national assessments on the impact trade policies have on other areas, such as environment, food security, etc. To improve the interaction between the trade and environment communities, and other communities as well, it would be even better and more comprehensive to use other regular reporting mechanisms at the UN level. These could be used to address synergies and conflicts between trade policy measures and other policy areas in which Members have obligations under international law.

Some relevant fora include the following:

- the Commission on Sustainable Development (CSD), which has already started to discuss the interlinkages between trade policy and sustainable development;
- the ILO, which has been mentioned in the final documents from the ministerial meeting in Singapore as having importance; and
- the Subcommission on the Prevention of Discrimination and the Protection of Minorities, which drafted a resolution in August 1998 that all future trade and investment agreements should be assessed concerning their human rights implications.

These examples show some of the possibilities to improve interaction between the trade and other communities by using existing instruments. This should not be done in a hostile, competitive manner. It should be used to identify existing and potential synergies, and to identify potential conflicts. This will help to find timely and adequate solutions, increasing overall policy coherence at the international level.

Early assessment and early warning with respect to potential conflicts will be the most important elements in any strategy to improve the interaction between the trade and environment communities. One of the most precise ways of identifying possible conflicts is to give NGOs and other affected groups a forum for making complaints. Such a complaint or petition mechanism can start on an informal base. A similar instrument for opening a discussion on specific problem areas would be to nominate special investigators or rapporteurs, who would have a mandate to collect information and to prepare reports. Practical options like these could improve access of civil society groups to the system, and they could be started in the near future.

From a civil society perspective, the time-frame is of great importance, especially if a new round is to be started, with new complex issues within an increasingly complex system. Even now, all the consequences of existing agreements are not adequately understood, neither their possible consequences for the developing world, nor for the environment. The complexity of decisions within the dispute settlement procedure is increasing and time is needed to understand the linkages between different policy areas. Complexity should not stop us from developing multilateral disciplines, but it should be understood adequately before taking up new comprehensive obligations. Policy coherence toward sustainable development for all human beings is required so as to avoid conflict between the international obligations of states.

# Chapter 19

# Part I.  Trade and the environment

## 3.  Interaction between the trade and environmental communities

*Dr Taimoon Stewart**

The issue of the interaction between the trade and environment communities is about conciliation. In this discussion of the interface between civil society and the WTO there is a third party within both civil society and the WTO, and that is the south. To move towards conciliation you have to understand the fears and concerns of all parties, including the south. You have to respect the point of view of all parties, and then you have to find ways of moving towards a position of compromise.

I would like to point to two issues of the south which, by implication, may have been referred to in other chapters, but which need more elaboration. First, their incapacity is a very real issue for south countries. You may notice that the south countries are taking almost opposite positions where the WTO is concerned. On the one hand, they are the greatest defenders of the WTO rules and don't want any changes in Article 20, etc. Yet this is because they see these rules as their only protection against unilateralism, protectionism, obstacles to trade and market access. On the other hand, for instance, the TRIPS Agreement is viewed as unfair to south countries, so they have to take this difficult position between a rock and a hard place.

Another problem is that the WTO rules have been politically interpreted for purposes in the Cartagena Agreement that did not come to pass. Two examples make clear this issue of lack of capacity and the need for sustainable development to include building capacity. Many of these small economies in the south have annual budgets that are probably less than some of the larger NGOs. A single person might be sitting at one desk in a ministry of trade to deal with all the WTO issues.

How can these smaller countries of the south cope when, even in the larger countries, even in the industrialized countries, they still have problems coping. I think that the issue of small economies, the issue of developing countries, particularly poor developing countries, has to be made central in terms of capacity building for the south.

The delegate from Iceland made a point about having a fisheries industry without subsidies though their fisheries industry is being threatened by competition from industries that are subsidized. The issue of fair trade has to be put on the table in that context. A similar argument applies to Caribbean bananas where small farmers producing bananas, supporting their families and keeping the economy going, are up

---

* Research Fellow, Institute of Social and Economic Research, University of West Indies, Trinidad and Tobago.

against large multinational corporations using very low-paid labour on large-scale production.

On another issue, south countries do not want harmonization of environmental standards. I would like to draw your attention to the *shrimp-turtle* case. Long before it became a WTO issue, sanctions were imposed on countries in the Western hemisphere – including the Caribbean. Trinidad and Tobago complied with the requirement to include TEDS, the turtle excluder device, in their shrimp trawlers' nets. Yet, we never thought of bringing the case to the WTO, because there are asymmetrical power relations in the world system. A small country like Trinidad and Tobago is not prepared to take on the might of the USA and the WTO. Later, it became a big issue with 40 countries involved.

However, when investigated, it was found that in the area where shrimps are harvested in Trinidad and Tobago, the water is very brackish and there are no turtles there. Meanwhile turtles do come to the east coast, one of the favorite areas for the nesting of ladderback turtles where, in fact, their greatest danger is being attacked by human beings who like their meat and eggs.

The government had to channel scarce resources into compliance with the US requirement which could have been put into programmes to protect the turtles on the east coast. Furthermore, in the TED requirement the dimensions of the opening were such that the ladderback turtle could not get through – it was too small. This is a very clear example where environmental standards from one country may not apply to another and may, in fact, be environmentally harmful, and where the resources are directed in a way which is not in the best interests of either the country or the environment.

# Chapter 20

## Part I.  Trade and the environment

### 3.  Interaction between the trade and environmental communities

*Fernand Thurmes, acting for James Currie\**

The discussion of "interaction between the trade and environment communities" is missing the key element of "development". In the European Union we attach a high priority to the establishment of effective channels for dialogue and for cooperation between trade, environment and development officials.

This is essential in order to ensure policy coherence and to develop positive synergies. These three policy areas will be considered in an integrated manner in the sustainability assessment of the new Round that the Commission has decided to undertake.

In his chapter, the WTO Director-General Mr Ruggiero called for "globalization with a human face". This requires integrating a strong environmental and development dimension in the new round. Trade liberalization can favour environmental efficiency and promote the integration of developing countries into the world's economic system. At the same time, environmental protection is essential to promote sustainable growth. High environmental standards are an incentive for investment and growth.

This being said, I will briefly address two issues:

- cooperation between the WTO and other international bodies, including multilateral environmental agreements; and
- the need for transparency in the WTO activities.

## COOPERATION BETWEEN THE WTO AND OTHER INTERNATIONAL BODIES

The WTO is an influential and powerful organization with a very comprehensive mandate. It is also a dynamic organization that has, in a very short time, demonstrated its ability to address new tasks and challenges. However, the WTO cannot work in isolation from other international bodies. There is a particularly strong need to establish effective cooperation links with other international organizations in the field of trade and environment.

---

\* Director-General, Directorate for Environment, Nuclear Safety and Civil Protection, European Commission, Brussels.

The outcome of Rio showed that in order to promote mutual supportiveness of trade and environment policies in favour of sustainable development, it was necessary to bring together the work conducted in various international fora. Organizations like UNEP, UNCTAD, the CSD, and the OECD have important contributions to make in this area.

Similarly, institutions like UNDP, and also the financial institutions, can usefully contribute to capacity building in developing countries and help address new trade and environment challenges. In this context, the efforts undertaken by UNEP to become more actively involved in the international debate on trade and environment are particularly welcome.

It is also necessary to enhance cooperation between the WTO and the multilateral environment agreements. The ongoing informal dialogue between the MEA secretariats and the Committee on Trade and Environment is playing a useful role in enhancing mutual confidence and understanding.

Also in this area there is a strong interaction between trade, environment and development. In the absence of international controls, trade in some categories of products can have detrimental environmental effects, especially in developing countries. Several MEAs are specifically aimed at addressing the concerns of developing countries. This is an additional argument in favour of a balanced and mutually supportive relationship between MEAs and the WTO agreements.

The recent evolution of WTO case law is encouraging. The recognition that WTO agreements cannot be interpreted in isolation from international law should contribute to increasing legal certainty and coherence. Dialogue between trade and environment policy-makers at the national level can also help promote coherence between MEAs and the WTO agreements, and more generally between trade and environment policies.

However, this is a difficult area. The latest case in point was the lack of agreement in Cartagena on the relationship between the bio-safety protocol and WTO agreements. This shows the imperative need to develop a consistent framework to clarify this issue.

## THE NEED FOR TRANSPARENCY IN THE WTO ACTIVITIES

In the European Union there is a broad consensus that it is no longer feasible to conduct economic negotiations in a closed room with only some ex-post information being provided to the outside world. Transparency is an essential requirement that should be integrated in the activities of the WTO. This is not only a democratic imperative – secretiveness is actually counterproductive. The experience of the Multilateral Agreement on Investment negotiations demonstrates that the lack of transparency generates tensions and social resistance.

The WTO has a responsibility for ensuring transparency in its work and activities, but I think we should agree that it does not carry the primary responsibility in this area. This is very largely a task for individual WTO Member states. They must develop mechanisms for public consultation, listen to the concerns of civil society and integrate those concerns into their national positions.

In Brussels we have already launched a process of dialogue with non-governmental actors including business, unions and NGOs. The European Union is also working to improve transparency in the WTO, notably through a policy of broader and more rapid access to documents, including dispute settlement reports, as well as more general openness in WTO processes.

As regards the WTO itself, transparency is a horizontal requirement that should apply to all WTO bodies, though not all WTO work attracts the same level of public interest. Demands for transparency and public consultation on trade and environment are particularly pressing. Citizens want to know how trade liberalization will impact on the environment and on their quality of life.

The WTO Secretariat has so far played a very useful role in promoting transparency in the work of the CTE. These initiatives are very valuable, but other complementary mechanisms will be needed. Once the new Round is launched, the environment will, and should, become a mainstream concern in these negotiations. A mechanism to promote transparency and input from civil society in this work will therefore be needed.

We welcome growing support for the idea of sustainability and environmental reviews of the new WTO negotiations. Several WTO Members, including the EU, will be conducting such studies, so we should clearly compare notes as we develop our work programmes and ensure transparency and dialogue with non-governmental actors.

A process of this kind would help achieve a better collective understanding of the interlinkages between trade liberalization, environmental protection and sustainable development. At the same time, it would provide an opportunity for consultations with, and input from, civil society.

# Chapter 21

# Part I. Trade and the environment

## 3. Interaction between the trade and environmental communities

*Gary Sampson\**

At the close of the Trade and Environment Symposium, the two most important questions now facing participants are:

- first, what process will permit the issues that have been raised here to be constructively addressed between now and the Seattle Ministerial Meeting and beyond?; and
- second, what are the priority issues for consideration in the forthcoming negotiations and when should they be taken up?

In short, where do we go from here at a time when ambitions and expectations have been raised by what has been a productive dialogue between representatives of non-governmental organizations and WTO member governments?

I see the coming months – and the period after Seattle – as a window of opportunity where many of the concerns that have figured in the trade and environment debate in recent years can be resolved. To achieve this objective, however, the channels of communication that have been opened by meetings such as this should not only be kept open, they should be intensified. But while expectations have been raised, it is important to be not only ambitious, but realistic. While some issues can be dealt with quickly and without negotiation on the part of governments, others requiring rule change can only be dealt with through protracted negotiations in the context of a broader multilateral round. Changing rules in the GATT, and now the WTO, is a rare event and the simple reality is that the WTO is seen by many to be doing what it is supposed to do very well according to the existing rules. As the WTO is a consensus-based organization, all countries will have to agree if there are to be far-reaching changes in the manner in which it functions.

Bearing this in mind, I would like to concentrate on substance rather than process. In my view, there are at least five areas which could be considered as priorities where real results are achievable in the foreseeable future.

The first involves improving the transparency with which the WTO operates. While there have been considerable advances in this area in recent times, I feel quite strongly that an organization only needs to be non-transparent when it has something to hide. The WTO has nothing to hide. The rules of the WTO are well

---

* Visiting Academic, London School of Economics, UK.

known, and while the results of the application of the rules may not please some, this is not a reason for delaying or restricting information relating to their application. Subject to very limited exceptions, I can see no reason why secretariat documents, government submissions and summary records can't be made immediately available to the public. It is not immediately apparent why, if a decision has already been taken to de-restrict certain documents, they should be kept for an arbitrary period before being made publicly available.

Similarly, it is hard to see why the Dispute Settlement Body can't have the same degree of openness that domestic court hearings have. Also, it is difficult to see why the findings of panels can't be made available to the public as soon as they are available in the WTO working languages.

Secondly, discussion in the Committee on Trade and the Environment has made clear that there are sectors where the removal of trade restrictions and distortions is not only beneficial to the environment in the importing country, but it can also lead to the expansion of exports of developing countries. The sectors have been identified where such "win-win scenarios" exist and the NGO community has played an important role in drawing attention to them. In this context, the work of WWF with respect to fisheries as presented at this symposium has shown how constructively a non-governmental organization can work with the WTO rules to promote policies that can address long standing global environmental problems.

What needs to be done now, however, is to identify the specific products within the priority sectors that can be negotiated with a "win-win" outcome in mind. To move ahead we need more information on the products within sectors, as well as the political will to carry out the negotiations and there is an important role for both governments and NGOs in providing this information.

Thirdly, the relationship between the rules of the trading system and those contained in multilateral environmental agreements has been extensively discussed in the CTE. The potential problems are well known and all options for dealing with such problems have been fleshed out. While it is perhaps time to take a decision, I am sympathetic to those governments who hesitate, as they are not convinced that a problem exists. Why change rules and face what may lead to an uncertain outcome if no problem has yet emerged? Having said that, greater clarity is required with respect to the relationship between these two bodies of international law. The commercial significance of the climate change and biosafety agreements, for example, means that a coherent relationship between their rules and those of the trading system is imperative and a framework for this relationship should be established.

Fourthly, the current interpretation of the concepts of like products and product/non-product related production processes underpins much of the application of WTO rules. The spectrum covering the implications of the present interpretation extends from a lack of clarity with respect to the WTO status of voluntary labeling (e.g., the WTO legitimacy of eco-labels) to differing views on the use of trade restrictions to enforce the adoption of preferred domestic standards in exporting countries (e.g., restricting imports to promote the use of certain fishing practices). Irrespective of the views held with respect to the current interpretation of these concepts, it has to be acknowledged that they constitute one of the critical pillars of the WTO, namely, the conditions under which foreign products can be discriminated against. Changing the current interpretation would greatly change the nature of the WTO. Matters such as this are not for negotiation, but for consideration at the highest level by a group of persons who can place systemic considerations above national interests.

Finally, the work of the Committee on Trade and Environment has been of enormous importance. It is frequently criticized and its work is greatly underrated. In my view, because of the extensive groundwork completed in this committee, the stage is set for a serious consideration of many of the most important trade and environment issues in the coming negotiations. But while the work of the committee has been useful, the question to address is has it completed its work as defined by ministers, and if so, what could be the future role of the CTE? It is now some years since its terms of reference were established. In the light of the discussion that has taken place in the committee, and the concerns expressed by the NGO community, it is time to rethink its role. It may well be found, for example, that the CTE could provide the channel of communication between governments and NGOs that has been sought after in both the WTO General Council and by NGOs.

I would like to close with two final comments. First, the WTO is an intergovernmental organization. A number of governments are concerned that, by opening up the WTO, by making it more transparent, we are, somehow, going to undermine its role as an intergovernmental organization. To be very clear, governments negotiate on behalf of their constituents and things should stay that way. Notwithstanding that, there should be a supporting process at the multilateral level to help governments convince their domestic constituents that what they are doing is in the national interest. The WTO must become more transparent and responsive to public concerns.

Secondly, I agree with Sylvia Ostry's comments that she is familiar with the well known principle of *laissez faire* but not *laissez litiger*. The WTO is unfortunately becoming a house of litigation. Some of the most important issues that will define the nature of the WTO in the next millennium are presently the subject of litigation, not policy discussion. The extraterritorial application of domestic standards through trade restrictions, the receipt of *amicus* briefs and the interpretation of legal implications of preambular language should not be the subject of litigation. They are matters of policy and should be treated as such.

# Chapter 22

# Part I. Trade and the environment

## 3. Interaction between the trade and environmental communities

*Hajime Ohta\**

Mankind's spirit of inquiry and desire to improve have advanced civilization and brought that advance to our daily lives. But the widespread effects of civilization have also resulted in the deterioration of our planet. Indeed, we are all agreed that environment is one of the highest-priority global issues confronting us. We must pay attention to this issue and make every endeavor at all levels of society to improve the environment.

But we have not yet reached a sufficient consensus on a blueprint for solving environmental problems. Furthermore, there have been no simple conclusions as to the most appropriate social and economic systems to which human beings should aspire. The course of general economic activities cannot help affecting nature around us. The impact of inter-country trade inevitably leads to some degree of environmental deterioration.

Though there is a need to monitor the relationship of trade and the environment, we have no monitoring system in place. Given the current situation, where each country has its own environmental policy and objectives, there is no international consensus on how to monitor trade in an environmental context.

I think the WTO should treat those multilateral environmental agreements – such as the Basel Treaty, Washington Treaty and Montreal Protocol – that represent a consensus achieved through the efforts of international society, as being exempt from the application of WTO principles.

At the same time, the WTO should be able to deal with these types of issues without achieving international consensus, or without placing emphasis on objectivity or universality. But the WTO is a forum created to deal with trade, so achieving progress on environmental issues by approaching them from a trade-related point of view is quite difficult. It is like trying to get a huge dog to move by merely tugging on its tail.

An international agreement is reached through the trial and error process of inter-action between individual citizens, industry and national governments. The details of that agreement should then be made a part of international rules.

The matter of international consensus gives rise to complicated questions. Apart from the MEAs I mentioned previously, there is another form of consensus that was

---

\* Executive Counsellor, Keindanred, Representative, Japan Economic Federation of Industries, Japan.

reached at the conference on climate change held in Kyoto. There, developed nations successfully made an international commitment to the mitigation of climate change.

To follow up on this commitment, Japan's national Diet passed two bills, one of which was the reform of the Energy Conservation Act. In this act, a system has been introduced to reduce the energy consumption of motor vehicles, home appliances and the like. In this approach, the energy efficiency of each device must be higher than that of the most efficient product currently on the market. The same energy conservation standard will be applied, not only for domestic products, but also for imports. This might affect trade to some extent.

Although international society has reached an agreement on the common goal of reducing greenhouse gas emissions, concrete measures undertaken to realize this aim might invite future discussions on trade and environment.

As one example of the steps that can be taken by industries in developed and developing countries, I would like to share with you our activities on the environmental issues. In 1991, before the Earth Summit put out its global environmental charter, we recommended that each industry make industry-wide voluntary action plans defining objective criteria and strategies. We then announced our voluntary action plan on the environment, and established a continuous framework in which virtually all the industrial sectors would participate in implementing, reviewing and improving measures to protect the environment. Within this framework, each participating association sets targets, reviews progress annually and makes those review results open to the public.

For example, the electric power industry has set its targets for reductions in $CO_2$ emissions per unit of output, pledging to achieve a level in 2010 for the electric power industry that is about 20 per cent lower than the 1990 level.

Furthermore, we have announced that total $CO_2$ emissions for the industrial and energy conversion sectors, as a whole, should be brought below their 1990 level by the year 2010. The first review was made in the fall of last year and its result was made public. Our voluntary action plan on the environment is now an important part of the Japanese Government's package to mitigate the changing climate.

Meeting the challenge of climate change, and other environmental issues, will require creative responses at all levels of the global community. Our initiatives, as well as voluntary activities in other countries, will hopefully serve as models for other countries to enact similar options.

# Chapter 23

# Part I.  Trade and the environment

## 3.  Interaction between the trade and environmental communities

*Konrad von Moltke**

I would like to make a few comments about the commonality of the trade and environment community, a few comments about the differences and then raise two basic points which I think need consideration.

I think it is worth bearing in mind that the single greatest political force today in favour of globalization is the environment. I have yet to find anybody, anywhere, at any time, who denies that environmental management requires international cooperation.

One of the paradoxes of the relationship between trade and environment policies, and perhaps one of the reasons why we have been engaged in this exercise for the last eight years, is that the economic outcomes of environmental policy and trade policy are identical. Both lead to structural economic change – though not the same change. Fundamentally, the purpose of environmental policy is to promote activities which are less environmentally harmful, and to restrain activities which are more environmentally harmful. If that isn't a description of what trade policy does – namely to promote efficient producers and to restrain inefficient producers – what is? So, to some extent, when we argue it is like a squabble among siblings.

Let me talk about some of the differences. I think we need to understand that when we talk about the environment we are talking about an abstraction. Environmental policy is many things. It is widespread. There is a good reason why no country in the world has a true environment ministry. Most countries have ministries which are called environment ministries, but if you look carefully there is somebody who is responsible for some significant aspect of environmental policy sitting in the finance ministry, the transport ministry, the agricultural ministry, the ministry of public health – heaven knows where!

So it's all over the place and, frankly, given that I can't understand why we think we can have a world environment organization. It's not going to work.

Those of us in the environmental area are basically what I would call policy retailers. We have got to deal with the specifics of specific situations, that is if we don't protect the turtles on the east coast of Trinidad and Tobago it isn't good

---

* Senior Fellow, World Wild Life Fund, Washington, and Institute for International Environmental Governance, Dartmouth College, USA.

enough, no matter if it's a good policy. That is the kind of problem we should deal with, and when we don't we have bad environmental policy.

I would argue that the trade community are policy wholesalers – big rules for everybody, all the time. It's not how we work. The environmental policy community is what I would call a policy scavenger. We use anything we can. Part of that is it's so difficult to map the environment into human institutions. We are dealing with something we don't control – the natural environment. We are trying to map it into policy, and basically we take anything we like. We see something, we ask "is that an opportunity?" Trade policy makers are principled people. A rule-based system. It's not how we tend to look at the world. So there are real differences.

And the third point is, we have created over the last 20 years, the most elaborate, extraordinary and remarkable structure of international regimes to deal with the environment. There are hundreds of them, many of them invisible, many of them ineffective, but the total effort is completely extraordinary. I think it is worth keeping that in mind for those of us who sometimes despair that anything will happen.

If you think of these similarities and difficulties you get some sense of why we have the disputes we have. I tend to think a good argument is a good thing, but it has got to be settled in the end.

Now two basic problems. First, I think those of us whose concern is primarily the environment have utterly failed to make our case successfully to the developing countries. I think the responsibility for that lies, in large part, with people like myself, who are outside of governments. It is not the business of governments to tell other governments what to do, but I think there is a complex argument here, which needs to be made, which isn't made. Let me make just one point in this area, at this moment.

I think southern countries come to this issue with a very acute sense of the fact that commodity markets – when they internalize environmental costs and it increases their costs – don't honor that activity. They don't get anything for it. Perhaps they are wrong, but we haven't disproved them. It is worth keeping in mind that if we solve that problem it is indisputable that they will have a larger part of the total economic rent that is available.

Let me give you an example, that of the banana dispute. At one level, the banana dispute is the unsavory spectacle of two OECD countries fighting to control the rent of a product produced in developing countries. But the interesting thing from my point of view is, as far as I can tell, the farm gate price for bananas is almost everywhere about eight to ten cents a pound. In the ACP countries as well. I'm told by banana producers that it will take four cents a pound extra, four cents a pound, that's all it will take, and every banana traded in the world would be produced organically.

Now how can it be that we have increased the price of bananas to European consumers by a billion and a half dollars and we can't get this problem solved? I think those are the kinds of issues we have really got to deal with.

Now, let me make one last comment which may surprise you. Let me ask the question: "What is it that economic policy makers and trade negotiators can learn from the environmental community?"

I think there are things to be learned from our experience and I think recognizing that will help the debate. As you move into issues which require policy retailing, that is where you need to make individual decisions on specific cases of investment or competition, I think you will need to learn how to do that from our experience.

That is why we in ISD feel very strongly about our warning not to include investment in the trade regime. If you look at the experience of the MAI they did everything wrong that they could have done wrong, and I think next time you have got to get it right. These are some of the things which come out of the relationship between the environment and the trade community, which I still think constitute an agenda which requires a good deal of work.

# Chapter 24

# Part I.  Trade and the environment

## Conclusion

*Renato Ruggiero**

I believe the Trade and Environment Symposium has shown that the trade and environment debate is entering a new phase. We are moving – and must continue to move – from identifying our differences towards identifying solutions.

We have heard a great number of ideas and proposals. It is impossible to mention all of them, so I will only try to refer to the main points.

## SUSTAINABLE DEVELOPMENT

Many speakers have underlined that our discussion should include, not only trade and the environment, but also development issues in order to address sustainable development in a comprehensive way. This means, among other things, improving market access to developing-country exports, capacity building, technical assistance, technology transfers, and debt relief. It seems to me we all agree that we must avoid a situation where the trade and environment debate opens up a new North/South divide.

## TRADE RESTRICTIONS AND DISTORTIONS

The removal of trade restrictions and distortions – in particular, high tariffs, tariff escalation, export restrictions, subsidies, and non-tariff measures – has the potential to yield "win, win, win" synergies for trade, for the environment and for development.

## TRANSPARENCY

Many of us see transparency from different points of view – though I think there has been an appreciation of the progress we have already made in this area. But we can all agree that this symposium has shown how governments and civil society can meet around the same table to share a frank exchange of views.

---

* Director-General, World Trade Organization, Geneva.

## ENVIRONMENTAL REVIEWS

The idea of conducting environmental reviews of trade agreements was supported by a number of speakers.

## MEAs

There was broad agreement that MEAs are the best and most effective way for governments to tackle transboundary environmental issues. However, there are still strong views over Article XX and how it should be applied. We do not yet agree about how – or whether – the issue of PPMs should be addressed in the trading system. Many doubts have been raised about whether trade restrictions are the most appropriate instrument to advance environmental policies. Many have underlined that environmental problems are best addressed at their source – which means, as various speakers have noted, internalizing environmental costs.

## COOPERATION BETWEEN THE WTO, UNEP AND OTHER AGENCIES

More coherence is needed in economic, environment, and development policy-making – on this point, there was no disagreement. First and foremost, this policy coordination must take place at the national level. But we also need greater coordination between WTO and UNEP, as well as with UNCTAD, the World Bank and others. I welcome UNEP's Klaus Topfer's commitment to continue strengthening these bridges. I also welcome the ideas we have heard for coordinating the global voice of the environment, and for strengthening its institutional foundations.

I have heard a number of voices today and yesterday expressing impatience with our progress. I frankly share your impatience. After all, it is impatience which helped to move the idea of a high-level dialogue forward. And it is impatience which will energize our work in the months ahead. So on that thought, let me not only declare this symposium closed. Let me declare our new dialogue open.

# Part II.
# Trade and Development

# Chapter 25

# Part II. Trade and development

## Introduction

*Renato Ruggiero\**

This meeting must offer the prospect of a real improvement in the situation of the developing countries. We can continue to complain about how unacceptable the world is today – and it certainly is. We can continue a sterile polemic in which the north and south blame each other. But this will not address the very serious problems we all face. It will not feed the millions of children who are hungry. It will not give these children the education and skills they need so their families – and their countries – can move confidently into the 21st century.

In some ways the dialogue we enter today is an old one. Development was one of the central goals of the original GATT architects. Over the years, our system has incorporated a number of rules, provisions, and initiatives for developing countries – all with the idea of recognizing and safeguarding their special needs and interests, as outlined in the WTO Secretariat background paper.

Yet in other ways the dialogue about trade and development is very new. First, because the level of inequality between countries and people is becoming more and more unacceptable. Two billion people, a third of humanity, live on less than $2 a day and 1.5 billion people still lack access to fresh water. One hundred and thirty million of our children have never gone to school. In a world made ever smaller by televisions, telephones and the Internet, the idea that billions are mired in poverty, while millions grow richer, is not just unsustainable. It is unconscionable.

Secondly, because the constituency, the trading system, has changed profoundly. When the GATT was born there were just 23 members, and only 11 of these were from the developing world. Today the WTO has 134 members of which 80 per cent are developing, least-developed or transition economies. Of the 30 candidates negotiating to join, practically all are developing economies or economies in transition.

Thirdly, because developing countries are becoming more and more important to the health of the world economy. In 1970 trade, as expressed as a share of developing-country GDP, was slightly less than 20 per cent. Today it is over 38 per cent. Between 1973 and 1997 the developing country's share of manufactured imports into developed markets tripled – from 7.5 per cent to 23 per cent. What these figures reflect is the developing world's truly remarkable integration into the global economy over the past three decades – even if this progress has profound inequalities which must be corrected. These figures also reflect the reality that the development

---

* Director-General, World Trade Organization, Geneva.

challenge is no longer a challenge just for developing countries – it should be a concern of the advanced economies as well.

I do not pretend, in these introductory remarks, to lay out an agenda that could meet this formidable challenge of our time, but I do want to underline one priority. Clearly we need to devote particular attention to the least fortunate in the world economy. The least-developed countries, several developing countries, and many of the world's "small states", are currently facing economic stagnation and poverty. They are not sharing in the benefits that others are reaping from global economic integration. The collapse of world commodity prices has darkened once again the prospect of a sustained improvement in their economic situation. We have to recognize that this is a most unacceptable situation in today's world economy. We must all give priority attention to this problem.

Over a year ago the WTO hosted a high-level meeting on the trade issues facing the least-developed countries. This was the first important sign of a new attention which the world trade system was finally giving to this dramatic aspect of the global economy. Building on that meeting, let me highlight three initiatives which I propose as main objectives of our discussions.

First, improved market access. Since the G-7 summit in Lyon in 1997, I have urged governments to provide bound free access for the export products of the least-developed countries. A number of WTO members have taken steps in this direction, and I congratulate you. The elimination of all obstacles to trade between all advanced economies and the least-developed countries – and between all advanced economies and the most dynamic developing countries, though using a different timetable – must be key objectives of future negotiations. The time for real action is now.

Secondly, capacity building. Trade alone certainly cannot solve all the problems of the least-developed countries. Eliminating trade barriers will not be enough unless we also reduce the very serious supply-side barriers these countries face: from infrastructure and institution building to health care, education, and social policy. This is why we have launched – together with UNCTAD, the ITC, the World Bank, UNDP, and the IMF – a new approach to technical assistance. This calls for an integrated framework where these international institutions ask the countries themselves to design a results-oriented programme tailored to their needs.

We need to build upon this new approach. But let us be frank. To do so, we need more financial and human resources in the WTO. We have to correct a situation where only 20 per cent of the resources for technical assistance come from our budget, and all the rest is generously provided by a small number of countries who do not even represent the world's largest trading powers. This is unfair, especially for the donor countries. It is also unsustainable.

Thirdly, debt relief. I want to underline the great importance that least-developed countries attach to debt relief – and to personally endorse their efforts to resolve this central issue, even if it is not in the mandate of the WTO. Advanced economies should accompany free market access with an initiative to cancel foreign debt for as many of these countries as possible. Several proposals have been made recently. They should be given careful consideration, and we should send a message of solidarity to those who want to move forward. A creative approach to debt relief, full market access and capacity building can provide the three pillars of a new strategy for bringing least-developed countries into the mainstream of the multilateral trading system.

The development challenge is really part of a much broader challenge – how to manage this increasingly global world? We need a new approach, a new vision of global governance which not only embraces more nations – at the highest levels of international decision-making – but also more issues and concerns.

We need a vision which addresses:

- capital movements and trade liberalization;
- development priorities;
- environmental and social concerns;
- human rights, gender equality, labour standards, health and education – especially the role of new technologies; and
- poverty eradication, cultural diversity, ethical concerns, and the fight against corruption.

All these must be embraced in an improved concept of global cooperation, first and foremost among international organizations. This is also the approach of my friend Jim Wolfensohn, President of the World Bank, and I fully endorse his important ideas on how to improve global governance.

Today we are no longer threatened by a Cold War nuclear confrontation. The new global threat is hunger, poverty, ignorance, inequalities, unemployment and the prospect of environmental collapse. And yet we also live at a time when mankind has reached a level of material and human progress unmatched in history – when we are all moving into a new world of unprecedented opportunities given to us by the revolutionary power of new technologies.

The fusion of computers and telecommunications is linking the world's people together, improving access to health care and education regardless of geography and distance. The reach of mobile phones into even the most remote villages is not only reducing physical marginalization, but can also make the difference between life and death. We in the WTO are already linking ourselves to the least-developed countries through a special Internet site. With electronic commerce we are opening up the opportunity for every nation, and every person, to be part of a world market for their services, their products, and their ideas.

I very much hope that this meeting can send a new message to our leaders and our people. A message of determination to promote a common strategy – among international institutions, national administrations, and civil society – to eradicate poverty and reduce inequalities in the world in 20 years. A common strategy to achieve a sustainable global environment – in developing and developed countries alike – in 20 years. Also, in the same period of time, a common strategy to eliminate the greatest part of global trade barriers – at least reflecting on a multilateral level, what governments have already agreed in regional arrangements.

All this is within reach. This should be part of the human face of development – using interdependence and globalization to resolve these fundamental problems of inequality, poverty and under-development; and to boost growth and employment everywhere. Let us not waste this great opportunity.

# Chapter 26

# Part II. Trade and development

## Introduction

*H. E. Ambassador Ali Said Mchumo*\*

This symposium will examine crucial aspects of the trade and development relationship – and will search for optimal approaches – in our collective endeavour to ensure that there is a meaningful development dimension to international trade issues; and that solutions are found to address the trade-related concerns of developing countries.

Development was one of the central goals of the founding fathers of GATT, and it has remained so in the philosophical framework of the Uruguay Round agreements, and of the World Trade Organization (WTO) established to monitor their observance and implementation.

For most, if not for all of us, trade is not an end in itself. For developing countries, trade must be an engine for growth in both quantitative and qualitative terms in order to eradicate poverty and ensure development with equity for all their peoples. Thus, trade would be an empty endeavour for developing countries if it lacked the development dimension. This symposium will examine the scope of that dimension, and the challenges and opportunities for its realization.

Over the years, we have created a multilateral trading system of which the WTO is the latest version of its embodiment. When the system began there was the perception that it was an instrument of a few rich countries, but we now believe that the system must serve us all, and that it must be particularly sensitive to the plight of the weakest amongst us. The WTO is no longer seen as a device imposed from above, but a structure and a system in which we must all participate for our common good. With a membership predominantly composed of developing countries, it is natural that the system must be geared to address the issues of concern to them, especially those who are the most disadvantaged. That is the main reason why developing countries are members of the WTO – they expect to benefit from it. Indeed, we owe it to ourselves to ensure that developing countries can identify a stake in the multilateral trading system which serves their interests if we are to prevent disenchantment and the divisive culture of "they" versus "us".

The WTO Director-General has highlighted what needs to be done to address the plight of developing countries, especially the least-developed countries, not only within the narrow context of trade but within the broader context of sustainable development – improving their market access, addressing their supply side

---

\* Chairman, WTO General Council, Tanzania.

constraints and enhancing their capacity to produce and export, and providing debt relief, among other measures.

Of course these measures and solutions go beyond what the multilateral trading system, and the WTO, can provide. However, the WTO cannot be, nor is it, insensitive to the problems that have arisen from our common interdependence. I share the desire for an overall global architecture to address the many complex problems that face the international community. No one organization can solve all the world's problems. This is why coherence and co-operation are required amongst institutions and policies, particularly in the areas of finance, trade and development.

Let me remind you of the four characteristics which define the multilateral trading system.

- First, it is a rules-based system. The balance of rights and obligations are of fundamental importance to all member states, developing and developed. The system is not based on the arbitrary exercise of the application of force and power, but on the rule of law with precisely defined rights and obligations.
- Secondly, it contains the principle of non-discrimination, which finds expression in provisions for most favoured nation (MFN).
- Thirdly, it has a corpus of other principles and provisions, including the principles of transparency and of binding tariffs.
- Fourthly, there is the dispute settlement system which has, to a great extent, shown that all WTO members can obtain remedies and satisfaction for the nullification or impairment of benefits or rights under the system.

Nonetheless, as we all know, the multilateral trading system is not a perfect one. It is the obligation of all of us to make the system work as it was intended, and to make its aims and ideals a practical reality to the benefit of all.

1999 was an eventful year of significant challenges for several reasons. At the Third Ministerial Conference in Seattle, member states were expected to decide on the way forward as far as their trading relations are concerned; while the global financial and monetary crises have shown that the best chances for recovery and growth lie in maintaining the multilateral trading system, while ensuring that protectionist sentiments and policies neither take hold nor prevail.

The world is entering a new millennium and people in all countries are entitled to enjoy the benefits of growth, prosperity and development. Poverty and inequity are unacceptable and must be eradicated. Developing country members are determined that the multilateral trading system should address the development dimension of international trade issues and trade-related concerns of developing countries, including the least-developed countries.

For all these reasons, the Symposium on Trade and Development should contribute to the following:

- facilitating the integration of developing countries in the multilateral trading system;
- building coherence amongst trade, finance and development policies and institutions;
- improving the participation and reducing the vulnerability of the least-developed countries in the trading system; and
- developing the role of the WTO in supporting the developmental objectives identified in the Marrakesh Agreement.

# Chapter 27

# Part II.  Trade and development

## Introduction

*Rubens Ricupero**


It is now more than a year-and-a-half after the beginning of a most serious crisis of development. It is still going strong: after devastating South-East and East Asia and Russia, it has just prostrated Brazil and Latin America. And no one can tell whether it has run out of regions to further ravage. As the crisis has not been exclusively linked to a single country, region or aspect, what could we call it? Asian, financial, economic, global? I prefer to describe it as "the crisis of development". There are three main reasons for doing so.


## DEVELOPING COUNTRIES HIT HARDEST


First, it not only started in a developing country – Thailand – but, so far, it has reserved its malignant force for the developing or transition regions of the world, those weak economies whose immune systems are particularly vulnerable. The industrialized countries have been largely spared from the vicious contagion. On balance, they have even benefited: they gained from the unprecedented collapse in commodity prices; cheap manufactured imports from countries forced to devaluate their currencies; a substantial improvement in their terms of trade with developing countries; and the boost to their equity markets from financial flows running away from emerging markets in a "flight to quality". The overall impact of these elements goes some way to explain why it has been possible to maintain the miracle of continuous expansion in industrialized economies without incurring economic overheating and a return of inflation.

In contrast, significant parts of the developing world have seen the fruits of decades of economic growth and poverty reduction evaporate in a matter of weeks. Practically all the developing nations have been touched. Those, like China or countries in South Asia, which were relatively unscathed in the first stages, are already feeling the pinch of a slowing-down. The net result is that, in 1998, growth in the developed world exceeded that in developing countries for the first time for many years, at 2.3 per cent against 1.5 per cent (if China is included). If China is excluded, average growth in developing countries was down to only 0.4 per cent.

If the hope of development lies in the possibility of growing more rapidly, thus narrowing the gap that separates rich and poor, this reversal of the trend represents

---

* Secretary General, UNCTAD.

a defeat for the entire international community. It also produces strong grounds to question the process of development in its present form.

Secondly, and another reason to call this a crisis of development, or at least one of certain modalities of development, is that paradoxically events have shaken some of the most advanced among the developing countries. In effect, the extremely weak and poor economies of the world were not among the more seriously hit because, in the first place, they had never had much access to the private financial markets and had been largely unable to take advantage of the expansion in world trade.

Those more at risk have been the 29 countries listed by the Institute of International Finance as so-called "emerging markets". These include not only the more successful developing nations but also the economies in transition. If development is a process that should steadily reduce the degree of vulnerability of economies to external shocks, how then can one explain that some of the worst-affected have been precisely those countries that were so advanced that they were generally regarded as having graduated to OECD ranks? Or else they have been countries in the avant-garde of development like Malaysia, Thailand, Indonesia, Brazil, or in previous crises, Mexico and Argentina?

Is the reason because these economies were more integrated into the international economy, or because their successful integration into the world trading system had not been matched by an equally successful integration in the world of globalized finance? As regards the latter, is the explanation largely one of failures in their national policies of financial regulation and supervision? Yet, if this seems true in some cases, in Asia, how can one explain the case of others, like Chile, where all the fundamentals were in the right place; there is a sound banking system and prudent regulations; and yet, nonetheless Chile posted an extremely high current account deficit last year?

We should not push the argument too far or be tempted to overstate the point. Korea is showing signs of renewing growth (although not yet employment) and Chile has "only" been forced to slow down from an annual growth rate of 7 to approximately 3 per cent. After all, development was not in vain and those countries are still better off now than they would have been in the past.

Thirdly, far from being a rare situation, the "stop and go" performance of developing economies is becoming more and more frequent. The current problems have nothing to do with the downward curve in the business cycle that regularly befalls capitalist economies, usually generating short recessions followed by more or less long periods of resumed growth. They are, in fact, more similar to the structural crisis that deeply disorganized the world economy in the inter-war period when more than 45 per cent of the 20 years corresponded to phases of recession or depression.

In a lecture delivered in Rome at the end of 1995, Michel Camdessus remarked that, at that time, in the space of a little over ten years, the world had gone through four important financial crises: the Latin American foreign debt crisis of the 1980s; the 1987 equity market crash; the 1992 EMS crisis; and the Mexican crisis of 1994–1995 – and more was still to come. Since then, events have proved him right. In the face of such increasing frequency, intensity and destructive power of monetary and financial crises, is it reasonable to stubbornly refuse to acknowledge that there is something wrong with the system itself, that we are not dealing with episodes of turmoil brought about only by faulty national policies but with structural instability and volatility resulting from deep changes in the international system? Is it sensible to insist that the world economy will finally stabilize around a system of floating exchange rates when, almost 30 years after it was introduced in the wake of the breakdown of the Bretton Woods system, it is still causing wild gyrations in value among main currencies, sometimes of near 20 per cent in less than a month, as we recently saw between the yen and the dollar?

There was a brief moment in September and October last year when the fall-out of the Russian collapse, and the near failure of a major US hedge fund, made even the USA fear for its economic life. It already looks like old history, but it was less than six months ago that Alan Greenspan made his famous speech about the disappearance of liquidity, something that he had never seen before in 50 years of monitoring the US economy. For a few weeks it appeared that the need for a new financial architecture was going to be widely acknowledged, that a looming catastrophe – or an "optimal crisis", in the words of Fred Bergsten – would finally conquer inertia and catalyse a concerted reaction. Alas, it was but an illusion. As soon as the cuts in interest rates performed their magic, we were back to business as usual on Wall Street.

## DELAY AND DENIAL

Thereafter, two basic attitudes have dominated the debate on the issue – delay and denial. It is true, as one of Parkinson's Laws states, that delay is the deadliest form of denial; and there has been no shortage of delaying tactics: a proliferation of meetings, inflation of communiques, multiplication of groups and fora. Some participants in this debate, perhaps heartened by the perverse selectivity of this crisis, do not shrink from stating that there is nothing wrong with the architecture, nor the foundations. At the most, there may be a small matter of improving the plumbing or fixing the electricity, possibly just the paint on the facade.

Those amongst us who participated in the Uruguay Round will have the feeling that they have already seen this film. To be precise, during the discussions in the FOGS group, when all attempts at building a solid bridge to assure coherence between trade, currency and finance were met with the same cosmetic action – with the consequences that we are now reaping. Even fixing the electricity or the plumbing may end up being too much for the advocates of denial. Changing the metaphor, they may find themselves rearranging the furniture on the deck of the Titanic, or playing the transparency waltz for passengers drowning for lack of a lifeboat.

I was doing some research for this piece when I came across an old Financial Times clipping from the end of 1995. The article started with the following words: "The strongest period of sustained trade growth for 30 years will buoy the global economy for the rest of this decade, according to an international forecast from the London Business School". Actually, the reverse has taken place; for it was the global economy, or at least its financial component, that felled the growth of trade. Trade growth collapsed from almost 10 per cent in 1997 to about 3.7 per cent last year.

One of the lessons of the crisis was to remind us of something that we should have known all along – that trade is not an autonomous force acting in a vacuum, one which permits us to pull ourselves up by our own bootstraps. Trade can do wonders, growing, for instance, at two to three percentage points above world output, as it has been doing for the past three decades. It cannot, however, perform miracles. When country after country is forced to sharply cut down on imports, in some cases by almost one third, as in the five most affected Asian countries, or by 10 per cent, as in Japan last year, something has to give. And do not believe that the worst is over. After a fall of 6 per cent in 1998, Brazil is expected to further reduce imports by 30 per cent this year. In January, Japan saw a plunge in imports of over 20 per cent compared with one year ago.

Adjustments in current account balances is, therefore, being achieved by the worst possible means, not through a virtuous circle of export expansion leading to import growth, but through a vicious circle of import repression generating deceleration in export volumes. Even when volumes expand, their value is diminished because of the combined deflationary effects of demand contraction, excess supply and currency devaluations. Adjusted for changes in the value of the dollar, the price index for commodities other than oil has fallen by more than 60 per cent since 1960. The populations of countries that achieved independence during the 1960s and early 1970s, and remain heavily dependent on one or two export crops, have seen their real buying power decline by almost two-thirds in the space of one generation. Under these circumstances, no significant pick-up in the pace of world trade is likely to come about this year.

Another worrying trend is the worsening of huge swings in current-account balances. Whereas, in 1998, the current-account deficit amounted to $294 billion in the USA and $52 billion in Latin America, the counterpart lay in the surpluses built up with $128 billion in the OECD countries of Europe, with $122 billion in Japan, and with $58 billion in the emerging markets of Asia (excluding China). This is fertile ground for the return of protectionism and trade conflicts, which we are witnessing with such a vengeance.

## INDUSTRIALIZED COUNTRIES SHOULD ACT

Implicit in this overview of the economic scene should be the conclusion that there is not a great deal that can be expected from developing countries in order to overcome the crisis. By contrast, industrial nations still enjoy considerable scope and freedom for expansionary policy actions. As UNCTAD has recently suggested in a paper prepared for ASEAN, one possible policy response could be the direct injection of liquidity into developing countries through official channels to raise demand, imports and growth. Japan and the EU are in a position to play an important role in providing a direct liquidity injection by recycling part of their surpluses in various ways to developing countries, in order to revive global demand, boost trade and accelerate growth. Given that the more advanced developing countries have, relatively speaking, a higher propensity to spend and import in terms of their effect on global trade and growth, such schemes could prove to be superior to domestic fiscal expansion in the surplus countries themselves.

Other means of producing a direct increase in liquidity in developing countries should also be explored. One possibility would be to remove the debt overhang of highly indebted poor countries (HIPCs) through a rapid write-off of their unpayable official and multilateral debt. The recent German proposal for debt forgiveness is a welcome development, not only on its own merits but also because its implementation under conditions of a global slowdown would enhance the impact on trade, growth and development. Similarly, a substantial new SDR allocation to developing countries could provide support not only to those countries facing a threat of contagion but equally to current-account and trade financing, at a time when not even middle-income developing countries have access to private finance at reasonable costs.

Thus, there is no shortage of concrete ideas about what to do. Those that I have just outlined fall under the jurisdiction of international financial organizations or major industrial countries, not the WTO. But what can be done here? What do developing countries expect and what do they want from future trade negotiations? The question can be answered in the same way that Samuel Gompers replied when urged to say, in a few words, what the US trade union movement wanted: "More", he said. More, we should say, and in two senses: more access and more flexibility.

## DEVELOPING COUNTRIES NEED MORE

More access to markets for developing country goods and services. But also more access to "greenfield" investment which generates additional export capacity and shared skills; more finance for development needs; and more access for their skilled labour to global markets for services, and to new techniques and knowledge.

Here is where we should finally address the cumulative "unfinished business" of the Tokyo and Uruguay Rounds:

- tariff peaks and tariff escalation in the food, textile, clothing, footwear and leather industries;
- the postponement until 2005 of economically meaningful removal of restraints on developing countries' exports of textiles and clothing;
- the very embryonic liberalization of trade in agriculture;
- the abuse of anti-dumping procedures; and
- the problem of rules of origin, phytosanitary measures, technical standards, and environmental barriers in those areas in which developing countries have become successful exporters.

More flexibility should be granted to developing countries, to use a variety of policies and instruments to promote such an extraordinarily complex and difficult process as development. No one should underestimate the daunting challenge faced by the poorest among the poor to absorb, let alone implement and use, trade agreements. Those countries need more, not less flexibility; more, not less assistance to succeed. It is hard to understand why developing countries seeking to accede to WTO are being asked to give up even the flexibility enjoyed by members.

We must resist the tendency to use trade negotiations as an instrument for the kind of global governance that denies developing countries the active policies to acquire competitive advantages. This, above all, when the same industrialized nations have widely and successfully used similar policies during their own historic process of development. As recently as the Uruguay Round, major industrialized countries have maintained for themselves the right to continue massive agriculture export subsidies.

How to achieve these goals? First of all, it is necessary that organizations like WTO and UNCTAD help developing countries become active protagonists in future negotiations, the conscious subjects and not passive objects of decisions that will condition their destiny. This requires a pro-active, positive agenda for developing countries' trade negotiations, a constructive and affirmative strategy in all issues under negotiation that should arise from the vigorous initiative and unity of purpose of developing countries themselves.

It is our duty to cooperate with the governments of developing nations in this endeavour by providing them with the research, analytical and conceptual inputs that are indispensable to the formulation of their negotiating positions in the light of their own trade interests – taking into account the possibility of coalition-building with like-minded partners, developing or developed alike. They will also need to acquire negotiating skills through a substantial programme in commercial diplomacy if they are to become aggressive proponents of an improved trading system. This includes, of course, continuous assistance for the implementation of agreements. Last but not least, they need help in dispute settlement which has often proved to be as important a way of gaining market access as negotiations.

When all is said and done, however, imbalances will still remain. Power will prevail in a world of men, not of angels. In this case, I refer to market power, that is the managed opening of one's own market in order to gain access to other people's markets. As markets present huge differences in size and purchasing power, how can we avoid the fact that the inevitable asymmetry in the use of market power will tend to aggravate excessive inequality?

I suggest that the answer lies in a redefinition of competition in the light of development. Almost all trade questions revolve around competition in one way or another. On the other hand, competition has many analogies to games, as can be seen from the application of game theory to trade negotiations. Up to now, we have tended to reduce competition to the two first requisites of any game: rules and arbiters. In our case, fair rules of trade agreements and the impartial arbitration of the dispute settlement process. We have so far largely overlooked a third, and absolutely indispensable, element of games and competition: learning, education, training and preparation. We did so because we believed that the best way to learn how to do something is by practising it. This is true, but it presupposes that there will be someone to tell us whether we did things the right way, how to correct our faults, and that during this process we would be spared being crushed by our trainers and teachers. In other words, one needs a breathing and learning space, a reinvigoration of special and differential treatment to successfully confront the dynamic changes in the global economy driven by rapid technological advance.

There is a need to bring this concept up to date, not only in terms of preferential tariffs and transition periods. We must now go beyond, and draw the lessons from the historical changes that are making knowledge and information, instead of capital, labour or resources, into the decisive elements of the economy and development. Information economics, a new branch of economics, is teaching us that, far from having a zero or negligible cost, information does have a substantial cost, part of the so-called transaction cost. In the past, technology was essentially embodied in machines. Technology is now embodied in human beings. We now require an incomparably greater effort to teach countries, particularly the least developed, the small, weak and vulnerable, how to produce and broaden their supply capability in goods and services; and how to compete effectively and use modern, electronic means in an increasingly demanding environment; how to take advantage of opportunities provided by the trading system.

An essential component of this effort has to be a massive programme of trade-related technical cooperation. Here we have a good example of the need to "put our money where our mouth is". It is no longer tolerable to continue the hypocrisy of stressing the role of trade as being the central ingredient of development and then allocating only 2 per cent of technical cooperation to trade-related activities. Programmes like the UNCTAD/WTO/ITC Joint Integrated Technical Assistance Programme for Least-Developed and Other African Countries, should be substantially reinforced if we are to meet the legitimate expectations of the apprentices of world trade.

## ENLIGHTENED SELF-INTEREST

In conclusion, as the founder of UNCTAD, the late Dr Raúl Prebisch, used to say, it is not only an imperative of justice or charity, but a matter of self interest to give the poor the necessary conditions to prosper, export and thus increase in a progressive and sustainable way their capacity not only to import but to pay for their own imports. Yet self interest, the soul of the market, is not enough. We have to put some heart into it, to add solidarity to self interest, to rededicate ourselves to the moral commitment of assisting the disadvantaged, because in the end it is only the belief in the basic unity of humankind, in a sharing of responsibilities and benefits, that will give legitimacy and enduring force to our endeavour.

# Chapter 28

# Part II.  Trade and development

## Introduction

*H.E. Ambassador F. Paolo Fulci\**

If development is the goal of human society, trade is its life-blood. Trade is the engine of growth. High growth generates new trade opportunities and new prosperity.

Trade and development reflect two crucial realities. First, there are several multi-lateral organizations dealing with both these issues in and outside the United Nations system. Each has its own mandate and competency. But these specific mandates and competencies are really complementary tools for our common goal: to create conditions for growth and development to the benefit of all the peoples of the world.

Secondly, to achieve this goal, the United Nations, the World Trade Organization and the Bretton Woods institutions are indispensable partners – a fact that is becoming increasingly clear to the Economic and Social Council (ECOSOC). The Council (i.e. ECOSOC) starts its deliberations each year with a one-day high-level policy dialogue with the heads of the international financial and trade institutions, including the WTO. Right from the start, the Council has recognized the importance of trade in promoting development. Historically, it was an initiative taken by ECOSOC that led to the adoption of the Havana Charter in 1948 and the eventual creation of GATT, the predecessor of WTO. Fifty years later, in 1998, ECOSOC addressed this issue once again and adopted a Ministerial document entitled, "Market access: developments since the Uruguay Round; implications, opportunities and challenges, in particular for the developing countries and the least developed among them, in the context of globalization and liberalization". The adoption of this short, policy-oriented communique, the first of its kind in the history of ECOSOC, shows the importance our Council attaches to the issue.

It has become a matter of fact that trade liberalization and market access are essential to any strategy for promoting growth and development and alleviating, and ultimately eradicating, poverty. Unfortunately, policy makers do not always pay enough attention to ensuring greater consistency among trade, aid, financial and environmental aspects of policies. Unless our policies serve the same ends, the goals of development and poverty eradication will remain elusive. The need to achieve greater coherence among these policies was clearly recognized in the Marrakesh Declaration. The UN global conferences of the 1990's (New York, Rio, Vienna, Cairo, Copenhagen, Beijing and Rome), all highlighted the need for policy coherence in the economic, social and environmental spheres, at the national and

---

\* President, Economic and Social Council (ECOSOC) of the United Nations.

international levels, to achieve the overarching goals of poverty eradication and sustainable development.

Bringing the various policy strands together is one of the major challenges for the 54 members of ECOSOC, a forum where the economic, social, environmental and humanitarian aspects of development issues are addressed in a comprehensive manner. This does not mean that the Council has the potential, or the intent, to get involved in highly technical issues. Rather, the Council's added value lies in providing broad political signals to negotiations carried out elsewhere. As ECOSOC noted at the end of its high-level segment in 1997, "In the current economic environment, the question of policy coherence has emerged as a critical one for all participants in the global economy".

These words were written just before the financial crisis broke out in Asia and elsewhere. The crisis brought home, dramatically, the need for integration and a comprehensive approach. To translate words into action, in spring 1998 ECOSOC held, for the first time, a special Ministerial meeting with the Bretton Woods institutions to address global financial integration and development. The meeting was so successful that the Council will hold it again, devoting it this time to the functioning of international financial markets and stability in financing for development. More than that, just a few weeks ago, the President and 21 Executive Directors of the World Bank came to the ECOSOC Hall in New York to address with us the challenges of development, and the need for increased partnership between the UN and the Bank. It was a rewarding experience, which we sincerely hope may be followed by similar dialogue with the International Monetary Fund and the World Trade Organization.

The key goal for ECOSOC in these gatherings is to promote a dialogue on *development and eradication of poverty*. Ensuring the provision of basic services, creating adequate infrastructure, and investing in human development are all necessary prerequisites for developing countries to benefit from trade liberalization and financial integration. In this endeavor, poverty eradication must be our top priority; and poverty eradication tops the Council's agenda for this year's session of ECOSOC in Geneva.

Let me reiterate what I said at the opening meeting of ECOSOC this year: Poverty remains indeed our main enemy. Poverty is born of, and generates, malnutrition, hunger and disease. Poverty produces ignorance, illiteracy and not education. Poverty causes a lack of jobs and opportunities. Poverty degrades the environment and the quality of life. Poverty breeds intolerance, hatred and, ultimately, social unrest and conflict. Above all, poverty inflicts almost incurable wounds on human dignity. Furthermore, to eradicate poverty is not simply a noble moral imperative. It is in the interest of everyone. It is also a critical strategic objective to bring about stability, stimulate productivity and opportunities, release resources and ultimately help us create a better world.

We have had enough – some would say too much – of documents, resolutions, declarations and paperwork on how to fight poverty. What we need is an indication of priorities, a precise agenda of things that can be done immediately, not impossible wish lists. It is with this in mind that we would like to see the Economic and Social Council adopt, this summer, a manifesto against poverty. This would embody a realistic concept of practical steps that could be taken in the immediate future to start turning the tide, to start bringing tangible results on the ground, not merely resolutions and reports. Action, deeds, not more talks and papers – that is what we need now.

Poverty ultimately breeds social unrest and conflict. Under such conditions, trade, let alone development, cannot flourish. Political instability is too often the result of economic and social processes. The Asian crisis has brought this out in tragic ways.

We are witnessing a historic transformation: the creation of a truly integrated global economy. We must help, not fight, the forces of integration. But globalization must have a human face. Partnership, and not impositions or hegemony, is the key element. Trade is one of the driving forces in this transformation. But trade must be inclusive if it is to promote broad-based and universally shared development. Governments and corporations must be socially and environmentally accountable in pursuing global economic integration. To begin with, we must enable the poor, the weak and the vulnerable to participate in the benefits of trade and development. Allow me to say it again: this is not only a noble moral imperative; it is in the real interest of all.

All of us should join and contribute actively to this endeavor. We owe it to ourselves, we owe it to the world, to its poor and forgotten masses. We owe it to our common future on this planet to work together in the fight against poverty. In this battle, we can and must do better.

# Chapter 29

# Part II.  Trade and development

## Introduction

*Shigemitsu Sugisaki\**

## INTRODUCTION

During the last 20 months, much of the world's attention has been focused on Asia, then Russia, and now Brazil. Many of these countries benefited from the adoption of a liberal trade regime, and from their ability to tap available foreign savings. In recent times, of course, these countries have also experienced significant difficulties following the reversal of private capital flows.

I would like to focus on another group of countries – the world's poorest countries – who have not only been shunned by private capital markets, but who have also not shared in the benefits of the progressive liberalization of the world trading system that has benefited the majority of WTO members.

One of the great disappointments of the last two decades has been the failure of living standards in the world's poorest countries to converge toward those of the richer countries. Over this period, average per capita incomes in the Least Developed Countries (LDCs)[1] have stagnated. Despite recent progress, per capita income in these countries averaged only $228 in 1996, the same level, in real terms, as in 1980. This disappointing performance, despite all the efforts so far, underscores the urgent need to look for far reaching bold solutions to enhance the growth prospects of the LDCs. There must be three critical components of such a strategy:

- action by the LDCs themselves to sustain and strengthen their own policies for growth and development;
- action by the international community to improve the external financial environment, particularly through appropriate debt relief and concessional assistance; and
- perhaps the most important in this forum in view of the close links between trade and economic growth, improved access to industrial countries' markets that would increase incentives for trade and investment activities in the LDCs.

---

* Deputy Managing Director, International Monetary Fund.
[1]  The term "Least Developed Countries" refers to a group of 48 countries classified by the United Nations as the world's poorest countries. However, many of the problems discussed in this chapter are shared by a somewhat broader group of relatively poor developing countries.

## THE POLICY FRAMEWORK

Despite the setbacks of the past two decades, recent economic performance of the LDCs has been encouraging. Real GDP growth improved markedly during 1995–1998, compared with the first half of the decade, allowing for an increase in real per capita incomes of almost 2 per cent a year. Moreover, average inflation has declined and other indicators of macroeconomic performance have also shown marked improvement. This improved performance, including performance in the context of IMF-supported programs, enhances the scope for further progress. Sustained growth with low inflation is central to addressing poverty and improving living standards. The events of the past 20 months have clouded the external environment: commodity prices are depressed; economic growth has slowed; demand for LDC exports has reduced; and external financing conditions have tightened. In these circumstances, it is essential that countries not turn away from open markets, but further invigorate market-oriented reforms. Only by embracing openness and liberal market-oriented policies will these countries share in the benefits of globalization.

To sustain and strengthen the improved economic performance of the last few years, the policy framework needs to be reinforced. LDCs must continue the momentum of policy reform aimed at high-quality growth. This entails the following.

- Prudent fiscal and monetary policies, and an appropriate and sustainable exchange rate regime that contributes to price stability, and to a sustainable external current account position. These are essential elements of an environment that encourages productive economic activity. But they are not sufficient in themselves.
- Supporting structural policies which are critical to the development of a strong supply response to export opportunities. Although the design of these must, obviously, be country-specific, policies that are particularly important include: a liberal open trade regime; the removal of subsidies and excessive regulations; appropriate government spending on the infrastructure; financial sector reforms; privatization; and institutional reforms to ensure property rights. Of these, open trade policies are particularly important to promote exports, remove anti-export bias, and attract investment.
- A high quality of governance and strict accountability in policy-making which is needed to make economic reforms successful in promoting long-run prosperity. Lack of transparency and accountability in public policy-making invites rent-seeking behavior and corruption. The impact of weak governance can also undermine macro-economic policy-making and implementation, and deter both domestic and foreign direct investment. A weak rule of law and failure to protect property rights also substantially undermines productive activity.

## EXTERNAL FINANCIAL ENVIRONMENT

Efforts of the LDCs to implement the kind of policies outlined above need to be supported by concessional assistance and debt relief. These are also critical inputs for achieving sustainable growth and development and for poverty reduction. On the part of the IMF, the adjustment efforts of many LDCs are being supported in the context of ESAF programs. This, however, is not enough.

## Debt relief

Enhanced debt relief is a much-discussed topic. Whatever the outcome of these discussions, enhanced relief, including debt forgiveness, will only be effective if it complements and reinforces the reform policies of debtor countries and leads to an increase in resource flows. It should augment, not replace, other concessional inflows and be linked to efforts to enhance domestic savings and investment.

For this reason, strong policy reform has been central to the Initiative for Heavily Indebted Poor Countries (HIPC), which the international community has been implementing for 20 years. Thus far, 12 countries have been reviewed for assistance under the Initiative; US$6 billion has been committed to seven countries, and assistance has been released to Uganda and Bolivia. Moreover, the initiative has been implemented flexibly: the track-record requirements for six out of the seven early cases have been shortened; programs supported by post-conflict emergency assistance can now be included as part of the track record; and in all cases targets have been set in the lower half of the debt-to-export target range.

The IMF, together with our colleagues at the World Bank, welcomes recent calls by the Group of Seven (G7) countries for a reassessment of the HIPC framework with a view to further strengthening the initiative. We have begun consultations with interested stakeholder member countries, other multilateral creditors, NGOs, religious groups, and other interested institutions. We will report to our respective executive boards shortly on this consultative process, and the issue is to be considered at the June G7 Summit in Cologne.

I should reiterate that the fundamental objective remains sustained poverty reduction. The experience of successful reformers shows that sustained policy implementation is required to attain this objective. This also requires strengthening the incentives to undertake the needed reforms. While we agree that debt relief should be provided to more countries, a general undifferentiated shortening of the required track record would not, by itself, strengthen the incentives to implement policies that promote growth and raise social spending. We do the people of the heavily indebted poor countries no favors by agreeing to earlier debt relief without the necessary supporting policies. In our view a better way of broadening eligibility for debt relief would be to reconsider some of the existing debt sustainability targets.

In discussing the possible enlargement of the HIPC Initiative, the constraints on resource availability must be taken into account.[2] Debt reduction competes with other elements of development assistance, and it is a major concern that the initiative in its current form is still not fully funded. The IMF welcomes the growing consensus in favor of limited gold sales as proposed by the Managing Director. However, even with such gold sales, further bilateral contributions by governments will be required to secure full funding of the IMF's contribution to the initiative.

---

[2]   A paper called "Tentative Costing of Illustrative Alternatives to the HIPC Initiative Framework" is available on the Fund web-site (http://www.imf.org/external/np/hipc/cost/cost.htm).

There is also a shortfall in the funding of the contribution of some other multilateral creditors, including the African Development Bank. This brings me to the subject of official development assistance (ODA).

## Official development assistance

The declining trend in ODA flows over the past several years is a major cause of concern. These flows have fallen steadily to a historically low level of about 0.22 per cent of GNP, well below the United Nations target of 0.7 per cent of GNP. Action is required to reverse this declining trend and increase ODA to support countries' efforts to strengthen development prospects and raise the very low living standards prevailing in the poorest countries. The impact of declining flows of concessional assistance partly offsets the beneficial impact of the HIPC Initiative.

Strengthening private capital inflows is, of course, critical and will be greatly enhanced by the adoption of the type of policy framework discussed above. But, for the poorest countries in particular, it will be some time before private flows increase sufficiently to effectively complement ODA. Private capital flows tend to be concentrated in a limited range of sectors in the relatively more advanced developing countries. They do not reach countries with the poorest infrastructure, and the most difficult social conditions. The need for reviving ODA flows has been reinforced by the financial crisis, which has underscored the challenges of sustainable development, and of reducing potential vulnerabilities of LDCs.

Official assistance is effective only when it complements locally-led efforts. Aid flows must be supported by a transparent policy framework aimed at achieving quality sustainable growth. The need is for an integrated approach to economic policy design, combining international financial support with better targeting of resources to priority development goals. Improving infrastructure, basic health and education, and governance, as well as environmental sustainability, have emerged as key areas requiring donor assistance. Donors must improve coordination with the authorities and strengthen their bilateral assistance to countries that have demonstrated a commitment to reform.

## Reforms in the global trading system

The third critical element of efforts to improve the growth performance and prospects of the poorest countries concerns trade. A growing body of empirical evidence and analysis demonstrates the close links between export performance and economic growth. Thus, enhancing export potential and incentives for productive trade and investment in the LDCs is an essential element of a growth-oriented strategy for those countries. Here, the rules and operation of the global trading system have a key part to play.

The marginalization of the LDCs in world trade justifies extraordinary efforts and actions on the part of the major beneficiaries of the global trading system. Moreover, the circumstances of the LDCs warrants exceptional treatment. Existing preference schemes have not been effective because they are complex, temporary in nature, and contain numerous exemptions and exclusions in areas of key interest to the LDCs. In the United States, for example, only some 1 per cent of imports entering under the Generalized System of Preferences come from the LDCs.

In view of the above, WTO Director-General Ruggiero has made a bold proposal in advocating across-the-board, duty-free access for the exports of the LDCs to the markets of the industrial countries. We endorse Mr Ruggiero's proposal. Enhanced access to industrial country markets for goods and services from the LDCs would substantially encourage them to undertake the domestic reforms necessary to exploit new opportunities. In this regard, the enhanced duty-free access should be bound in the WTO to give the necessary security to domestic and external investors. Such exceptional actions by the industrial countries to enhance export and investment incentives in the LDCs should, in our view, be matched by appropriately ambitious trade reforms in the LDCs, also bound in the WTO.

Reform of the global trading rules should also include a review of the "special and different treatment" accorded the LDCs in the Uruguay Round, which exempts them from certain trade rules and allows them to postpone the implementation of others. If certain rules, and the economic policies underlying them, are considered beneficial, then the LDCs should meet the same standards for these policies as other countries. Special and differential treatment for the LDCs should, instead, be a positive force. For example, the LDCs need special access to technical and financial assistance to raise their capacity to implement reforms, including multilateral obligations from which they may now be exempted. Here, I would note that the Fund and five other agencies are working together to strengthen our trade-related technical assistance to LDCs within the process agreed at the high-level meeting held here in Geneva in October 1997. Moreover, ways should be found for the LDCs to have better access to the dispute-settlement provisions of the WTO through lowering the costs involved.

Another key reform is to liberalize domestic policies and reduce barriers to trade against those products in which LDCs have the potentially greatest comparative advantage. Markets for agriculture in the world's richest economies remain highly distorted by import restrictions and export and production subsidies. Indeed, subsidies to agriculture in OECD countries average about 1.5 per cent of GDP. The Uruguay Round made important advances in this area, and these should be followed by further ambitious reforms. This would enhance LDC export potential. It would also be a significant benefit to the industrial countries themselves, through more efficient resource allocation, reduced budgetary costs, lower prices, and generally enhanced consumer welfare. Textiles is another area of LDC comparative advantage that remains subject to restrictive trade policies. Here again the Uruguay Round made important advances on the removal of quantitative restrictions, but implementation has so far been substantially back-loaded.

Lastly, the continued strengthening of the WTO and the rules-based system is also important to the LDCs. The WTO provides transparent and enforceable multilateral rules, broadly based on sound economic principles, that help ensure a level playing field for traders from all countries, rich and poor.

## CONCLUDING REMARKS

Let me again stress the need for extraordinary efforts to address the plight of the world's poorest countries, in order to raise significantly their living standards. We must encourage and facilitate the adoption of appropriate policies, and also ensure that when the countries concerned make the necessary efforts to integrate with the international financial and trade systems, these systems will work in their favor. This latter is an essential complement to actions by the international community to improve the external financing environment.

Together with debt relief and enhanced official development assistance, reforms of the multilateral trading system aimed at the integration of the LDCs would be important components of an international environment that would help ensure the success of domestic reforms in the countries concerned. Moreover, the trade reforms discussed in this paper would not be costly; the LDCs account for less than one half of one per cent of world trade. In our view, appropriate actions by all concerned in the areas outlined here would be the clearest example of policy coherence between the IMF, the World Bank, the WTO, and our member countries.

# Chapter 30

# Part II.  Trade and development

## Introduction

*Caio Koch-Weser\**


## INTRODUCTION

I would like to make four main points. First, for nearly two decades now, developing countries as a group have been in the vanguard of progress on trade liberalization, and this openness to trade has paid off not only in higher growth but also in providing a stimulus to the world economy as a whole.

Secondly, it is important that we protect these gains and resist a return to protectionism. There remains a large unfinished agenda in the trade and development area, and we need to move forward.

Thirdly, everyone has a role to play in moving this agenda forward, from the World Bank and other international institutions, to countries themselves.

Fourthly, trade alone cannot form the basis for lasting development; it must be part of a broader development agenda to invest in the poor and integrate them into the global economy.


## THE JOURNEY HERE

It's extraordinary how far the international community has come on trade liberalization over the past 50 years. In the industrial countries, average tariffs on manufactures have fallen from well over 40 per cent to an average of 2.5 per cent after the Uruguay Round.

For various reasons, serious liberalization in the developing countries started later. But even there, by the end of the Uruguay Round, average tariffs on manufactures had fallen below 15 per cent. While almost six times the level in the industrial countries today, it is only a third of the rate applied by the industrial countries at the beginning of GATT. I am pleased to say that the World Bank played a role in this process. During the critical years, from 1981 to 1994, the bank made 238 loans to 75 countries that supported liberalization of trade or foreign exchange policy. These loans affected imports of over $600 billion, including roughly $400 billion from industrial countries and $200 billion from developing countries. These loans helped

---

* Managing Director, The World Bank.

bring about more liberal trade regimes in developing countries and helped them participate more fully in the Uruguay Round.

The evidence that a liberal trade regime enhances long-run economic performance is now quite overwhelming. Jeff Sachs and Andrew Warner estimate that developing countries that liberalized grew at 1.33 percentage points per year faster than those that remained closed – a growth dividend large enough to make a big dent in poverty within a generation. Most of the dramatic export growth of the last 20 years from developing countries has been in labor intensive manufactures, creating millions of jobs, particularly for women.

Trade liberalization can also play an important, positive role in the adjustment to financial crises. By lowering the cost of capital goods, it can help re-establish investment flows and renew the capital stock. Despite the crisis, East Asia is still a good example of how relatively open economies achieved high growth rates that lifted millions from abject poverty. Some of the worst-hit countries, notably the Republic of Korea and Indonesia, have rightly taken this opportunity to liberalize their trade regimes further. The bottom line is that developing countries are better equipped to meet the basic needs of their citizens if they embrace the nettle of liberalization, rather than shrink from it.


## CHALLENGES AHEAD


Let's face it: the severity of the financial crises affecting developing countries has made many people wary about global integration. Some have painted trade liberalization with the same brush as poorly-implemented financial market liberalization. But clearly they are not the same. Open trading systems do not carry the same risks as open financial systems. Indeed, openness to foreign commerce has been shown, time and again, to be the best path to raising incomes and living standards. On every continent open economies have fared better than closed ones. Think of Chile, Korea, or Mauritius.

In tackling the challenges ahead, we must keep in mind another lesson from the past, since global integration, and unease about it, is not new.

More than a century ago, trade barriers were very low, and 90 per cent of the world's population lived in countries with convertible currencies. But by the time the First World War was over, many countries had forgotten the benefits of free and open trade and investment. International cooperation broke down, leading to financial instability, protectionism, and ultimately, to war. We must not forget the lessons learned from that episode, lessons that led to the formation of the GATT, the IMF, and the World Bank as well.

Even though the Uruguay Round was a major achievement, and provided a framework for liberalization, it made only very tentative steps towards liberalization in many areas. We need to build on this framework in a number of key areas.

In agriculture, we need to lower the high rates of protection in industrial countries so that developing countries can have access to large markets and earn sorely needed foreign exchange.

We are also keen to see manufactures trade included in the next round of negotiations. Most developing countries now rely heavily on exports of manufactures; because of this, they stand to benefit the most from liberalizing manufactures trade.

(Of course to ensure that they capture these gains, the developed countries must honor their commitments to phase out the infamous Multifibre Arrangement quotas against developing country exports of textiles and clothing.)

Developing countries can gain enormously by further liberalizing services trade in areas of export interest, such as construction and movement of natural persons, and in areas like infrastructure and power, where they can benefit from foreign expertise.

## OUR PARTNERS AND OUR ROLES

The agenda I have just outlined cannot move forward without action from developing and transition countries, who make up over 80 per cent of WTO membership, and all of the 30 or so countries in the accession queue.

A great deal needs to be done to help developing countries, particularly the least developed, to participate fully in the multilateral system, which may help them to win new market opportunities, and tame the special interests that might otherwise close their economies to the world.

Many of the items on the new trade agenda involve comprehensive reforms of domestic regulatory policies. In order to make bound commitments in these areas, developing countries may also need bound commitments of assistance to implement them.

The World Bank, working in cooperation with the WTO and other partners, can help through advice and lending programs. For example, bank-supported technical assistance allowed 17 countries, including Bangladesh, Ghana, Indonesia, Jamaica and Senegal, to join the WTO Agreement on Basic Telecommunications.

A 1996 reform and development loan to Jordan helped them to adopt new customs laws, increased use of computers by customs, and raised product standards. Similarly, technical assistance lending to Lebanon supported a move to an automated customs clearance process.

To underpin this operational work, we've begun a program of research, capacity-building and dissemination that we hope will prove useful in preparing developing country policy makers for the new negotiations.

We are doing this in collaboration with staff from the Secretariat, and with regional research agencies from around the world. We are preparing a series of research papers on key themes for the negotiations, and a handbook for developing country negotiators. We are also arranging a number of workshops around the world. In September, we hope to release key findings from this process at conferences in Washington and Geneva.

We also are partnering with the IMF, WTO, UNCTAD, UNDP, and ITC under the Integrated Framework for Trade Related Assistance to Least Developed Countries.

The goal of the Integrated Framework is to make trade a more effective vehicle for development. It is completely demand-driven, and is tailored to individual country needs. The bank's contribution focuses on increasing basic capacities' infrastructure, human and enterprise capacities, whatever is needed to efficiently produce internationally-tradable goods and services and to participate fully in the WTO process. For example, our work in Ethiopia and Uganda is focused on helping them to overcome their country-specific obstacles to trade, such as poor roads and railways, unreliable access to power and water, and limited telecommunications.

I don't mean to suggest that trade liberalization rests solely on developing country shoulders. Even the best intentions and the best plans will fail if developed countries don't adhere to the very policies they want developing countries to follow. Wealthy countries can't abandon their commitment to international trade as soon as imports increase. The recent outbreak of protectionism in the steel industries of developed countries provides a sobering warning of the continuing strength of protectionist interests.

## THE BROADER DEVELOPMENT AGENDA

No matter how successful our trade liberalization efforts are, trade alone can't spur lasting development. Increasingly, we in the World Bank – indeed all of us in the development community – are seeking a balanced approach to the problems of development. To respond to this concern, Jim Wolfensohn has developed what he calls the Comprehensive Development Framework – a more holistic approach to development assistance that draws on our many years of varied experiences and evolving thematic emphases. Broadly, this approach seeks to integrate the macroeconomic, trade and financial sides of development with the structural, social and human sides.

The essential point is that equitable and sustainable development cannot take place if either side is considered separately from the other. A key part of this framework is to help developing countries build the institutions that form the foundation for a market economy. These foundations are the social and institutional underpinnings of a market economy that developed countries now take for granted, but took generations to develop. The foundations include: strong public institutions and a system that fights systemic corruption; strong laws and a justice system that can guarantee that laws will be enforced; well regulated banks, stock exchanges and capital markets; and strong social safety nets to protect the most vulnerable.

The World Bank is very active in helping countries to build effective institutions. For example, we are involved in a very successful project to modernize the Supreme Court in Venezuela. We are also currently piloting National Institutional Reviews in five countries – Armenia, Bangladesh, Bolivia, Ethiopia, and Indonesia – to assess the quality of their institutions and to propose an overall strategy for institutional change.

Such a Comprehensive Development Framework involves more than getting exchange rates right, or fixing fiscal or monetary policy, or even getting trade reform implemented.

As important as these elements are, they are not enough. Development requires a totality of effort that ensures that developing countries have good health facilities and an education system available to boys and girls equally; sufficient infrastructure and access to clean water and power; environmental protection; and strategies for the special challenges of rural and urban development.

In the context of this broader framework of development, some of the "new" trade issues, particularly labour and environment, become a concern. Raising labour standards and preventing environmental degradation are serious development issues and should be treated as such. Such issues must not be allowed to become a weapon in the hands of the still strong protectionist lobbies in many industrial countries.

# CONCLUSION

Historical experience and economic analysis have shown, time and again, that trade is a vital ingredient of development policy. But opening markets alone is not sufficient for development. More is needed, including the creation and strengthening of institutions at domestic and international levels.

There is so much at stake. We must use the opportunity of new negotiations to rise above parochial interests, and to set the stage for transforming the global economy in the 21st century. It is an opportunity that must not be missed.

# Chapter 31

# Part II.  Trade and development

## Introduction

*T. N. Srinivasan\**
*Samuel C. Park Jr\*\**

The debate on the role of openness to international flows of goods, technology and capital in the development process is as old as economics. After all, Adam Smith praised the virtues of openness and competition in *The Wealth of Nations*. A moment's reflection should be enough to convince anyone that the sources of economic development are essentially three: the growth in inputs of production; improvements in the efficiency of allocation of inputs across economic activities; and innovation that creates new products, new uses for existing products, and brings about increases in the efficiency of use of inputs.

Being open to trade and investment contributes to each of the sources of growth. By allowing the economy to specialize in those activities in which it has comparative advantage, efficiency of the allocation of domestic resources is enhanced. By being open to capital, labour and other resource flows, an economy is able to augment relatively scarce domestic resources and use part of its abundant resources elsewhere where they earn a higher return. Clearly, efficiency of resource use in each nation and across the world is enhanced by the freedom of movement of resources. Finally, the fruits of innovation anywhere in the world become available everywhere in such an open world.

While the potential benefits of openness from the perspective of growth and development and world welfare have been obvious since Adam Smith, if not earlier, appreciation of this potential in full measure has been slow in coming. Even now doubts persist about the potential. The recent financial crises, resulting from volatility of short-term capital flows in some of the erstwhile rapidly growing and outward-oriented economies of East Asia, have revived skepticism about outward orientation. I would argue that the case for outward orientation in trade and investment remains strong, financial crises notwithstanding.

Let me briefly recapitulate the history of the developing countries in the multilateral trading and financial system that emerged after the Second World War. This system, which consisted of the GATT, the IMF, the World Bank and later the UNCTAD, was influenced very much by the disastrous experience in the interwar period with the world trading and financial system.

---

\* Professor of Economics, Department of Economics, Yale University, USA.
\*\* Chairman, Department of Economics, Yale University, USA.

It is worth recalling that the First World War ended a world in which man-made barriers to trade and capital flows were minimal, currencies were tied to gold so that exchange risk was absent, no passport and visa requirements impeded the flow of people seeking a better life elsewhere. According to some economic historians, the so-called globalization of the recent years is, in many ways, a resumption of the same process that was rudely interrupted by the First World War. Let me quote from Lord Keynes' eloquent description of the pre-World War I golden era of globalization:

"What an extraordinary episode in the economic progress of man that age was which came to an end in August 1914! ... The inhabitant of London could order by telephone, sipping his morning tea in bed, the various products of the whole earth, in such quantity as he might see fit, and reasonably expect their early delivery upon his doorstep; he could at the same moment and by the same means adventure his wealth in the natural resources and new enterprises of any quarter of the world, and share, without exertion or even trouble, in their prospective fruits and advantages; or he could decide to couple the security of his fortunes with the good faith of the townspeople of any substantial municipality in any continent that fancy or information might recommend. He could secure forthwith, if he wished it, cheap and comfortable means of transit to any country or climate without passport or other formality, could dispatch his servant to the neighbouring office of a bank for such supply of the precious metals as might seem convenient, and could then proceed abroad to foreign quarters, without knowledge of their religion, language, or customs, bearing coined wealth upon his person, and would consider himself greatly aggrieved and much surprised at the least inference. But, most important of all, he regarded this state of affairs as normal, certain, and permanent, except in the direction of further improvement, and any deviation from it as aberrant, scandalous, and avoidable."

Keynes, as referenced in Sachs and Warner, 1995, p. 9.

The attempt to return to the pre-war gold parities in the radically different economies of the post-war failed, disrupting trade and capital movements. The great depression, escalation of tariffs and competitive devaluations by major trading nations ended any possibility of a resumption of the process of global integration interrupted by the war.[1]

## FIRST MOVES

The GATT, an agreement to reduce tariffs, was the result of the initiative of the United States. It was an agreement among 23 contracting parties which consisted of independent customs jurisdictions rather than independent nations. It was to be subsumed in a formal International Trade Organization (ITO). The United Nations Conference on Trade and Employment, which met in Havana during November 1947 to March 1948 after the conclusion of the GATT, agreed on a draft charter for the ITO but – primarily because the US did not ratify the charter – the ITO did not

[1] The same Lord Keynes sang a very different tune after the depression (Keynes, as referenced in Sachs and Warner, 1995, pp. 10–11): "I sympathize, therefore, with those who would minimize, rather than with those who would maximize, economic entanglements between nations. Ideas, knowledge, art, hospitality, travel – these are the things which should of their nature be international. But let goods be homespun whenever it is reasonably and conveniently possible; and, above all, let finance be primarily national."

come into being. In the meantime, the GATT, which was brought into force through a provisional protocol of application, became the only framework for governing international trade until it was subsumed and replaced by the WTO in 1995. Even though, as the eminent scholar of international trade law, John Jackson (1989), put it, the GATT limped along for nearly five decades without a formal constitution, it sponsored eight rounds of multilateral negotiations which have succeeded in reducing trade barriers significantly. And the result has been an unprecedented growth of world trade substitution exceeding the growth of world output in the last five decades.

Although more than 11 of the original 23 contracting parties of the GATT were developing countries, they did not effectively participate in it, or deem it as a framework that would promote their interests. Indeed, in the Havana Conference the most heated discussions were about trade and development, with the developing countries denouncing the Charter that was eventually passed with their agreement, as inimical to development. In the GATT, until the introduction of Part IV on Trade and Development in 1964, only Article XVIII on governmental assistance to development was the principal and only provision dealing with problems of developing countries.

After the incorporation of Part IV in 1964, the next major GATT event from the perspective of developing countries was the grant of a ten-year waiver from the "most favoured nation" (MFN) clause with respect to tariff and other preferences favouring trade of developing countries. This so-called Generalized System of Preferences (GSP) was later included under the rubric of the "enabling clause" of the Tokyo Round that formulated the Differential and More Favourable Treatment of developing countries in the GATT.

The Tokyo Round, concluded in 1979, was the first round in which the developing countries participated in strength and with cohesion. But it produced outcomes that were not in their long-term interest, primarily because their demands continued to be driven by the import-substitution ideology.

The formal incorporation of a Special Differential and More Favourable Treatment of the developing countries triply hurt them:

- first, through the direct costs of enabling them to continue their import substitution strategies;
- secondly, by allowing the developed countries to get away with their own GATT-inconsistent barriers (e.g. the Multi-Fibre Arrangement (MFA) in textiles) against imports from developing countries; and
- thirdly, by allowing the industrialized countries to keep higher than average MFN tariffs on goods of export interest to developing countries.

The experience of developing countries in the GATT, up to the conclusion of the Tokyo Round, could be interpreted in two diametrically opposite ways. On the one hand, it could be said that from the Havana Conference on, the developing countries had been repeatedly frustrated in getting the GATT to reflect their concerns. Tariffs, and other barriers in industrialized countries on their exports, were reduced to a smaller extent than those on exports of developed countries in each round of the MTN. Products in which they had a comparative advantage, such as textiles and apparel, were taken out of the GATT disciplines altogether. Agriculture, a sector of great interest to developing countries, was also subjected to a waiver and, thereafter, largely remained outside the GATT framework. "Concessions" granted to developing countries, such as inclusion of Part IV on Trade and Development and the Tokyo Round enabling clause on special and differential treatment, were mostly rhetorical, and others, such as GSP, were always heavily qualified and quantitatively small. In sum, the GATT was indifferent, if not actively hostile, to the interests of developing countries.

The other interpretation is that the developing countries, in their relentless but misguided pursuit of import-substitution as the strategy of development, in effect "opted out" of the GATT. Instead of demanding and receiving what turned out to be "crumbs from the rich man's table", such as GSP and a permanent status of inferiority under the "special and differential" treatment clause, they could have participated fully, vigorously, and on equal terms with the developed countries, in the GATT. Had they adopted an outward-oriented development strategy, they could have achieved faster and better growth.

## URUGUAY ROUND

After initially resisting the initiation of the Uruguay Round 1986, and the inclusion of non-traditional issues such as services and intellectual property rights in the negotiations, the developing countries did participate vigorously in the negotiations. In the final agreement they took several steps to move away from being exceptions to multilateral disciplines. They succeeded in ensuring the phasing out the infamous MFA, an egregious violation of the principles of GATT.

On the whole, the quantitative gains to developing counties form the trade liberalization of the Uruguay Round are not only modest but unevenly distributed. (Gains to sub-Saharan African countries are very small, if there are any at all.) One reason for the modest gain is, in part, due to the fact that tariffs in industrialized countries on exports of developing countries were reduced to a relatively smaller extent. Another reason is that the dynamic gains to developing countries from liberalization is difficult to quantify. Also, the net gains from GATS, TRIMS (Trade-Related Investment Measures), TRIPS (Trade-Related Intellectual Property Rights) and the strengthening of the Dispute Settlement Mechanism are virtually impossible to quantify.

Before turning to the unfinished agenda of the Uruguay Round and agenda for a possible new millennium round, let me endorse what the Director General Ruggiero (1999) has already emphasized: the growing importance of the developing countries in the WTO membership and in world trade. From 23 contracting parties of the GATT in 1947 of whom 11 were developing countries, membership in WTO as of March 1999 stands at 134. Nearly four-fifths of WTO members are developing countries.

Growth in world trade has continued to outstrip that of world output. Between 1950 and 1964, merchandise trade grew at about 8 per cent per year, 40 per cent faster than output. Between 1964 and the first oil shock of 1973, trade grew at 9.2 per cent per year, double the rate of growth of output. Although growth of trade and output slowed down after the oil shocks, nonetheless trade grew faster than output except during a brief period between 1980 and 1985. As the Director General of the WTO (Ruggiero, 1999) has noted, the developing countries shared in this growth.

The share of trade in developing country GDP, which was less than 20 per cent in 1970, roughly doubled to 38 per cent in the last year, though the increase was unevenly distributed among countries. Between 1973 and 1997 the developing countries' share of manufactured imports in developed markets tripled, from 7.5 to 23 per cent, reflecting the remarkable integration of the developing countries into the global economy in the last three decades. This makes it all the more essential that the world trading order will continue to provide a conducive world trade and financial environment for developing countries to catch up and converge to the levels of income of today's developed world.

The post Uruguay Round agenda includes the review of TRIPS and the Agriculture Agreement and negotiations on left-over items of GATS agreement, such as on movement of natural persons and maritime services. I am afraid that developing countries, led by Brazil and India, by initially refusing to discuss intellectual properties and eventually giving in to the inclusion of the issue in the WTO as the TRIPS agreement, made a colossal mistake. This has opened the door for demands for linkage of market access to enforcement of objectives which have little or no relationship to trade. The prime examples are labour and environmental standards.

## STICKING TO THE MANDATE

Overloading the WTO with responsibility in areas not related to trade would be very unfortunate. As the late Nobel laureate, Jan Tinbergen argued in his well known work on policy assignment, there has to be at least one policy instrument per objective, and using the same policy instrument for achieving more than one objective is a sure prescription for achieving none of the objectives efficiently and in full measure. The same logic applies equally to assignment of responsibility to international institutions. The World Bank, the International Monetary Fund (IMF) and International Labour Organization (ILO) have their own mandates. So does the WTO. By going beyond the mandates of each and using it to achieve objectives unrelated to its mandates is inappropriate.

In the arena of intellectual property there is the World Intellectual Property Organization (WIPO) and the Paris and Berne Conventions; for labour there is the ILO; and for environment there is the United Nations Environment Programme (UNEP). There is no reason why these specialized agencies could not be used as fora for negotiating, and for creating effective multilateral disciplines on intellectual property, labour and environmental standards.

Even now it is not too late to use the forthcoming review to take TRIPS out of the WTO and to put it in a redesigned WIPO. In the first two ministerials of the WTO, the ministers firmly resisted bringing labour standards into the WTO and insisted on ILO as the appropriate forum to handle the issue. The WTO Committee on Trade and Environment has thus far not recommended any unfortunate linkage between trade and environment. The sooner this committee is wound up, and the issue taken to UNEP or a similar forum, the better it would be.

Agricultural trade was liberalized, but not fully brought under GATT disciplines in the UR agreement. Indeed the tariff process, by which all forms of intervention were to be converted in tariffs and then reduced on an agreed schedule, was scandalously abused by all countries. Some countries, such as Japan and Korea, even managed to stall any early and major reduction of their sky-high barriers to rice imports. The case of the EC is another. It is absolutely essential that in the negotiations that will begin next year, agricultural trade is finally and fully brought under WTO disciplines.

Let me also draw your attention to the fact that the General Agreement on Trade in Services (GATS) is not the analogue of GATT in terms of non-discrimination and national treatment. Nonetheless it is a step forward. The agreements in tele-communications and financial services that have since been concluded are impor-tant. Yet on the movement of natural persons, in which the developing countries have a significant interest, progress towards an agreement has been slow. This has to be rectified.

The strengthened Dispute Settlement Mechanism (DSM) is undeniably in the interest of all members of the WTO. The provisions in the UR Agreement that make available the services of the WTO Secretariat, if needed, to enable the devel-oping countries to avail of the DSM, are to be welcomed. Yet, realistically speak-ing, the administrative and information-gathering capabilities of many developing countries are likely to prove inadequate, even with the assistance of the WTO Secretariat, to present a strong case before the DSM. Nonetheless the experience thus far with the DSM is encouraging even though unilateralism, which the strength-ened DSM of the WTO was meant to curb, has not disappeared.

The continuing use by the US of Section 301 of its domestic trade legislation to put countries on a watch-list for their weak enforcement of intellectual property rights, and the recent action against the EU by the US, even before the final pro-nouncement by the Dispute Settlement Body, on the extent of damage to the US of the EU Banana import regime, are unfortunate examples of unilateralism.

## ISSUES FOR THE NEXT ROUND

Let me now turn to the issues that need to be taken up in the next round of multilat-eral negotiations.[2] The Director-General of the WTO, Mr Ruggiero has rightly emphasized the importance of the full implementation of liberalization commit-ments agreed in the Uruguay Round. He drew attention to the claim by developing countries that the industrialized countries have not lived up to the spirit of agree-ments such as those relating to textiles (Ruggiero, 1999). Understandably many developing countries are reluctant to enter into a new round of negotiations when the commitments given in the prior round do not seem to have been kept. Those with a long memory will recall the failed attempts in the past by developing coun-tries to get the developed countries to stand-still and roll back GATT-inconsistent measures employed by them. While the reluctance is understandable, the stakes are too high to postpone a new round for too long.

Let me take an example. The late, unlamented European Commission recom-mended the imposition of anti-dumping duties against imports of grey cotton cloth from some developing countries such as Egypt, India and Pakistan, even though

---

[2]   See also Bhagwati, 1996.

such imports are restricted by quotas under the infamous MFA and, as such, exporters cannot hope to gain market shares by dumping! Fortunately the EU ministers rejected the Commission's recommendation. I would argue that economic rationale for dumping has never been very strong and having anti-dumping measures as a WTO legitimate instrument only encourages its abuse. Unlike safeguard measures, the ADMs can be applied to exports from a particular country or even from a particular firm. No wonder they have become the preferred means of protection. Sadly, many developing countries have also begun to use ADMs. Some have suggested that the use of ADMs be made harder, for example, by raising the threshold of injury to domestic industries before ADMs could be invoked. But at the risk of sounding utterly naive politically, I would call for the removal of ADMs from the list of permitted trade policy instruments in the next round. In my view, ADMs are the analogues of chemical and biological weapons in the arsenal of trade policy instruments.

Since the start of the Uruguay Round, there has been a disturbing and unfortunate increase in the number of discriminatory regional trade agreements that have been concluded. Many more have been proposed. Contrary to the expectation of some, the successful conclusion of the Uruguay Round did not stop this trend – on the contrary, there is some evidence of acceleration. Many developing countries are already members, or are eager to become members, of such Preferential Trade Agreements (PTAs). This eagerness might also lead them to accept deleterious agreements on labour standards in PTAs that are not necessarily in their interest.

I should also stress that though many developing countries are eager to enter into regional PTAs this does not necessarily mean that it is in their best interests to do so.[3] Even at the time the GATT was negotiated, the incompatibility of the principle of non-discrimination (that is the foundation of GATT) and the PTAs was recognized. Article XXIV, by placing rather stringent conditions before pronouncing any proposed PTA to be compatible with GATT, was an attempt to reconcile the irreconcilable. Another effort to make discrimination sound benign is the proposal for open regionalism, a proposal that has been embraced by the Council of Economic Advisers to the President of the United States (CEA, 1995), the World Bank (Burki and Perry, 1997) and Secretary General Ruggiero, among others (WTO, 1996). The most enthusiastic advocate of this proposal is Bergsten (1997). I have argued (Srinivasan, 1998c) that open regionalism is more an oxymoron than a fruitful concept. Openness with respect to membership cannot make a regional PTA non-discriminatory.

Given that political, rather than economic, considerations were (and are) the driving forces behind PTAs including the most enduring of them all, namely the EU, it is not surprising that in the past the GATT working parties on PTAs looked the other way when Article XXIV ran up against political goals. Out of 89 working parties established by GATT during its 47-year existence to examine proposed PTAs, 15 did not complete their work before GATT was subsumed in the WTO, five did not report and out of the 69 which reported, only six explicitly acknowledged the conformity with Article XXIV of the agreements they examined. This six

---

[3] On the implications of the proliferation of PTAs for the multilateral trading system, see Panagariya and Srinivasan (1998) and Srinivasan (1998c).

most notably did not include the EU; in other words, no GATT working party has pronounced on the compatibility or otherwise of EU with Article XXIV.

Given the discriminatory nature of PTAs, the enormous complexities of the rules of origin that PTAs (other than customs unions) necessarily involve, the dismal record of the working party mechanism for examining the compatibility of any proposed PTA with Article XXIV and the political basis for many of them, it would seem that instead of attempting to modify the Article as some have suggested, a far better course would be to ensure that all PTAs (regional or otherwise in their membership) are temporary. In other words, Article XXIV should be replaced with the requirement that preferences granted to partners in any PTA should be extended on a MFN basis to all members of the WTO within a specified period, say, five to ten years.

Mr Ruggiero also drew attention to the importance of investment and competition policy. Again, a convincing case for going beyond making such policies transparent is yet to be made. Harmonizing them across countries and industries and enforcing them through linkage to market access are at best premature and, at worst, not in the best interests of the countries involved. For most developing countries which do not have market power in most world markets, openness to trade is the best competition policy. Investment issues involve sovereignty in an essential way and, as such, cannot be treated lightly.

There is a legitimate concern for the development of the "least developed and less dynamic developing countries", to use Mr Ruggiero's terminology. While recognizing that trade alone cannot solve their, or for that matter, any country's problems, he has been urging WTO members to provide duty free access for the export products of least developed countries. It is true that no single policy can solve the deep rooted problem of poverty in these countries. Yet the important lesson from the development experience of the last five decades is that rapid growth is the only effective instrument of poverty alleviation; and openness not only promotes more rapid growth but also makes the growth more poverty-alleviating since it enables the more efficient use of the only asset that the poor own, namely their labour.

Yet I must respectfully voice a note of dissent on preferential access to markets: whether part of regional trading agreements, or special favours granted to particular countries or country groups such as least developed countries, they are inherently discriminatory, distort trade and reduce the potential growth benefits accruing from trade. Once granted, producers and countries will invest resources expecting that the favourable treatment will continue indefinitely.

Withdrawal of favours then would impose a terrible burden of adjustment on such producers and countries. The EU's banana regime is an example – the Caribbean countries will face significant adjustment problems if it is dismantled in a short time as is being demanded. It is a bit ironic that the ten-year back-loaded phase-out of MFA will provide ample time for industrialized countries to adjust, while relatively poor banana exporters of Caribbean economies will have a much shorter time to adjust if the preferences they enjoy in the EU are phased out in a very short time.

I am afraid that policies of preferential access to markets such as the GSP are inappropriate instruments for accelerating the development of the least developed countries. Offering them preferential access will, on the one hand, have limited effect on accelerating their development while, on the other, it will create a false sense of complacency in developed countries of having done enough. Surely, we can do much better by turning, instead, to the necessary task of providing resources and technical assistance to these developing countries, while ensuring that they become equal partners in the world trading system.

## SUMMARY AND CONCLUSIONS

The third ministerial meeting of the WTO will be held in Seattle, USA, in October 1999. It is widely expected that a proposal for a comprehensive new round of multilateral trade negotiations (dubbed the "millennium round") will be adopted at the meeting. In addition, as part of the built-in agenda of the Uruguay Round: the TRIPS agreement is up for review; a mini-round of negotiations on agricultural trade to complete the process of fully integrating this vital sector into the WTO is to be initiated; and the postponed negotiations on maritime services as part of the GATS will finally get underway – all three to take place during 1999–2000.

I have argued that the developing countries have to participate effectively in all the forthcoming negotiations – particularly in the Seattle ministerial that is most likely to launch the next round of multilateral negotiations – in order to ensure that their interests are well served. There are a number of issues on which developing countries have to define their interests clearly and fight for them.

First, as I have argued above, an unfortunate mistake was made in the Uruguay Round in bringing TRIPS into the WTO. There were other fora, notably the World Intellectual Property Organization (WIPO) and also the Berne and Paris Conventions, which could have been the natural arena for negotiating agreements on intellectual property and related concerns. Yet it was agreed to bring TRIPS into the WTO and this agreement has opened the door for demands to bring even less trade-related issues such as labour and environmental standards into the WTO. The forthcoming TRIPS review should be used to consider taking TRIPS out of the WTO and put in the WIPO, if necessary, after strengthening its enforcement mechanism.

Secondly, an agreement on movement of natural persons should be concluded at the earliest time. This is an unfinished item of GATS.

Thirdly, although the interests of agricultural (particularly food) exporters and importers among developing countries do not necessarily coincide, their overall interests are better served if agricultural trade is fully integrated into the WTO. In particular, developing countries should insist on the elimination of export subsidies and the phasing out of interventions in agricultural trade such as through the Common Agricultural Policy of the European Union. The horror show that was the process of "tariffication" of agricultural supports in the Uruguay Round should not be allowed to take place again in the mini-round in other areas. Once and for all, the disciplines that apply to trade in manufactured goods should be extended to agricultural trade, with tariffs bound at reasonable levels and reduced substantially. Existing non-tariff barriers have to be phased out and new ones not allowed. In particular it must be ensured that sanitary and phytosanitary restrictions do not become non-tariff barriers.

Fourthly, anti-dumping measures, which have become the preferred protectionist device of all countries, developing and developed, should be made WTO-illegal.

Fifthly, the ministers from developing countries should insist at Seattle that there be no further discussion of labour or environmental standards at the WTO and that, in the future, the ILO should be the forum for negotiations on labour standards. With respect to environmental issues, the United Nations Environmental Programme could be the negotiating forum. The ministers should also propose that the Committee on Trade and Environment at the WTO be wound up.

Sixthly, the ministers should replace Article XXIV of GATT 1994 with the requirement that all preferences granted to partners of existing, or proposed, future preferential trading agreements, such as free trade or customs union agreements, regional or otherwise in geographic coverage, should be extended to all members of the WTO on a MFN basis within a ten to 15-year period of the coming into force of such agreements.

Seventhly, it seems premature, at least from the perspective of developing countries, to negotiate and conclude a Multilateral Agreement on Investment and related issues such as competition policies. An agreement to make current policies transparent should be the first step.

Finally, the legitimate concern of the community of trading nations for accelerating the economic and social development of the least developed and less dynamic countries should be channelled into providing them with resources, knowledge and technology so that they are enabled to grow faster and reap the benefits of being integrated with the global economy. Offering them preferential access to world markets, besides having only a limited beneficial effect on their growth will not only create a sense of complacency on the part of rich countries of having done enough for them but also, more seriously and deleteriously, enable the rich countries to persist in maintaining trade barriers that are detrimental to developing countries as a whole. Indeed, by demanding and receiving a special and differential treatment in the GATT and agreeing to the creation of the Generalized System of Preferences which are exceptions to the GATT's fundamental principle of non-discrimination, developing countries had in the past enabled the industrialized countries to get away with their own GATT-inconsistent trading arrangements such as the MFA. Developing countries should not fall into that trap again. They have much to gain by participating fully and as equal partners with the developed countries in a liberal world trading system.

## REFERENCES

Bergsten, C. F. (1997), "Open Regionalism," *World Economy*, Vol. 20, October, pp. 545–565.

Burki, S. J. and G. E. Perry (1997), "Towards Open Regionalism," in Burki, S. J., G. E. Perry and S. Calvo (eds.), *Trade: Towards Open Regionalism*, Proceedings of the Annual World Bank Conference on Development in Latin America and the Caribbean, Montevido, Uruguay.

Council of Economic Advisers (1995), *Economic Report of the President 1995*, Washington, D.C.: CEA.

Jackson, J. (1989), *The World Trading System*, Cambridge, Massachusetts and London: The MIT Press.

Ruggiero, R. (1999), "The New Multilateral Trade Negotiations, the European Union and its Developing Country Partners: An Agenda for Action," Geneva: WTO Press/122, 19 February.

Sachs, J. and A. Warner (1995), "Economic Reform and the Process of Global Integration," *Brookings Papers on Economic Activity*, 1.

Srinivasan, T. N. (1998), "Regionalism and the World Trade Organization: Is Non-Discrimination Passe?" in A. O. Krueger (ed.), *The World Trade Organization as an International Institution*, Chicago: The University of Chicago Press, pp. 329–349.

WTO (1996), "The Road Ahead: International Trade Policy in the Era of the WTO," *The Fourth Annual Sylvania Ostry Lecture*, Ottawa, 28 May, Geneva: WTO Press/49, 29 May.

# Chapter 32

# Part II. Trade and development

## 1. Linkages between trade and development policies

*C. Fred Bergsten\**

## THE GLOBAL TRADING SYSTEM AND
## THE DEVELOPING COUNTRIES IN 2000

1999 is likely to be a watershed year for the world trading system. The Ministerial Conference of the World Trade Organization in Seattle in November/December hopes to chart a course for global trade policy in the early part of the twenty-first century. The European Union, Japan, the United States and Canada – the Quadrilateral Group that functions as an informal steering committee for the system – as well as many other countries, have already agreed to use that occasion to launch a Millennium Round of multilateral negotiations to liberalize trade further, and to write new rules to govern additional types of economic transactions among nations.

At the same time, a substantial backlash against globalization is clearly gathering force in some quarters. If successful, that backlash could both derail the effort to commence new international liberalization initiatives and promote the creation of new protectionist pressures around the world.

Some of the backlash can be found in developing countries. Surprisingly, however, very little reaction against trade liberalization has surfaced in the East Asian countries that have been hit hardest by the global financial crisis (and even their pullback from full participation in global financial markets has been quite limited). The most worrisome tendencies are in fact emerging in the United States, despite the continued strong performance of its economy. This must be of deep concern to all trading countries because of America's pivotal role in both world trade and the functioning of the global trading system.

The developing countries have a very strong interest in the outcome of these global economic debates. "Outward orientation" has become a central tenet of virtually every successful development strategy. Trade has grown twice as fast as world output over the past decade or more. Nineteen of the world's top thirty exporters, counting the European Union as a single entity, are now developing countries. Seven of the top twenty recipients of foreign direct investment are in the developing world.

---

\* Director, Institute for International Economics.

165

"Outward orientation" itself is not a sufficient condition to assure development success. High rates of national investment, stability of macroeconomic policies and resilient domestic political institutions are crucial as well.[1] But "outward orientation" appears to be a necessary component of effective development strategy and a key explanation of why some countries have done better than others. Its maintenance, and indeed expansion, is thus a central consideration for global development.

This in turn means that an open international trading system has been of central importance for the development successes of the past several decades. "Outward orientation" in individual developing countries would never have succeeded, indeed would probably never have been attempted, in the absence of relatively open markets around the world. Hence systemic openness is also a crucial component of any effective global approach to development.

A number of others at this symposium will address the linkages between trade and development in some depth. Following the principle of comparative advantage, I will focus instead on the outlook for the global trading *system* and how its evolution may affect the prospects for development. In particular, I will analyze a series of threats to the prospects for continued openness, suggest how they might be countered, and recommend ways in which the developing countries themselves can contribute to maintaining a global trading system that will permit their own national development strategies to flourish.

In addressing these issues, and devising a strategy for the Millennium Round and beyond, it is first essential to sketch the pattern of global trade policy that has been evolving over the past couple of decades. I will then analyze the contemporary threats to the trading system, with considerable emphasis on the trade policy of the United States, and propose a strategy to avoid a renewed slide toward protectionism around the world. Finally, I will attempt to draw out several implications for developing nations, proposing that they adopt a proactive role in both moving the global system in a constructive direction and pursuing their own national interests within that context.

## TREND TOWARDS FREE TRADE

A large part of the world has eliminated all barriers to trade, or is in the process of doing so. The fifteen members of the European Union have created a "single internal market". Australia and New Zealand have completed their free trade area. Several large groupings are en route to a similar outcome: the North American Free Trade Agreement (Canada, Mexico, United States), Mercosur (Argentina, Brazil, Paraguay, Uruguay) and the ASEAN Free Trade Agreement (Brunei, Indonesia, Malaysia, Philippines, Singapore, Thailand and now Vietnam).

In addition, a series of newer groupings have pledged to abolish all impediments to their international trade in the coming years. The European Union and the Mediterranean countries (EUROMED) have committed themselves to free trade by 2010. The 34 democracies of the Western Hemisphere agreed at their Miami

---

[1] Dani Rodrik (1999), *The New Global Economy and Developing Countries: Making Openness Work*, Washington: Overseas Development Council.

**Table 1    Regional free trade arrangements share of world trade, 1998**

| | |
|---|---|
| EU | 22.8 |
| EUROMED | 2.3 |
| NAFTA | 7.9 |
| MERCOSUR | 0.3 |
| FTAA | 2.6* |
| AFTA | 1.3 |
| AUSTRALIA–NEW ZEALAND | 0.1 |
| APEC | 23.7* |
| Total | 61.0 |

* Excluding sub-regionals.

summit in December 1994 to work out a Free-Trade Area of the Americas (FTAA) by 2005 and negotiations to that end began last spring. The 21 members of the Asia Pacific Economic Cooperation (APEC) forum – which account for half of world output and include the three largest national economies (United States, Japan, China) – decided, via their Bogor Declaration of November 1994, to establish free trade and investment in the region by 2010 for their higher income members that make up 85 per cent of their commerce, and by 2020 for the rest.

Over 60 per cent of international commerce now takes place within these existing or planned free trade regimes (see Table 1). This share is rising rapidly, both because of the creation of new arrangements and because trade expands more quickly under such conditions. The question thus arises: why not eliminate all trade barriers throughout the world? Why not launch a movement toward *global* free trade at the upcoming WTO Ministerial Conference in Seattle?

## COMPETITIVE LIBERALIZATION

In answering these questions, it is first essential to understand why so many countries, in so many different parts of the world, with such different economic systems, at such different stages of development, have all headed in the same direction. There are of course different national circumstances which explain the detailed strategies and timing of the individual initiatives. The overarching force, however, has been the process of competitive liberalization.

The rapid increase of global interdependence has induced virtually all countries, whatever their prior policies or philosophies, to liberalize their trade (and usually investment) regimes. Economic success in today's world requires countries to compete aggressively for the footloose international investment that goes far to determine the distribution of global production, and thus jobs, profits and technology. Most countries offer direct incentives to foreign investors but an open trade and investment regime is even more critical for this purpose. Mexico was traditionally a

very closed economy (and was extremely wary of embracing its northern neighbour), for example, but decided to liberalize and propose NAFTA when it became
convinced that doing so was essential to avoid losing out in the global competition
for capital.

Moreover, success in today's global economy requires countries to compete effectively in international markets rather than simply at home. This is true no matter
how large the domestic market. Some of the world's most self-contained economies
including Brazil, China, India and perhaps most notably the United States – which
maintained extensive quotas on automobiles, machine tools, steel and numerous
other products less than fifteen years ago – have joined the competitive liberalization race.[2]

Competitive liberalization is pursued by countries that until recently had deeply
entrenched protectionist traditions. France is a dramatic case in point. So is
virtually all of Latin America, which embraced import substitution doctrines as
recently as two decades ago. The most stunning reversal of all comes from many of
the former command economies of the Communist world, ranging from China
through Central Europe to parts of the former Soviet Union and now Vietnam.

An intellectual and ideological sea-change underlies this historic development.
Import-substitution, and even autarkic models of development and national economic strategy, were reasonably respectable into the 1960s and even the 1970s. But
their shortcomings were then exposed, including the Third World debt crisis of the
1980s, and they were replaced by a new consensus of "outward orientation".[3]

The Asian, now global, financial crisis has interrupted neither these policy
actions nor the intellectual trends. To be sure, there has been some East Asian reaction against short-term capital flows (though even Malaysia *liberalized* its treatment
of foreign direct investment, including short-term transactions within multinational
firms while, at the same time, it imposed new barriers to hot-money flows). But
there has been very little recourse to new trade barriers. The ASEAN countries have
even decided to accelerate the timetable for achieving free trade under their
ASEAN Free-Trade Agreement (AFTA).

This change in basic thinking does not, however, explain the onset of regional or
other *international* trade arrangements. Why didn't the new attitude simply produce
a spate of *unilateral* trade liberalization, which textbooks recommend as the most
direct route to maximizing trade benefits for an individual country? The answer lies
in the politics of trade reform.

## POLITICAL ECONOMY OF TRADE REFORM

To be sure, some unilateral liberalization has taken place. This has been especially
true in East Asia and Latin America. Most of the 100 or so instances of "unilateral

---

[2]  For the latest compelling evidence on the relationship between trade openness and growth, see
Sebastian Edwards (1998), "Openness, Productivity and Growth: What Do We Really Know?," *The
Economic Journal*, Vol. 108, No. 444, March.
[3]  The intellectual history is traced in A. O. Krueger (1997), "Trade Policy and Economic Development: How We Learn," *American Economic Review*, Vol. 87, No. 1, March.

liberalization" over the past couple of decades were adopted within the context of IMF or (especially) World Bank adjustment programs, however, suggesting that "reciprocity" in the form of foreign financial assistance played an important role in those decisions.[4]

In most cases, domestic political opposition blocked countries from abolishing their traditional barriers. Entrenched interests fought hard, and frequently with prolonged success, to maintain their protected positions. The politics of economic reform were difficult and contentious in virtually every case.[5]

The standard strategy for achieving trade reform was to mobilize enough pro-trade interests to overcome the forces that resisted further market opening. These included beneficiaries of imports such as consumers and industrial users of imported inputs.[6] However, such groups are rarely organized and their gains from liberalization are both modest and widely diffused. Hence they typically produce little political counterweight against those who would be adversely affected by increased foreign competition.

To overcome such opposition, it became necessary to appeal to exporters and others who gain directly from the opening of markets abroad. The political economy of trade liberalization in individual countries thus rested heavily on parallel liberalization in partner countries. The most assured technique for achieving such parallel action was to insist on reciprocity, through the negotiation of trade agreements, with enough existing or potential markets to tip the internal balance in favour of the desired liberalization.

The United States agreed in the Uruguay Round to get rid of its textile quotas, which was of course of enormous benefit to many developing countries, by negotiating concessions from the rest of the world on intellectual property rights and agricultural distortions. Through that same negotiation, Japan and Korea began to open their rice markets, another benefit for many developing countries, by appealing to the export interests of their (especially high-tech) manufacturers. It is not only respectable but essential, for even the wealthiest economies in the world, to use external pressures for liberalization in order to overcome internal political resistance.

*Negotiated* liberalization thus turns out to be far more feasible than *unilateral* liberalization. The key becomes a country's ability to persuade its foreign partners to proceed in tandem with it. Large trading entities, such as the United States and the European Union, obviously have the most leverage in this context because of the attraction to others of the opening of their markets.

Another key variable is the stage of liberalization at which a country finds itself. Initial reductions of very high tariffs can be relatively easy because they put few dents in the real level of protection and thus can often be implemented unilaterally.

---

[4] Dixon, H. (1998), "Controversy: Trade Liberalization and Growth: An Introduction," and Greenaway, D., W. Morgan and P. Wright (1998), "Trade Reform, Adjustment and Growth: What Does the Evidence Tell Us?", both in *The Economic Journal*, 108, September.

[5] An excellent analysis of the political requirements for successful reform can be found in Williamson, J. (1994), *The Political Economy of Policy Reform*, Washington: Institute for International Economics, January.

[6] See Destler, I. M. and J. S. Odell (1987), *Anti-Protection: Changing Forces in United States Trade Politics*, Washington: Institute for International Economics, September.

But most countries have found that they must apply the traditional political econ-omy approach to engineer the later, and most difficult, phases of the process.

All these considerations apply to developing as well as industrial countries. They too can deploy the domestic political economy of trade reform – through participating in reciprocal trade negotiations – to overcome resistance to further "outward orienta-tion". In many cases, their markets are large (and dynamic) enough to provide them with real leverage in international negotiations – especially if they work together effectively. Since trade barriers in many developing countries have now come down to levels that are difficult to reduce further, invocation of the political economy of international trade has become especially important – and especially promising.

## REGIONAL VERSUS GLOBAL LIBERALIZATION

In seeking reciprocal liberalization, countries could turn either to their respective geographic region or to the global trading system as a whole. The global approach is fundamentally superior because it maximizes the number of foreign markets involved and avoids the economic distortions (and political risks) of discrimination among trading partners. Indeed, the succession of GATT "rounds" throughout the postwar period has made a major contribution to the freeing of global trade.

As the urgency of competitive liberalization accelerated over the last decade or so, however, the regional approach has played an increasingly prominent role. It has turned out to be less time-consuming and less complicated to work out mutu-ally agreeable arrangements with a few neighbours than with the full membership of well over 100 countries in the WTO. Moreover, regional groupings are demon-strably willing to proceed much more boldly: many of them have decided to adopt totally free trade, as noted above, whereas none of the global conclaves to date has even considered such an ambitious goal. The rapid growth in the membership of the WTO, whose predecessor GATT had fewer than 50 members though the first sev-eral postwar negotiations, added to this change in the calculation.

Desires to overcome traditional political rivalries have also been a driving force in the success of several of the regional economic arrangements. The cardinal goal of the European Union was to end the historic hostility between France and Germany. Mercosur sought to end the arms race, including its nuclear dimension, between Argentina and Brazil. A successful APEC would reduce the risk of intra-Asian and trans-Pacific conflicts, which have been so prevalent over the past century. A success-ful South Asian FTA would presumably help ease tensions between India and Pakistan. Regional trade arrangements are thus often motivated by priority national security concerns. This is another reason why they frequently move more quickly and more boldly.

Much of the political economy of competitive liberalization in recent years has in fact played itself out in the dynamic interaction between regional and global initiatives to reduce trade barriers. The United States initiated the Kennedy Round in the 1960s to counter the discrimination inherent in the creation of the European Common Market (as well as for broad foreign policy reasons); and the Tokyo Round in the 1970s to counter the additional discrimination from the Community's expan-sion to include the United Kingdom. The Europeans cooperated in both ventures and thus enabled the regional and global efforts to "ratchet up" the scope and pace of liberalization.

The positive interaction between the two strategies accelerated sharply in the 1980s and 1990s as competitive liberalization became the norm and countries searched for tactics to obtain the needed domestic support. The United States reversed its traditional aversion to regionalism by embracing free trade agreements with Israel and Canada after the European Community blocked the launch of new negotiations in the GATT – to which the EC responded by dropping its veto and permitting the Uruguay Round to begin. When the Round faltered in the late 1980s, the three North American countries launched NAFTA and the Asians initiated APEC.[7] When the Round almost failed to meet its final deadline in December 1993, APEC's initial summit in Seattle in November 1993 induced the Community to finally agree because, according to one top European negotiator, it "demonstrated that you had an alternative and we did not." The regional initiatives also reinforced each other: APEC's Bogor Declaration was instrumental in galvanizing the Miami summit, a few weeks later, to commit to free trade by a date certain in the Americas.

This positive interaction also extends to the sub-regional level. President Bush's offer in 1990 to negotiate free trade pacts throughout the Western Hemisphere led to an explosion of bilateral and plurilateral agreements across South and Central America as countries sought to prepare themselves to qualify for free trade with North America. In Asia, AFTA has accelerated its timetable and substantially broadened its coverage to stay ahead of APEC. AFTA and Australia/New Zealand have discussed possible linkages between the groups.

Hence regional and global liberalization initiatives have been mutually reinforcing throughout the past three decades or more. The fears of some observers that regionalism would derail globalism have been demonstrably overcome.

It is probably noteworthy that many of these regional institutions have been driven by developing countries: NAFTA by Mexico; a Free Trade Area of the Americas by a number of Latin American countries; APEC's "free trade by 2010/2020" commitment by Indonesia and several other Asian countries; and of course the "South–South" agreements (such as AFTA and Mercosur) themselves. Indeed, the North–South cooperation manifest in many of these trade agreements stands in marked contrast to the confrontation, and even hostility between North and South that was prevalent as recently as the 1970s. Broader political as well as trade, development, and other economic objectives have been well served by these initiatives.

## THREATS TO THE TRADING SYSTEM

But determined leadership has been required to avoid conflicts between regionalism and globalism. Doing so has also required the maintenance of effective *global* trade rules to provide a framework that would deter conflict between the regional arrangements, including rules that apply to the arrangements themselves, and an institution to enforce them. Even so, there have been some close calls – especially when the global system faltered. The new regional arrangements spawned by the missed deadlines of the Uruguay Round were intended to serve as alternatives to the global

---

[7] See Funabashi, Y. (1995), *Asia Pacific Fusion: Japan's Role In APEC*, Washington: Institute for International Economics, October.

regime if needed. An ultimate failure of the Round, which almost occurred, would have discredited the entire global system and raised a real spectre of competing blocs.

Moreover, the European Union frequently seems to focus so heavily on its regional agenda that it forgets its global responsibilities. The United States is sometimes viewed as preoccupied with NAFTA or APEC. By joining East Asia and North America, APEC has eliminated any possibility of the evolution of the three-bloc world that was so widely – and rightly – feared a few years ago; but a failure to work out accommodations with Europe could instead create a two-bloc world that would convey substantial dangers as well. South America might decide to halt its liberalization once Mercosur has consolidated, and Brazil might be happy to leave its new leadership of that region undisturbed for at least a while. Countries not participating in any of the major regional pacts, such as India, correctly see a risk of increasing discrimination against them if regionalism were to become the dominant form of trade liberalization. There is a constant need to keep the global/regional interaction on a supportive course. This is one key reason why a new initiative is now required to consolidate the regional liberalization initiatives into an agreement to achieve *global* free trade in the early 21st century.

There are other risks to the continued progress of competitive liberalization that need to be met by a new global initiative. The most threatening of these challenges do not arise in the countries that have rejected openness most strongly in the recent past – some developing countries and the former command economies – although some of them do harbour lingering doubts that could again assume ascendance. Paradoxically, the strongest pressures to reverse the liberal course can be found in the countries that created, nurtured and championed the postwar order: the United States and the European Union.

Two structural changes dominate the evolution of the American economy over the past generation. One is globalization: the share of trade has almost tripled in a generation and now exceeds the same share in the European Union as a group and (especially) in Japan. The other is the stagnation of real incomes and a regressive shift in income distribution: the United States has created tens of millions of new jobs but the median family income, despite a pickup in the last couple of years, is still lower today than a generation ago and only the top 20 per cent of the population is unambiguously better off.

The central question for present purposes is the degree of causality between the two phenomena. Globalization, like any dynamic economic change, of course creates losers as well as winners despite its net positive effects on the economy, and virtually all economists agree that it has contributed to some of the problems cited. The majority believes the relationship accounts for only 10–20 per cent of the problem and that a retreat into protectionism would make it worse.[8] But at least a few serious studies attribute a larger part of the country's chief economic difficulties to globalization and call for a shift in trade policy as a result.

American politics frequently reflect this tension. Only extremists of both right and left have launched frontal attacks on the bipartisan trade policies of the past 60 years and all their nation-wide campaigns have been decisively rejected. But

---

[8]   As summarized and enlarged upon in Cline, W. R. (1997), *Trade and Income Distribution*, Washington: Institute for International Economics, November.

organized labour and its allies have succeeded in stalemating US trade policy for the past four years, persuading the Congress to deny the President any new trade-negotiating authority despite the strength of the American economy. Labour and its allies remain implacably opposed to any new trade (or international investment) liberalization, and are indeed seeking new protection in steel (and perhaps other sectors in the near future). Especially when cyclically adjusted, US trade policy is in serious trouble.

Moreover, the US trade and current account deficits are likely to exceed $300 billion in 1999 and to continue growing for the foreseeable future. These numbers are double the previous record of the middle 1980s and are approaching those deficits' record share of the total economy. During that previous episode, the dollar dropped by over 50 per cent against the other key currencies, and the Congress almost passed massively protectionist trade legislation (and did substantially tighten the anti-dumping statutes and enact the infamous "Super 301" provision). Any significant slowdown in the US economy, and concomitant rise in unemployment, could turn US trade policy in a protectionist direction.

The situation in Europe is fundamentally similar if quite different in its details. Europe's chief economic problem is high unemployment, which has risen from 2 to 3 per cent a generation ago to above 10 per cent now – from well below the American norm to more than twice as high. But average wages and incomes in Europe have risen substantially over this period, in sharp contrast to their stagnation in the United States.

These two great industrial areas have thus made very different social choices. By limiting its social safety net and permitting firms to downsize to boost profits, the United States forces its displaced workers to find new jobs at whatever wage is available – pricing its labour competitively and thus maintaining full employment. Europe has by contrast become a generous welfare state with extremely rigid labour laws, discouraging new hires from both the supply and demand sides while maintaining social peace through government transfers of a large share of its higher incomes to the poor.

The bottom line is that neither Europe nor the United States has been able to generate a steady increase in the number of well-paying jobs. Europe has rising incomes but high unemployment. America has low unemployment but flat incomes. Perceptions and politicians in both could come to treat trade as a major source of the problem, or even *the* major source of the problem, and thus pave the way for a massive reversal of global liberalization.

The Asian giants, Japan and China, also pose major threats to the continued openness of the trading system. The political economy of liberalization succeeds in winning domestic support, even in a country as large as the United States, only when its major foreign markets (especially if they are also its toughest competitors) are seen as joining the process and contributing their fair shares to the process. Japan has grudgingly participated in all the GATT rounds but access to its markets remains extremely truncated (and it single-handedly blocked APEC's latest liberalization initiative).[9] China has not yet committed to the minimum reforms necessary

---

[9] Sazanami, Y., S. Urata and H. Kawai (1995), *Measuring the Costs of Protection in Japan*, Washington: Institute for International Economics, January 1995. The authors conclude that the consumer costs of these barriers total at least 3–4 per cent of Japanese GDP and that they block at least $50 billion of imports annually.

to join the World Trade Organization. Protectionists in other countries, with some justification, will use the reluctance of Japan and China to liberalize to oppose further reduction of their own nations' barriers.

## RESTARTING THE BICYCLE

Why do all these threats to future liberalization matter? International trade and investment continue to flourish, if at a modestly slower pace due to the financial crisis. Does business simply need to be assured that no new impediments will be erected?

The problem with this "stand pat" scenario is its instability. The history of trade policy teaches forcefully that failure to move steadily forward toward liberalization condemns the trading system to tip over in the face of protectionist pressures – the "bicycle theory". For example, protectionism scored major successes, especially in the United States, during the prolonged periods when the GATT became moribund immediately after the successful conclusion of the Kennedy Round in the late 1960s and the Tokyo Round in the early 1980s. It is no accident that protectionism is on the rise in the United States, despite the strength of the overall economy, in light of the current trade policy vacuum.

One of the great advantages of the contemporary regional initiatives is that they have kept the "bicycle" moving forward after the conclusion of the Uruguay Round. The Round itself also helped by scheduling future negotiations in a number of sectors, and the three subsequently successful sectoral agreements – on telecommunications services, information technology and financial services – also maintained the forward momentum. But no additional agreements are in sight and none of the regional negotiations are making headway. *No serious trade-liberalizing effort is underway anywhere in the world at this time.* Hence, it is necessary to launch a new global strategy that will simultaneously keep the "bicycle" moving forward and avoid the centrifugal risks of drifting into conflicting blocs.

The substance of a new global initiative should include elimination of all remaining tariff and non-tariff border barriers. The Uruguay Round set up these remnants of traditional protection for decisive action by converting agricultural quotas into tariffs, removing quota protection from textiles and apparel, and obtaining bindings of most duties. One more major effort could condemn these practices to the dustbin of history.[10]

In addition, new negotiations are needed to enable the global system to catch up with some of the "new problems" that are plaguing international trade relations. Protectionists in all countries are ingenious in staying "one step ahead of the judge" and the system needs continuous updating to stay within reach.

For example, most American (and others') complaints about Japan no longer relate to that country's border barriers. They focus instead on the anti-competitive behaviour of its firms with their exclusive supplier or distributor arrangements (vertical *keiretsu*, as in auto parts and film, respectively) and domination of particular markets (horizontal *keiretsu*, as in glass or soda ash). The United States has,

---

[10]   This case is made persuasively in Whalley, J. and C. Hamilton (1996), *The Trading System After the Uruguay Round*, Washington: Institute for International Economics, June.

unfortunately, but perhaps necessarily, been using trade measures, such as Section 301, to address non-trade problems. There is an urgent need to work out new international agreements on competition policy and corporate behaviour.

Investment is a second area in which the international rules have lagged far behind commercial practice. Investment is now an essential element of international trade, especially in services but in traditional manufacturing as well. Aside from a few very modest covenants on trade-related investment measures agreed in the Uruguay Round and APEC's inadequate "nonbinding investment principles", however, there are virtually no multilateral agreements on investment.[11]

Since developing countries are both major recipients of direct investment and legitimately concerned that they reap a fair share of its benefits, addressing it in the new Round should be high on their priority lists. New research shows that many of the devices used by host countries in an effort to maximize their gains, such as local content, joint venture, and technology transfer requirements are, in fact, counterproductive because they discourage the firms from transferring their best know-how and integrating the covered subsidiaries into their best-practices global networks. Nor can most developing countries compete with the industrial countries in offering investment incentives. On the other hand, export performance requirements may be quite effective and economically justified. Hence developing countries have a high stake in working out new and better international rules in this area, trading their residual desire to impose domestic content, joint venture, and technology transfer requirements for limits on the rich countries' use of locational subsidies and investment incentives.[12]

Another pending issue is regionalism itself. The GATT article that governs such arrangements is extremely weak and its implementation has been even weaker: of the 100 or so "free trade agreements" that have been notified to the GATT, none have been rejected and only a very few have been approved. Now that regionalism is so prevalent, the WTO needs to adopt much stronger provisions and procedures to make sure that they evolve in an open manner.

A number of other topics must be addressed as well. The numerous linkages between environmental measures and trade must be sorted out in ways that both protect the environment and avoid providing new excuses for protecting against trade. The relationship between trade and labour standards needs to be resolved as well.

A broader yet clearly related issue is international monetary arrangements. The current regime of flexible exchange rates periodically permits sizable and prolonged misalignments of major currencies, such as the huge overvaluation of the dollar in the first half of the 1980s and its more modest overvaluation now, and the large undervaluation of the yen in the late 1980s and again until quite recently. These misalignments in turn lead to large trade imbalances that intensify protectionist pressures in the deficit countries by tilting the domestic political balance against exporters and in favour of import-competing industries. The WTO will not solve this problem but should push the International Monetary Fund, and the G-7 as

---

[11] See Graham, E. M. (1996), *Global Corporations and National Governments*, Washington: Institute for International Economics, May.

[12] These findings and recommendations derive from Moran, T. H. (1998), *Foreign Direct Investment and Development: The New Policy Agenda for Developing Countries and Economies in Transition*, Washington: Institute for International Economics, December.

its informal steering committee, to improve the functioning of the monetary system to reduce some of the pressures on the trade regime.[13] Such trade-monetary linkage featured prominently in the original planning for the Tokyo Round in the early 1970s and, to a lesser extent, in the planning for the Uruguay Round in the middle 1980s.

The need for the WTO to address a series of new trade issues also replicates the earlier postwar history. The Kennedy Round produced a major reduction in the high tariffs that were the major tool of protection in the early postwar period. The Tokyo Round then attacked government procurement, subsidies and other non-tariff border barriers. The Uruguay Round turned to major behind-the-border problems such as intellectual property rights and services rules. Each of these reforms exposed a new set of constraints on market access that required a further initiative to bring the international rules up to date, and the present period is no exception.

It would be possible to address all these issues in a series of separate regional negotiations. Indeed, some of the regional agreements have innovated successfully in addressing new topics in the past: the Canada–United States Free Trade Agreement provided a model for some of the services talks in the Uruguay Round, Australia and New Zealand successfully meshed their competition policies in a manner that also enabled then to eliminate anti-dumping duties, and NAFTA has pioneered in forging effective rules on investment. There would be a serious risk of inconsistency if such issues were addressed differently in the different regional fora, however, and it would be much more efficient to derive worldwide approaches that could be applied by all. The case for globalism is again compelling.

## THE "GRAND BARGAIN"

The members of the WTO should therefore agree to consolidate the free trade arrangements that have already been set at the regional level, covering more than 60 per cent of world trade as described at the outset, into a global commitment to achieve worldwide free trade by a "date certain". The date could be 2010, on the APEC and EUROMED models, with a possible extension to 2015 or 2020 for the poorer countries. Implementation of the agreement would keep the bicycle moving forward for some time. It would thereby provide maximum support for the development goals of the poorer countries by maintaining an open multilateral trading system that would enable them to successfully pursue their "outward orientation" strategies.

Such a commitment would have to rest on a "grand bargain" between two groups of countries: the high-income mature economies of North America and Western Europe and the rapidly growing, lower income countries that make up most of the rest of the world plus Japan. As noted, the lower income fast growers (and Japan) owe much of their success in recent decades to the openness of the world economy that enabled them to pursue "outward oriented" development strategies. Hence they need insurance against any reversion to protection by the "old rich", especially

---

[13] Specific proposals can be found in Bergsten, C. F. and C. Randall Henning (1996), *Global Economic Leadership and the Group of Seven*, Washington: Institute for International Economics, June.

in the wake of the adverse impact on those countries' trade balances of the financial crisis.

There is a second component of this "insurance motive" in a number of developing countries: insurance that their domestic successors will not reverse the liberalization of their own economies. Such reforms can be "locked in" by binding the country's liberalization in international agreements, regional and/or global. Such bindings apply only to international trade and investment policies, and directly related domestic measures, but it would be difficult to reverse most domestic reforms if it were impossible to raise new external barriers to support a reversion to *dirigisme*.

The Asian and Latin American countries have been predominantly concerned about a possible reversion to protection in the United States, by far their largest market, and hence have emphasized trade deals with that country. They are also concerned about Europe, however, so are pursuing that dimension as well: Mercosur through a pending trade agreement with the European Union; East Asia through its new summits with the Europeans. Neither of these arrangements are likely to produce much substance, however, so East Asia and Latin America – which are still likely, despite their current difficulties, to be two of the fastest growing parts of the world economy over the coming decades – would benefit greatly from engaging Europe and Japan in the same kind of free trade commitments they have already elicited from the United States. This can probably be done only through a global effort in the WTO.

The second part of the "grand bargain" would provide the higher income countries with increased, and eventually full, access to the markets of the lower income but rapidly growing countries around the world (and Japan). Most countries of this latter group, despite their impressive liberalizations over the past decade or so, retain substantial trade barriers.

This part of the bargain would be attractive to the rich countries because they too are heavily dependent on integration into global markets. Such dependence is nothing new for Europe but, as noted above, has only evolved in a major way for the United States over the past two or three decades. This rich-country interest focuses primarily on countries with large and rapidly growing markets that still maintain substantial access barriers. Hence the United States and Europe would benefit greatly from the proposed "grand bargain".

There is nothing new conceptually in this proposal for the "old rich" to pledge to avoid new barriers while the "rapid growers" commit to eliminate theirs. Such asymmetric liberalization has lain at the heart of the agreements on NAFTA, the FTAA and APEC, the European Union and even the Uruguay Round itself. In these versions of the "grand bargain", the poorer countries have bought assured continued access to the markets of the rich countries by agreeing to catch up over time with those countries' prior liberalizations. There is rough justice in the proposed asymmetry because the willingness of the rich countries to facilitate the "outward-oriented" growth strategies of the poor, by reducing their barriers much further and much faster, enabled some of the latter to start catching up with the income levels and standards of living of the former.

The novel element here is to shift the context to the global plane via the WTO. This would consolidate and link the existing regional agreements. It would also bring South Asia, the former Soviet Union, Africa and the few other uncovered parts of the world into the deal. It would keep the bicycle moving forward for some time.

# IMPLICATIONS FOR DEVELOPING COUNTRIES

Developing countries clearly reaped important gains from the Uruguay Round of multilateral trade negotiations. The phase-out of the Multifibre Arrangement will provide a substantial boost to their exports. They gain from the total ban on voluntary export restraint agreements (VERs) that was concluded in the Round. The creation of the World Trade Organization (to replace the GATT), and especially its Dispute Settlement Mechanism (DSM), provides substantial protection for countries with smaller levels of trade.

As in any reciprocal negotiation, developing countries of course made several "concessions" in the Uruguay Round. Most of those "concessions," such as reduction in tariffs, in fact benefit their own economies on balance by reducing costs to consumers and to industrial users. Nevertheless, like the United States and all other countries, developing countries experience some costs from trade liberalization and some elements of society may, on balance, lose from the phenomenon. Hence domestic policy must provide for these contingencies, helping to smooth the required adjustments and to equip all segments of society to benefit from globalization rather than feel victimized by it.

Looking to the future, it is clear that the developing countries have a major interest in an early launch and successful completion of the Millennium Round. Failure to turn back the rising threat of protectionism, especially in the United States and the European Union, by restarting the "bicycle" of liberalization could levy substantial costs on their exports through a proliferation of anti-dumping cases and other new barriers. It could even jeopardize implementation of the complete phase-out of textile/apparel quotas agreed to in the Uruguay Round.

Moreover, a failure to pursue new multilateral liberalization could lead to renewed emphasis by the largest industrial countries, the United States and the European Union, on their regional arrangements. Many developing countries could thus suffer the double loss of renewed barriers and renewed discrimination.

Needless to say, developing countries should vigorously press their own priority interests in pursuing the new Millennium Round. This observer would suggest a few possibilities:

- elimination of the high tariffs that will remain, especially in the United States, on many apparel and textile exports after the phase-out of quotas under the MFA;
- elimination of the very high tariffs on agricultural imports in many industrialized countries;
- new agreements on foreign direct investment that would both expand its levels and help developing countries achieve a fair share of its benefits, as described above;
- tougher disciplines on the use of anti-dumping duties, especially by the United States and the European Union – though linking this issue to competition policy in a new negotiation on that topic, which has considerable intellectual appeal, is politically unacceptable to the United States and would thus be likely to kill any prospect of progress in either area;
- liberalization of movement of natural persons, where many developing countries have a strong competitive advantage, under the General Agreement on Trade in Services;

- elimination of preferential tariffs in regional arrangements, including the EU and NAFTA, that discriminate against exports of many developing countries; and
- further strengthening of the DSM to help protect the rights of countries with smaller trade levels.

In short, developing countries have a great deal to gain from a new multilateral Round. Pursuing these goals actively would seem to be far preferable to seeking re-negotiation of the Uruguay Round, as some developing countries are considering, which would clearly jeopardize phase-out of the MFA as well as the other gains cited above. It is certainly a better strategy, and far more likely to succeed, than try-ing to block the launch of a new Round pending full implementation of the Uruguay Round agreements, which will surely occur before the commencement of implementation of the outcome of a new Round. Such a negative course would replicate the futile effort of some developing countries to block the Uruguay Round, which discredited them in international trade circles for a prolonged period and would have turned out to be against their own interests. Developing countries should avoid any push for renewed "special and differential" treatment (which was effectively terminated by the creation of the WTO and never paid off for them any-way), but should seek full and active participation as an equal partner in the trading system.

## LAUNCHING THE MILLENNIUM ROUND

A wide variety of considerations thus point in a single direction: the launching later this year, at the Seattle Ministerial Conference, of a new Millennium Round in the World Trade Organization, perhaps in the context of a decision to achieve global free trade by a "date certain" in the early part of the 21st century. Such initiatives are needed to keep the "bicycle" of competitive liberalization moving forward. They are essential to provide effective multilateral means to deal with the trade and other international economic disputes that will inevitably increase as economic interdependence grows. They are necessary to avoid the risk that the rapidly prolif-erating regional arrangements could turn into hostile blocs with adverse effects on international security as well as global prosperity.

From the standpoint of the developing world, new trading opportunities would result from such an initiative. Outward-oriented growth strategies could be sus-tained and accelerated with an assurance that the rich industrial markets would not turn inward. The proposed "grand bargain" would indeed globalize the enormously encouraging progress in bridging the North–South gap that has been pioneered in recent years by the key regional agreements – the European Union, NAFTA, APEC and the FTAA – and which began at the global level in the Uruguay Round. The developing countries, which account for the bulk of the world's population and vir-tually all of its population growth, would become increasingly enmeshed with the "old rich" in a web of cooperative and mutually beneficial economic arrangements. There could be no better investment in securing future peace as well as prosperity.

# Chapter 33

# Part II.  Trade and development

## 1.  Linkages between trade and development policies

*Dr Keith Bezanson**

There is a need for a new global Round of trade negotiations. The interests of development urgently require such a Round.

About 40 per cent of the world is currently in recession and the immediate prospects are for an increase in that percentage. Latin America, for example, is likely to fall into recession this year. Six of the world's major countries are experiencing economic contractions of 6 per cent or more. The United States ran a current account deficit of about $200 billion in 1998, a figure that will likely reach $280–300 billion this year. This represents a more than doubling of the annual current account deficit since 1997. In the meantime, Japan, the euro zone and emerging Asia will run a 1999 current account surplus of just over $300 billion. This represents a trebling since 1997.

It is the rising United States deficit over the past 18 months – the surge in US private spending – that has allowed the world economy to accommodate the Japanese deflation and the massive outflow of capital from East Asia. Were it not for that huge and rising deficit, the 40 per cent of the world now in recession would be much, much higher. This imbalance is exceedingly dangerous as the US role, both for political and economic reasons, may prove unsustainable. There are some worrying signs that this may be happening. There is increasing recourse in the United States to anti-dumping measures and growing number of calls for expanded protectionism.

This is not the first time in recent years that we have encountered such a global imbalance. One of the powerful reasons for starting the Uruguay Round in 1985 was to limit the protectionist pressures arising from an exploding US deficit. The current situation gives strength and urgency to the calls for a new global trade Round.

The issues and risks I have just sketched are of central concern to development. Whatever may be said about the defects, dangers and negative consequences to development of economic openness, there is little doubt about the fact that a new era of protectionist trade policies, of economic closure, emanating from the United States would severely damage the prospects of poorer countries.

The first point I want to make, therefore, is that global stability in trade policy is central to development prospects. A new trade Round directed to confronting the

---

* Director, Institute of Development Studies, and Senior Fellow, International Institute for Sustainable Development.

current turbulence and imbalances is of profound importance to development. I associate fully, therefore, with the position presented by Fred Bergsten, although some of the reasoning behind our shared position is not entirely identical.

Trade policy, however, is only a part of development policy. Trade policy is *not* a substitute for development policy.

Beyond this point, however, Fred Bergsten and I are not in agreement. He essentially places all developing countries into a single category, and argues that they need only to open their doors fully to trade and investment and that development will follow. This view is similar to that of many economists over the past ten to 15 years and involves the presentation of trade liberalization as a panacea to development. The standard hypothesis claims, in essence, that trade and financial liberalization are inevitably growth-enhancing. This is usually presented as a self-evident truism. This is a seductive oversimplification and, moreover, it is not supportable on the basis of fact. Vastly exaggerated claims on the links between trade and development have become commonplace on the part of economists and politicians. Dani Rodrick correctly notes that:

"During the 1950s and 1960s, when import-substitution was in vogue, there was excessive optimism about what government interventions could achieve. Now that outward-orientation is the norm, there is excessive faith in what openness can accomplish."

This is in no way an argument against openness to trade and investment. I have already indicated my strong agreement with Fred Bergsten on the need for a new Round of global trade negotiations precisely with a view to avoiding a new wave of protectionism. Moreover, it seems to me pretty clear that openness in trade and to FDI, *under certain circumstances can* contribute to development benefits (e.g. inflow of needed investments, access to capital and intermediate goods not available domestically at comparable cost, ideas and technology).

The essential point is that development and development policy are much more complex, variable and uncertain than trade policy. Good trade policy may be an important ingredient – indeed it may be a central ingredient – to good development policy. But trade policy and general economic openness are not substitutes for development policy.

For many of you, this observation may seem to fall into the category of the blindingly obvious. For the better part of two decades, however, the ruling dimension in the international counsel handed out to the poorer countries in the world has involved the presentation of openness as the panacea of development.

Good theory must accord with fact – with the evidence. The fact is that we now have a reasonable body of empirical evidence, and that evidence simply does not accord with the optimism and exaggerated claims for the relationship between economic openness and development. There is now ample, although not always conclusive, literature on the actual relationship between trade/capital openness and growth. This literature shows us that the standard hypothesis needs to be strongly and carefully qualified. (See, e.g., UNCTAD's 1997 Trade and Development Report which takes a hard look at a vast quantity of available data and concludes that policies of unfettered openness have led to greater inequality within and between countries.)

More generally, the history of development over the past quarter century tells us clearly that the countries that have done especially well have shared a number of policy characteristics:

- they have generated above average rates of domestic savings;
- they have invested a high percentage of GDP;
- they have maintained macro-economic stability; and
- they have invested heavily in the development of human resources.

By contrast, the history of successful development over the past 25 years shows unclear and unconvincing relationships between degree of economic openness and growth. Again, I am in no way arguing against openness or for a return to whole-sale policies of import-substitution. I am arguing on the basis of what I conclude to be overwhelming evidence for the importance of formulating and using trade policies wisely in support of broader development purposes. In this regard, we need to be very mindful of another fact: development policies are susceptible to fashions and to dangerously oversimplified prescriptions. This is not a new observation, having been made forcefully by Albert Hirshmann in the mid-1960s.

If trade policy can contribute to development benefits *under certain circumstances*, as I have claimed, what then are the circumstances? What are the more complex sets of factors that need to be addressed? What are the recent and key lessons that we have learned about the linkages between trade policy and development policy?

Obviously, there are no simple answers here and no check list to effective development policy. Let me suggest for consideration seven factors.

*One*, it is the countries in East Asia, and a selected number from Latin America, that have benefited most from increased economic openness. Through development strategies involving large elements of import-substitution policies, these countries had reached a substantially higher level of industrialization and economic diversification *prior to* beginning an adjustment process to greater economic openness. This suggests the phasing of economic openness. (This, of course, is not a new suggestion and was very central to the polarized debate over the past 15 years between the proponents of "big bang" liberalization and "gradualism".) A hypothesis that merits examination is that, at least for very poor countries, initial policy emphasis on a selected balance of import-substitution policies may be more effective than export promotion. The hypothesis would further hold that a certain level of development is required for a country to compete effectively in international markets and to benefit from trade and financial liberalization.

*Two*, in respect of commodity exports, there is an urgent need to avoid the "fallacy of composition" problem. As matters now stand, there is a serious risk of a vicious circle, in which developing countries lose foreign exchange earnings when they (collectively) increase their export volumes, and respond to a decline in foreign exchange with policies which increase their export volumes further. The sole beneficiaries are consumers in importing countries. For developing countries and the producers of commodities in those countries, the result is "immiserising" growth (producing more and producing it more efficiently, but falling further behind). For much of the last two decades, the structural factors underlying this problem were actually reinforced by the policies embodied in the adjustment programmes of the IMF and the World Bank.

*Three*, liberalization is viewed by the asset markets as a positive signal. The effect of this is generally to push exchange rates in the wrong direction. This indicates a need for particular caution with regard to capital account liberalization. For low income countries, a more cautious approach to direct foreign investment may be called for, in view of the potentially high foreign exchange risk.

*Four*, the extent of competition for FDI flows (and portfolio investments), and the policies which have been adopted to attract them, have the potential to inflict negative social, developmental and environmental consequences in developing countries. This is the battle cry of many international NGOs and is usually presented as a "race to the bottom" argument. The NGOs are correct in being worried about the potential negatives. But, just as exaggerated claims of the development benefits of economic openness are damaging, many of the claims of negative consequences are likewise exaggerated and damaging. There is also evidence of a range of positive social and environmental consequences resulting from FDI through the adoption of ISO standards, and trans-national corporations have responded environmentally and socially to the watchfulness and global reach of the international NGOs themselves. We also need to be very watchful of disguised protectionism here in the form of strong Northern advocacy for high labour and environmental standards in developing countries. Such advocacy may be far more concerned with protecting Northern markets than in the welfare of developing areas. The risks and the potential combine, in my view, to suggest that a case can be made for a global institutional framework for dealing with issues relating to FDI and the operations of trans-national corporations. In principle, such an institution would apply a code of fair practices for TNCs (e.g. health, safety and environmental standards) and would also aim to ensure that host countries do not compete away the potential advantages of FDI (e.g. through tax concessions and the underpricing of natural resources).

*Five*, trade openness can exert a potentially important impact on both government revenues and government borrowing. On the revenue side, trade openness can reduce revenues substantially through the reduction of import tariffs and duties and export taxes. On the borrowing side, a move to trade and financial openness usually represents a shift from financing directed primarily to the public sector, to financing directed mainly to the private sector. This serves to limit the external financing available to government. The result is a significant increase in the fiscal constraints facing governments, unless and until the tax base can be broadened through tax reform. For low income countries, the scope for this may be exceedingly limited, both by relatively low levels of income and consumption, and by limited administrative and enforcement capabilities. This situation appears to be particularly acute in sub-Saharan Africa where government revenues have been strongly downward in recent years, and where the majority of countries (25 out of 42, according to recent data) rely on taxes on international transactions for 30 per cent or more of total government revenues.

*Six*, openness leaves countries vulnerable to external shocks and such shocks can bring about political turmoil and can revive ancient religious, ethnic and racial conflicts. External shocks have been part of the development horizon since the 1970s. They have come in the form of dramatic reversals in capital flows, inflation and high real interest rates in Western, developed countries and severe, negative shifts in the terms of trade. It seems unlikely that such shocks will disappear from the global landscape. Thus, countries that choose high degrees of economic openness are wise to ensure the ability to manage turbulence in the world economy. This raises institutional and human resources issues that appear to me to be central to the relationship between trade policy and development policy.

*Seven*, really a repetition of what has already been said, is to emphasize that economic openness for the poorer and developing countries is a mixed blessing. It needs to be carefully ordered, managed and nurtured in order to become a positive force for development. Openness is not, by itself, a reliable instrument to generate growth and national well-being. Those are the challenges and the tasks of a much more ambitious constellation of complementary development policies and institutions.

By way of concluding thoughts, let me note that the subject "Linkages Between Trade and Development Policy" is in no way new. The subject was discussed extensively by the classical economic thinker most often credited as being the godfather of economic openness, Adam Smith. In "The Wealth of Nations", Smith attacks the protectionism of the Navigation Act in harsh terms. He leaves no doubt about his thinking and he thunders forth that the protectionism of the Navigation Act results in taxes on the necessaries of life:

"Such taxes, when they have grown up to a certain height, are a curse equal to the barrenness of the earth and the inclemency of the heavens."

Don't you wish that economists today could write like that? But Smith does not stop at this point. He continues at much greater length, and for several pages, on the social and developmental costs of adjustment. He argues that removing barriers quickly must be avoided in order not to inflict major damage to the wider public good. He has this to say:

"...freedom of trade should be restored only by slow gradations, and with a good deal of reserve and circumspection. Were these high duties and prohibitions taken away all at once, cheaper foreign goods of the same kind might be poured so fast into the market as to deprive at once many thousands of people of their ordinary employment and means of subsistence ... The equitable regard, therefore ... requires that changes of this kind should never be introduced suddenly, but slowly, gradually, and after a very long warning. The legislature, were it possible that its deliberations could always be directed, not by the clamorous importunity of partial interests, but by an extensive view of the general good."

That is the challenge of building the link between trade policy and development policy.

# Chapter 34

## Part II.  Trade and development

### 1.  Linkages between trade and development policies

*Maria Livanos Cattaui**

As the world business organization, with members over many countries, we would argue that any new approach needs to take into account micro-economic aspects more fully. When we discuss developing countries there is little mention of local business – the strengthening of local business, the strengthening of local markets and, with that, the proper partnership with international business.

On a related point, most of us seem to agree that trade is an enormous help but not a sufficient condition for development. Some of the factors that are conducive to economic development also help a country compete in the international market for goods, services, capital, and technology. I would like to raise four points.

My first point is that one of the basic principles underlying the multilateral trading system is non-discriminatory market access, secured by bound tariff rates. This is a simple, straightforward principle but, regrettably, many protectionist policies continue to discriminate against the exports of the developing countries, especially in textiles and agriculture. This retards development.

Other factors enter into this. We carried out a business survey among our members in developing countries. It revealed that problems are not limited to pure trade and protectionist issues but, above all, involve practical issues that prevent businesses from being able to export into the developed countries. These issues range from technical standards and labelling to sanitary and phytosanitary measures.

Developed countries still spend a lot of money on development assistance. Meanwhile they deny market access to exports of developing countries, thus depriving them of the means through which they could forego such assistance. Hypocrisy seems to be alive and well in this domain. No doubt the denial of market access for goods and services that are crucial for developing countries is one of the most straightforward linkages between trade and development.

I have always felt that the banana dispute can only be dealt with more sensibly by trying to disentangle the trade and development aspects. Professor Bhagwati wrote an interesting letter to the FT, inspired by the ongoing banana war, in which he deplores our inability to come up with a compensation and adjustment programme that would adequately help the small banana exporters. He says:

"... nothing in the doctrine of free trade requires that we ride at breakneck speed and with reckless regard over the economies of the small and poor nations. It is time to recognise

---

\* Secretary General, International Chamber of Commerce, Paris.

that the WTO dispute settlement mechanism needs to be supplemented by co-ordinated efforts."

He is referring to the need for the World Bank and the IMF to ease the cost burden for developing countries of implementing binding trade decisions. Most of us could agree with that proposition but I think it needs to be placed in the proper context. The fact is that the WTO dispute settlement mechanism is supposed to protect the poor and weak members from the sometimes threatening and harmful unilateral actions of the bigger trading partners. To me this is all the more reason for developing countries to strongly support the WTO.

My second point is that the role of trade in promoting development should not distract from the essential preconditions of development. These we generally group under the umbrella of good governance. We know what they include – a stable political system and sound macro-economic policies, but also some practical things, like a solid framework of business laws, an independent judiciary and particularly the encouragement of entrepreneurial spirit and private initiative in the countries involved. Most importantly, development will falter without an efficient and honest bureaucracy. I have always maintained that an efficient bureaucracy is one of the biggest attractions for foreign investors, and is even a precondition facilitating trade. An efficient customs system lends a competitive advantage to developing countries.

My third point is that the same conditions that are conducive to domestic investment are good for foreign investment. Foreign investment is all too often criticized, but it is worth recalling what it really brings with it – what it should bring with it – i.e. management skills, technology, training of the workforce, but also the building of local supplier networks, and the best practices in the efficient use of resources, including attention to environmental factors. Above all, it should and does bring links to foreign markets.

I would propose that trade and investment have a very special role to play in the knowledge economy. What do we mean when we talk about a knowledge economy? Knowledge is a more important factor than land, labour, capital and natural resources, mostly because with knowledge we can acquire the other factors. Unfortunately, knowledge is expensive and time-consuming to create. This is exactly why I think that one way the developing and least-developed countries can acquire knowledge is through trade and investment.

Conversely, countries that block access to knowledge are likely to experience little effective trade and investment. Among other things this highlights the importance of appropriate domestic policies, which brings us back to the crucial role of good governance. We must not just focus on ideas, for instance, that telecommunications monopolies, whether public or private, are a source of political power. Instead, we must look beyond and admit that telecommunications help provide the realities of a knowledge economy. What is needed is more access to communications and (although it is just one small part) less fear of the Internet. I admit that knowledge can be threatening, but by cutting themselves off I fear that developing countries will only become further marginalized into know-not countries.

My fourth and last point is that some developing countries continue to entertain ideas of import substitution and the protection of infant industry, although adherents to the theory are dwindling. ICC strongly supports the view that developing countries have not taken full advantage of WTO rules and disciplines. Their aim must be active and equal participation. Paul Collier had an interesting footnote on this, which is that in many African countries we find a capital-hostile environment with local capital fleeing abroad. It is true that Africans hold a larger share of their wealth outside their countries than citizens of any other region. Among the factors to blame for this are highly restrictive trade policies.

The problem is that we continue to hang on to concepts that have become obsolete and which now start to militate against the objectives they were supposed to achieve. Perhaps we need to reconsider the concept of special and differential treatment for non-reciprocated trade concessions since it seems to result in less, not more, contact with international business, while reduced competitiveness makes exporting more expensive. These are the practical consequences that we in the business world see.

Let me close with some potentially good news, though it starts out on a discouraging note. Despite some excellent efforts, only a few of the developing countries have demonstrated that economic freedom, appropriate market reforms and well-timed trade openings can work. This is also true for Africa. Unfortunately, the negative attitude of companies in African countries is being reinforced, rather than encouraged, by inappropriate government action and neglect of the local business community. The good efforts are untold and unsupported.

For this reason ICC has entered into a work programme with UNCTAD and the developing countries for a benchmarking approach to investment and the development of investment guides. This includes workshops of our pilot series in each African country – bringing together the local business community, its international corporate partners, and the government authorities concerned. We have found that because of the low profile of the local business community in these countries and the lack of data and research analysis, potential investors and trading partners are simply not dedicating a high enough level of attention (and money) to preparing investment strategies. They spend much more time and resources to find out about investments elsewhere, but not in Africa. We mean to change this, intending to:

- correct the existing biases;
- work with local governments and local businesses to strengthen local entrepreneurial capacity;
- help build real and competitive markets; and
- support implementation of non-reversible reform policies in order to encourage firms to bring to the developing countries their best know-how, their best practices, their global business and market networks.

By changing the perception of acceptable risk in this practical and mutually beneficial process, business world-wide can contribute effectively to market development in developing countries.

# Chapter 35

# Part II.  Trade and development

## 1.  Linkages between trade and development policies

*Professor Wontak Hong\**

"Outward orientation" is a necessary component of an effective development strategy. I would like to focus on three aspects of outward-looking growth. I believe that if people have proper understanding of these aspects, it may be easier for us to search for the ways and means that will make developing nations more actively participate in the WTO system as equal partners.

The first aspect is about the linkage between trade and development. The experience of East Asian NICs shows that "export promotion and expansion of labour-intensive manufactures exports" serve as the engine of growth and catching-up. A rapid expansion of labour-intensive manufactures exports will tremendously increase employment opportunities, eliminate the foreign exchange constraints that frustrate growth efforts, and improve the overall production efficiency by re-allocation of labour from low-productivity traditional sectors to high-productivity manufacturing sectors. Perhaps the most important result of export-oriented growth is the enormous dynamic learning effects arising from the cost–quality competition at international markets.

The second aspect is understanding that the role of government is very important. We should not be too dogmatic about the virtue of *laissez faire* or Hong Kong style positive non-interventionist policy. There are plenty of market failures caused by external economies. There are more than 150 developing countries on the earth. All these countries have potential comparative advantage in labour-intensive manufacturing activities, but only about ten countries could actually take advantage of this potential comparative advantage and could actually realize massive exports of labour-intensive manufactures. The experience of East Asian NICs shows the importance of the role of government in one way or another.

The third aspect suggests the need for us to search for a more agreeable form of government intervention in markets, or the proper role of the government. For instance, the East Asian NICs had to choose between the regime of financial repression characterized by credit rationing on the one hand, and complete financial liberalization on the other. The latter may cause domination of the domestic financial sector by foreign banks and complete opening-up of the financial sector to a very volatile short-term foreign capital movement. The former is preferred by the politicians and bureaucrats of developing nations and the latter is preferred by advanced nations such as the US. The financial crisis of East Asian NICs suggests the need

---

* University of Seoul, Republic of Korea.

for advanced nations to think more carefully about the way they force developing nations to adopt certain kinds of institutional arrangements or policy measures. We can learn much more from the mistakes committed by East Asian NICs than their successful experiences.

I believe that the advanced nations and the WTO system have to tolerate a more active role of the governments of developing nations so long as they adopt policy measures that are fairly transparent, that are more non-discriminatory, and that are more universal rather than sector specific. I will give one example. Japan introduced a fixed exchange rate of 360 yen-per dollar in 1949. By the end of the 1950's, this rate had very much undervalued Japanese currency. However, by adhering to 360 yen-per dollar rate until the early 1970's, most Japanese industries became very much export-oriented. Undervalued yen enhanced the competitive power of Japanese manufacturing sectors at international markets and facilitated Japan's export-oriented growth. This is one example of transparent, nondiscretionary policy measure that a government can adopt.

Furthermore, the advanced nations should maintain some kind of benign neglect of very active government leadership, or intervention of the market in a developing nation, until the magnitude of its manufactured exports increases to, say, ten times its current magnitude. After all, their absolute magnitude is extremely small now. When export of the country becomes really substantial, then the WTO system can seriously regulate the extent of government intervention.

The advanced nations can provide expanded access of developing nations to their domestic markets. Of course a measure like this will be conducive for developing nations to participate more actively in the WTO system as an equal partner. But at the same time, WTO should search for a more agreeable form of government intervention for developing nations instead of simply imposing some policy-cum-institutional arrangements they prefer.

# Chapter 36

# Part II.  Trade and development

## 1.  Linkages between trade and development policies

*Professor Deepak Nayyar**

I would like to begin with three simple propositions. First, trade is a means, it is not an end. Second, development is not simply about economic growth, it is about improving living conditions of the people. Third, there is nothing automatic about development, for there are specificities in time and space. Hence, it should come as no surprise that there is no cause-and-effect relationship between trade liberalization and economic development. Forgive me for beginning in this pedagogic manner, but I do so for an important reason. In sophisticated debates, we often lose sight of simple truths. And these must not be forgotten.

I want to divide my presentation into two parts: first, the linkages between trade and development, which was meant to be the theme of this session; and second, the multilateral trading system and the developing countries, which has become the theme of this session. Let me consider them in turn.

## LINKAGES BETWEEN TRADE AND DEVELOPMENT

In the post-colonial era, which began soon after the end of the second world war, most underdeveloped countries adopted strategies of development that provided a sharp contrast with their past during the first half of the twentieth century. For one, there was a conscious attempt to limit the degree of openness and of integration with the world economy, in pursuit of a more autonomous development. For another, the state was assigned a strategic role in development because the market, by itself, was not perceived as sufficient to meet the aspirations of latecomers to industrialization. Both represented points of departure from the colonial era which was characterized by open economies and unregulated markets. But this approach also represented a consensus in thinking about the most appropriate strategy for industrialization. It was, in fact, the development consensus at the time.

It is almost fifty years since then. And it would seem that, in terms of perceptions about development, we have arrived at the polar opposite. Most countries in the developing world, as also in the erstwhile socialist bloc, are reshaping their domestic economic policies so as to integrate much more with the world economy and to enlarge the role of the market *vis-à-vis* the state. This is partly a consequence of

---

* Jawaharlal Nehru University, New Delhi, India.

internal crisis situations in economy, polity or society. It is also significantly influenced by the profound transformation in the world economy and political situation. The widespread acceptance of this approach represents a new consensus in thinking about development. It has come to be known as the Washington Consensus (even if somewhat shaken by the financial meltdown in South East Asia).

In spite of the shift in paradigm from the development consensus of the 1950s to the Washington Consensus of the 1990s, the degree of openness *vis-à-vis* the world economy and the degree of intervention by the state in the market have remained the critical issues in the debate on development. The past fifty years have, of course, witnessed a complete swing of the pendulum in thinking about these issues. But the complexity of the reality is not captured by either consensus – old or new. And we seem to have moved from one kind of fundamentalism to another.

The belief in free trade is almost a sacred tenet in the world of orthodox economics. Yet, from time to time, the profession of economics has recognized that there are reasons – orthodox and unorthodox – which may justify departures from free trade. Economic theory has analysed these exceptions to the rule, mostly in response to developments in the real world which have questioned the free trade doctrine.

In the era of classical political economy, even before the doctrine gained widespread acceptance, it was recognized that there are two critical assumptions underlying the strong prescription of free trade: first, that market prices reflect social costs and, second, that a country's trade in a good is not large enough to influence world prices. If these assumptions do not hold, free trade cannot ensure an efficient outcome. Market failure provides the basis of the infant industry argument, recognizing that free trade may prevent an economy from realizing its comparative advantage in manufacturing activities. Monopoly power provides the basis of the optimum-tariff argument recognizing that restricting the volume of trade may enable an economy to increase its real income at the expense of the rest of the world. These arguments were accepted as valid exceptions to the rule by Mill, thus providing the analytical foundation for legitimate departures from free trade. It must be recognized that this thinking was prompted largely by the concerns of late industrializers such as the United States and Germany who wished to follow in the footsteps of England and France. It was also motivated by the pursuit of economic interests rather than economic efficiency on the part of nation states.

More than a century later, at the beginning of the post-colonial era, the aspirations of underdeveloped countries were similar for they were latecomers to industrialization and wanted to accelerate the catching-up process. In the realm of politics, of course, the strong sentiment against free trade stemmed from the perceived association between openness and underdevelopment during the colonial era. In the sphere of economics, however, the argument against free trade was based on market failure. It had two dimensions. First, it was argued that there were significant positive externalities in any process of industrialization which were difficult to identify, let alone capture. Second, it was argued that imperfections in factor markets, both labour and capital, would pre-empt the realization of potential comparative advantage in manufacturing. The infant industry argument was, thus, generalized into the infant manufacturing sector argument. The industrial sector was protected from foreign competition and the pursuit of industrialization in most developing countries came to be based on the strategy of import substitution.

Recent developments in the theory of international trade which have relaxed the assumption of constant returns to scale and perfect competition, to model scale economies and market structures, have, once again, questioned the free trade argument. This literature on strategic trade policy, which surfaced in the industrialized countries during the 1980s, developed a theoretical case for government intervention in trade on the basis of assumptions which are different from those in orthodox theory but conform more to observed reality. In terms of positive economics, the new theories suggest that trade flows are driven by increasing returns rather than comparative advantage in international markets which are characterized by imperfect competition.

This has led to the formulation of two arguments against free trade in the sphere of normative economics. The first is the strategic trade policy argument which states that appropriate forms of government intervention can deter entry by foreign firms into lucrative markets, and thus manipulate the terms of oligopolistic competition to ensure that excess returns are captured by domestic firms. The idea is that, in a market which has a small number of competitors, strategic support for domestic firms in international competition can raise national welfare at the expense of other countries. The second is an old argument in a new incarnation which states that government should encourage activities that yield positive externalities. In a world of increasing returns and imperfect competition, such externalities are easier to identify in industries where research and development expenditure is large and firms cannot entirely appropriate the benefits from investment in technology and learning.

Economic theory has, from time to time, thrown up serious questions about free trade. The response of orthodoxy has been predictable. It has endeavoured to reduce the validity of the widely accepted arguments for protection to a set of stringent conditions. It has attempted to dilute the arguments against free trade, in the context of industrialization and development, by arguing that domestic economic policies provide the first/best corrective. It has coaxed the new trade theorists into an acceptance of free trade as the best policy by invoking the real world of politics. The exceptions, it would seem, have been explored to establish the rule.

Yet these exceptions have provided the rationale for departures from free trade in the real world of policy choices. The infant industry argument, sometimes generalized into the infant manufacturing sector argument, has shaped the strategies of most countries that were, or are, latecomers to industrialization, at least in the earlier stages of their development. It has, therefore, been the focus of an extensive literature and an intensive debate on trade and industrialization, particularly with reference to the experience of the developing world during the second half of the twentieth century.

In recent years, the new trade theories have revived the same issues and similar concerns by exploring the linkages between trade, industrialization and growth in a dynamic context. For one, these theories have emphasized, for the first time, the significance of market structures. For another, these theories have pointed to the inequalizing effects of trade, given the importance of initial conditions, so that even if trade is good more trade is not always better. Thus, unmindful of the conclusions reached by orthodoxy, economic theory has lent new dimensions to the discussion on trade and development or openness and industrialization.

The profound change in thinking, from the development consensus to the Washington Consensus, was strongly influenced by the actual industrialization experience of economies in Asia, Africa and Latin America, during the four decades which followed the second world war. The post-mortem of failures led to a diagnosis while the analysis of successes led to prescriptions. These lessons drawn from the experience of particular countries were sought to be generalized and transplanted elsewhere. Such an approach tended to ignore not only the complexities of the growth process but also the characteristics of economies which are specific in time and space.

Yet this approach came to exercise a profound influence on thinking about development. The bottom line was clear. Industrialization policies, which protected domestic industries from foreign competition and led to excessive or inappropriate state intervention in the market, were responsible for the high cost and the low growth in these economies. Inward-looking policies, particularly in the sphere of trade, were seen as the prime culprit. The prescription followed from the critique. More openness and less intervention would impart both efficiency and dynamism to the growth process. And outward-looking policies, particularly in the sphere of trade, were seen as the prime saviour. Thus, trade policies were perceived as critical in the process of industrialization and development.

It needs to be said that this approach to trade and development was narrow in its focus. It was not recognized that there is more to trade policies than the distinction between import substitution and export promotion or inward and outward orientation, just as there is much more to industrialization and development than simply trade policies. Even more important, perhaps, this approach was selective in its use of theory and history. For one, there was a striking asymmetry between the unqualified enthusiasm of policy prescriptions advocating freer trade, unmindful of the distinction between statics and dynamics or irrespective of time and place, and the formal exposition of the free trade argument in economic theory with its careful assumptions, proofs and exceptions. For another, the characterization of the success stories as economies which approximated free trade and *laissez-faire* was a partial, if not a total, caricature of history for their export orientation was not the equivalent of free trade, just as the visible hand of the state was more in evidence than the invisible hand of the market.

It would mean too much of a digression to enter into a detailed discussion on the industrialization experience, its neo-classical critique and the neo-liberal prescription. There is an extensive literature on the subject, which is characterized by a diversity of views that range from the orthodox through the heterodox to the unorthodox. Elsewhere, I provide a critical assessment of the neo-classical analysis and the neo-liberal prescription in terms of theory and experience. It would serve little purpose to do the same here. Instead, I would simply like to highlight some of the analytical limitations of the new orthodoxy on trade and development which now dominates thinking about economic policies.

First, it is a simple fallacy in logic to claim that if something (state intervention or protection) does not work, its opposite (the free market or free trade) must work. This is true only in a dichotomous world of two alternatives. In the world of economic policies, where there are always more than two alternatives, such a view is obviously false.

Secondly, the emphasis on trade liberalization, which assumes that international competition will force domestic firms to become more efficient, makes an elementary but commonplace error in the design of policies. It confuses *comparison* (of equilibrium positions) with *change* (from one equilibrium position to another). In the real world, economic policy must be concerned not merely with comparison but with how to direct the process of change. Thus, even if a reduction in protection can, in principle, lead to a more cost-efficient economy, the transition path is by no means clear. And the process of change should not be confused with the ultimate destination of an economy that is competitive in the world market.

Thirdly, there is a presumption that what is necessary is also sufficient. The management of incentives, motivated by the object of minimizing cost and maximizing efficiency at a micro-level, is based on a set of policies that are intended to increase competition between firms in the market place. Domestic competition is sought to be provided through deregulation in investment decisions, in the financial sector and in labour markets. Foreign competition is sought to be provided through openness in trade, investment and technology flows. It must, however, be recognized that policies may be necessary but are not sufficient, for there is nothing automatic about competition. Policy regimes can allow things to happen but cannot cause things to happen. The creation of competitive markets that enforce efficiency may, in fact, require strategic intervention through industrial policy, trade policy and financial policy.

Fourthly, the strong emphasis on allocative efficiency is matched by a conspicuous silence on technical efficiency. It is forgotten that low levels of productivity in most developing countries are attributable more to technical inefficiency than to allocative inefficiency. Inter-country differences, as also inter-firm differences, in technical efficiency are explained, in large part, by differences in technological (and managerial) capabilities at a micro-level. These capabilities determine not just efficiency in the short-run but also competitiveness in the long-run. But, given the nature of the learning process, such capabilities are both firm-specific and path-dependent. The new orthodoxy simply ignores this critical dimension on the supply side. In contrast, the heterodox literature places the acquisition and development of technological capability centre-stage in the story of success at industrialization. It also shows that the presumed relationship between trade liberalization and technical efficiency is dubious in terms of both theory and evidence.

In my reflections on the linkages between trade and development, I set the stage by explaining the rationale of departures from free trade in economic theory and by outlining the orthodox critique of the industrialization experience in developing countries. The latter highlights the sins of import substitution and state intervention to stress the virtues of openness and markets. However, the policy prescriptions derived are strong generalizations, which do not match orthodox theory in terms of rigour and do not recognize recent theoretical developments in terms of insights. What is more, the neo-classical critique and the neo-liberal prescription are both characterized by analytical limitations. Most important, perhaps, the mainstream literature on trade and development is narrow in its focus just as it is selective in its use of theory and experience.

The changed international context, attributable to globalization, has important implications for trade and development which must be recognized. An increase in the degree of openness of economies is inevitable, while the degrees of freedom for nation states are bound to be fewer. But it would be a mistake to consider this necessity as a virtue. Simplified prescriptions, which emphasize more openness and less intervention to advocate a rapid integration with the world economy, combined with a minimalist state that vacates space for the market, are not validated either by theory or by history. Economic theory recognizes, and economic history reveals, the complexities of the industrialization process. The degree of openness and the nature of intervention are strategic choices in the pursuit of industrialization, which cannot be defined (and should not be prescribed) once-and-for-all, for they depend upon the stage of development and must change over time. There can be no magic recipes in a world where economies are characterized by specificities in time and in space.

The irony is that, at the present juncture, when the disillusionment with the state is so widespread, given the reality of globalization, its role in the pursuit of indus-trialization and development is more critical than ever before. However, this does not mean, nor should it suggest, more of the same. Correcting mistakes and learn-ing from experience is vital. It is, therefore, essential to redefine the economic role of the state *vis-à-vis* the market, so that the two institutions complement each other and adapt to one another as circumstances or times change. That is what success at development is about.

# MULTILATERAL TRADING SYSTEM AND DEVELOPING COUNTRIES

The rules governing trade, which began life with the GATT five decades ago, have evolved over time, but the system has not quite kept pace with the changing reality and the increasing complexity of world trade. An increasing proportion of world output enters into the world trade. An increasing proportion of world trade is made up of intra-firm trade. Trade flows have moved much beyond the simple world of goods, just as trade barriers have moved much beyond the simple world of tariffs. Trade is more and more an arena for conflicts and claims from other spheres. In a world of unequal partners, where bargains are struck among the major players, a large number of countries are spectators, rather than participants, in multilateral negotiations.

In this world of unequal partners, it is not surprising that the rules are asymmetri-cal in terms of construct and inequitable in terms of outcome. The strong have the power to make the rules and the authority to implement the rules. In contrast, the weak can neither set nor invoke the rules. The problem, however, takes different forms.

First, there are different rules in different spheres. The rules of the game for the international trading system, being progressively set in the WTO, provide the most obvious example. There are striking asymmetries. National boundaries should not matter for trade flows and capital flows but should be clearly demarcated for tech-nology flows and labour flows. In effect, this implies more openness in some spheres and less openness in other spheres. The contrast between the free move-ment of the capital and the unfree movement of the labour is the most stark.

Secondly, the emerging rules which are asymmetrical, may significantly reduce the autonomy of developing countries in the formulation of economic policies in their pursuit of industrialization and development. The existing (and prospective) rules of the WTO regime allow few exceptions and provide little flexibility to coun-tries that are latecomers to industrialization. The rules on trade in the new regime will make selective protection or strategic promotion of domestic firms *vis-à-vis* foreign competition much more difficult. The tight system for the protection of intellectual property rights might pre-empt or constrain domestic technological capa-bilities. The possible multilateral agreement on investment, when it materializes, will almost certainly reduce the possibilities of strategic bargaining with transnational corporations. Taken together, such rules are bound to curb the use of industrial policy, trade policy and technology policy as strategic forms of intervention to foster industrialization.

Thirdly, the agenda for new rules is partisan, but the unsaid is just as important as the said. The attempt to create a multilateral agreement on investment in the WTO, which seeks free access and national treatment for foreign investors with provisions to enforce commitments and obligations to foreign investors, provides the most obvious example. Surely, these rights of foreign investors must be matched by some obligations. Thus, a discipline on restrictive business practices of transnational corporations, the importance of conformity with anti-trust laws in home countries, or a level playing field for domestic firms in host countries, should also be in the picture.

It need hardly be said that the nature of the solution depends on the nature of the problem. Where there are different rules in different spheres, it is necessary to make the rules symmetrical across spheres. Where there are the same rules for unequal partners, there should be some recognition of differences in the level of development. Where the agenda for new rules is partisan, it is imperative to redress the balance in the agenda.

There is a clear need for greater symmetry in the rules of the multilateral trading system embodied in the WTO. If developing countries provide access to their markets, it should be matched with some corresponding access to technology. If there is almost complete freedom for capital mobility, the draconian restrictions on labour mobility should at least be reduced. For countries at vastly different levels of development, there should be some flexibility, instead of complete rigidity, in the application of uniform rules. It is, in principle, possible to formulate general rules where application is a function of country-specific or time-specific circumstances, without resorting to exceptions. This is, of course, easier said than done. It implies a set of multilateral rules in which every country has the same rights but the obligations are a function of its level or stage of development. If the proposed multilateral agreement on investment is so concerned about the rights of transnational corporations, some attention should also be paid to their possible obligations.

It is clear that such correctives are possible only through more democratic structures of governance. I recognize that these may be difficult to construct in a world of unequal partners. But we must not forget that, in the world around us, political power is used (and will continue to be used) to foster economic interests. The multilateral trading system is no exception to this rule. Thus, developing countries must ensure that their political voice is heard in the WTO, for even if they do not have the requisite political power they do have economic interests to preserve and to promote. For this purpose, it is essential to find common causes in a world where there are many conflicts or contradictions, because groups of countries with mutual interest are more likely to be heard than single countries by themselves. It is possible for developing countries to register their voice if they decide to act in cohesion, say, in the WTO. At this juncture, for instance, developing countries could insist that they would not agree to a new round of multilateral trade negotiations until their concerns are recognized and essential correctives are introduced, not only in the agenda but also in the rules.

# Chapter 37

# Part II.  Trade and development

## 1.  Linkages between trade and development policies

*John Toye*\*

Dr Bergsten's chapter has in it four different types of argument. First of all, there are statements of principle concerning the relationship between trade expansion and development, and the benefits of a multilateral trade system. These arguments of principle are familiar, as are the rejoinders to them. The second type of argument is an argument about timing. It is a rather strong and specific claim about the pressures of the current conjunction. Dr Bergsten argues that, at the moment, US protectionist pressures are strong and that – if the international community does not move ahead with further trade liberalization – it is bound to fall back to a worse position than the current one. Like cycling, he argues, trade liberalization has a dynamic that requires continuous forward movement in order to avoid wavering and collapse. That is his timing argument for starting another Round. The third type of argument is about the size of the potential gains for developing countries, and the fourth is about the feasibility of securing those gains.

It is useful to keep these different lines of argument separate in our minds. The arguments of principle have been much discussed. I congratulate all the previous discussants for having raised a wide range of possible rejoinders. Little would be added by my commenting further on these rejoinders, and I do not propose to do so. I shall direct my remarks to the argument about timing, and the argument about the feasibility of the developing countries securing the potential gains of further trade liberalization. In particular, I shall pay attention, as Paul Collier has asked us to do, to the feasibility of the least developed countries securing the potential gains. How will they play a part in a new Round, especially if the timing argument is correct?

Before I do so, however, let me say this – as a recent arrival at UNCTAD, I am still learning the coded language of trade policy discourse. Much significance is clearly attached, in the discussion of these issues, to the term "special and differential treatment" for developing countries. It seems to me that this term is being used in a variety of ways, and we should distinguish the negative sense from the positive. I agree with those speakers who have said that special and differential treatment, in the sense of a general exemption from membership obligations of GATT/WTO, is no longer the right way forward for developing countries, if it ever was. As Mr Ricupero stated, it is important that the dialogue on trade policy be as full and inclusive as possible, and that is why having so many least developed

---

\* Director, Globalization and Development Strategies Division, UNCTAD.

countries outside the WTO is a problem. The aim should be, especially as far as the least developed countries are concerned, to enhance their proactive participation in a positive agenda of discussions.

At the same time, there is an acceptable meaning of the terms "special" and "treatment", identified with another code word – "flexibility", for which Mr Ricupero argued so eloquently. Flexibility means being willing to allow, within a set of general rules, certain exemptions so that least developed countries can do certain things necessary for their development which the more developed countries bind themselves no longer to do. This is difficult ground. However, as you have heard in the foregoing comments, temporary, selective and performance-related protection has been an important component of the trade régimes of some of the countries that have grown at historically unprecedented rates. Any general set of trade rules must be sufficiently flexible to permit this to happen in the future, in appropriate cases.

Undoubtedly, this poses a problem. We can look at the East Asian experience and see that their departures from free trade were developmentally positive. Yet we also know that what they did was very difficult to do. It is comparable to a high-wire act in the circus, in which the performer climbs a ladder, walks across the high wire and collects a bag of gold (the rewards of development). We know that most people who try to do this fall off the wire long before they reach the bag of gold. What is to be done? One way is to ask everyone, in the interests of health and safety, to foreswear the high wire. But since some people can walk the high wire, and benefit from doing so, what is the justification for preventing them? The key to the solution of this far from easy problem is to be found in the concept of flexibility. How to provide the right degree of flexibility is something that any new Round must address.

I come now to the questions of timing and feasibility. Mr Ricupero has pointed out that only 2 per cent of technical assistance world-wide is trade related. In these circumstances, he made a plea for the launch of a massive programme of trade-related technical assistance. Such a programme, focused around training in commercial diplomacy, would assist least developed countries to acquire the information they need to determine their best interests, the negotiating skills to caucus and to develop the negotiating positions which would enable them to use the leverage due to their share of the WTO membership. The mere fact that the developing countries have the largest share of WTO membership does not lead to the conclusion, and here I quote Dr Bergsten directly, that "... the global trade system cannot marginalize the developing countries". I wish that were true, and that it could become a new law of international political economy. But it was not true in the Uruguay Round, and if marginalization is to be prevented in a new Round, the numerical majority would have to be aligned behind pre-agreed negotiating positions.

Now I ask myself whether there is enough time to develop and implement a massive programme of technical assistance to assist the least developed countries to be ready for a new Round of negotiations? I would sympathize with any least developed country that felt that it was being hustled into a new Round, without enough thought being given to whether the technical assistance that it needs to avoid continuing marginalization can possibly be absorbed in time. We have heard the arguments of urgency ably put by Dr Bergsten. Now we need to consider whether they are consistent with the feasibility of adequate preparation for the effective representation of the interests of the least developed countries, their proactive participation in a positive trade agenda, and their securing in reality the potential gains of a new Round. I ask all of you here today to weigh this question, and decide where you think that the balance falls.

# Chapter 38

## Part II.  Trade and development

### 2.  Trade and development prospects of developing countries

*Carlos Alfredo Magariños\**

I am going to look at the prospects, the future, of trade and development based on my observations while I was a Minister of Industry in my own country, Argentina, and what I see now as Director-General of UNIDO.

If we look at the current situation, the medium-term prospects for the developing countries *vis-à-vis* trade and development are not very rosy. Viewing them is like looking through a glass darkly. Owing to the present international economic situation, these prospectives are not only matters of concern but are also the results of processes so recent and so unprecedented, that understanding them and their probable consequences has to be called a work in progress.

Until recently there were predictions that the developing world would be able to attain yearly growth rates of around 5 to 6 per cent and that their participation in world production if this tendency could be maintained could increase from 16 per cent in 1992 to 30 per cent in the year 2020.

But these predictions were made in the framework of an expanding world economy. Today, 25 per cent of the world economy is in recession and at least four of the major world economies are suffering an annual reduction of 6 per cent or more.

Private capital flows into the developing countries have fallen to less than half, from $325 billion in 1996 to $150 billion in 1998, and we could witness an even greater decrease during the current year. The Japanese economy does not, as yet, give signs of responding to the enormous stimulus that it has received. Even the United States and Europe are facing a decline in exports, and prospects of adjustment in the stock markets, as a result of a weaker world demand.

Only the United States economy has been able to remain solid, supported by a remarkable strength of personal consumption that rose by $38 billion in 1998, an amount roughly equivalent to the total yearly output of the mid-sized economies of Asia.

The situation is complicated and worrisome. But there are some positive signs. We can observe and at the same time recognize the differences between how Thailand and the Republic of Korea have dealt with the critical situation faced by their respective economies. Japan has announced that it expects to return to dynamic economic growth. At the same time China has acted with a great deal of prudence, caution and responsibility in a most delicate situation. As happened in 1995 in Mexico, the recent crisis in Brazil has had a limited contagious effect in the

---

\* Director-General, United Nations Industrial Development Organization.

region but, at least, it has not generated a domino effect in Latin America (even considering the fact that the Brazilian economy represents 40 per cent of the GDP of the region).

What I consider to be of paramount importance is that – despite the difficulties that the world economy is encountering, even in countries that have been mostly affected by those difficulties – there has not been a dramatic change of direction in the mechanisms of free trade and sound macroeconomic policies. Obviously, there have been critical assessments that have recognized emerging problems but there have been no dramatic calls for abandoning such mechanisms.

I am convinced that the developing countries should take advantage of this fact to move forward in the structural reform process, to make additional efforts to achieve an even freer trade despite the current difficulties. Once the international economic crisis is resolved, we will encounter even greater demands to solve the problems of social inequality, violence and poverty.

## ARGENTINA AND MERCOSUR

From my own perspective it is clear that sound macroeconomic policies and free trade could significantly contribute to the solution of these problems. In expressing this viewpoint, I would like to make reference to some of the conclusions I reached during my participation in the Argentinian Government and the process of negotiations towards the establishment of the Common Market of the South (MERCOSUR).

In 1989, yearly inflation reached 5,000 per cent in Argentina. After various failed attempts, in 1991 the government launched a dramatic and successful stabilization program within the framework of an equally successful structural reform. We were able to reduce inflation and the economy began to grow. Between 1991 and 1993, gross domestic product grew at an average of 6 per cent and, in 1994, the rate of growth was the third largest in the world, behind China and Singapore. Inflation was reduced to less than 1 per cent in a short time.

One of the main reasons why we were so successful is that we were able to tackle various fronts at the same time: implementing prudent fiscal and monetary policies; privatizing public enterprises and services; deregulating the market; and opening our economy to the world at large. I still remember that only four weeks before we instituted a currency board (I was entrusted with preparing the tariff reform in my capacity as National Director of Foreign Trade) we lowered the average import tariff – perhaps the most drastic reform of our recent economic history – from more than 40 per cent to 10 per cent.

Additionally, a strategic decision was taken at the same time to construct a free trade regime with neighbouring countries. This was a highly debated decision in view of the fact that previous attempts in Latin America towards trade integration had achieved limited results. The best known and widely applied trade policy was ALADI, the Latin American Integration Association which succeeded the Latin American Free Trade Association (LAFTA) that dated back to 1960 and that achieved some positive results of limited impact that cannot be ignored. Without overlooking the good results achieved by ALADI, and far from pretending a critical evaluation, one could say that MERCOSUR, established in the early 1990s, showed, in contrast, more rapid and substantial results towards enhancing the intra-regional growth in trade.

What makes the case of MERCOSUR relatively more successful? What is it that explains the difference? The answer can be found at two levels.

The first has to do with the overall economic framework that applies to the free trade agreement. The partners of MERCOSUR began by applying sound macroeconomic policies that stabilized the economy and generated sustainable growth on the demand side, based on reducing inflation and regaining access to credit. At the same time, prudent fiscal and monetary policies were applied. Competition was encouraged by deregulation and lowering tariffs. Also, an aggressive program was introduced aimed at reducing public expenditure, improving fiscal revenues and privatizing public enterprises and services.

These policies resulted in a straight-jacket for the private sector (local as well as international) obliging them to redefine their strategies. The fiscal and monetary policies resulted in the reduction and elimination of subsidies, while the regional and international trade agreements also prevented the application of protectionist policies. Additionally, consumer demand rose, thus increasing the need for importing, or otherwise accessing, technology to support and ensure market success.

The second level had to do with the overall strategy for integrating the Latin American common market. In comparison with ALADI, which concentrated on reciprocal concessions for reducing tariffs on a sector-by-sector or even product-by-product basis, MERCOSUR allowed, with the exception of a very few sectors, for automatic across-the-board reduction of tariffs. The scope for haggling and for exercising political pressure was therefore minimized. The commercial policy, and the commitment to pursue common policy objectives that trade organizations such as this one propose, had a positive impact on the performance of MERCOSUR. While it is true that, within MERCOSUR, tariffs were reduced to 0 per cent for 85 per cent of traded products, it is equally true that tariffs for the international market in general were also reduced significantly, as I already said when I referred to the tariff reform in Argentina at a time when the Currency Board was established. This is open regionalism, not the construction of a trade fortress or the establishment of a system that obstructs trade.

If we look at the impact of trade regimes on the structure of industry, we see that high tariffs and subsidies go hand-in-hand with the industrial policies associated with import substitution and state ownership of industry. Under those circumstances, firms tend to produce a wide range of products with a minimum of innovation and investment, confident that protection will provide them with a captive consumer market.

But what happens when tariffs are lowered in the context of a program of macroeconomic stabilization? From what I saw as Minister of Industry, companies adopt specialization as their new strategy. Many firms that were not so prominent in Argentina made an about-face and began to increase investment, with a totally different approach that included limiting their product range, focusing on their core businesses and including cost-effective imports as part of their production operations.

It is very important to understand that it was technological change, in that context, that made it possible to take advantage of the return to economic stability and open trade. Technology is changing the structure of industry worldwide and across many sectors. For example, it is the lowered costs of communications and transportation, which are the springboards of globalization, that have made plant size and location less important. Production costs are falling in relation to the costs of marketing, advertising and other service factors embedded in final consumer prices. Developing countries stand to benefit from the industrial restructuring that is brought about by these cost reductions. Argentina shows how a country and a region can profit from structural reform programs and an open trade regime accompanied by advances in technology.

It is not, I think, an exaggeration to say that all those recent changes made it possible to move from import substitution schemes, with high tariffs, to a strategy of specialization with open trade aimed at promoting economic and industrial growth.

The experience of Argentina and more broadly that of MERCOSUR seems to give us some guide posts. Trade that opens in the context of deep economic restructuring offers the possibility for a country to enter the international mainstream, especially when its regional trade is growing. Foreign direct investment not only grows but grows within the international framework. Technology is brought into the marketplace and competitiveness is enhanced.

But we must also recognize that regional economic growth, in the context of world economic expansion and growth in international trade at that time, created a favourable environment for economic expansion.

We must recognize that MERCOSUR profited from a conducive environment during a period of worldwide economic growth and trade expansion.

## PROSPECTS FOR TRADE

Most countries UNIDO works with do not have the type of industrial base on which a MERCOSUR arrangement could build. Also, we are at a time when the world economy might enter a significant downturn.

One of the most distressing pieces of information that has come to my attention, since I came to UNIDO fifteen months ago, concerns the trade impact of the Lomé Convention, particularly manufactured exports. Under the favourable trade concessions granted to developing countries under the Lomé Convention over the last ten years, manufactured exports did not increase. This tells us that trade concessions do not work, in terms of promoting growth and development, without the existence of an industrial base with sufficient critical mass. This is especially valid when trade barriers on manufactured goods are so low for most of the products that concessions are of little significance.

Looking at the global trade picture, it is not clear that the world will be able to keep to the path and speed of trade liberalization that has prevailed since the end of World War II under GATT. It is clear that, in general terms, much has been achieved. Most industrialized countries have already significantly lowered tariffs on manufactured goods. But it seems that we are on a plateau in terms of free trade. It will not be easy to go farther in trade liberalization for many reasons. One is that we have already reached a high level of openness in trade industrial goods, even though full Uruguay Round implementation will not be completed until 2005. This leaves little room for the kind of expansion seen in the last decade or more.

For example, agricultural trade appears to face difficulties in spite of the recent signals of reform in European agricultural policies. Also, services are not as easy to control as trade in goods. For one thing, it is not simple to identify increments in service productivity. Nonetheless, trade in services has been growing faster than trade in goods in recent years, and will doubtless continue to do so as industrialized country consumers demand more service-related products. The GATT on trade in services achieved in the last round is a good start, but I see no reason to believe that we will be able to advance more quickly in services than we did in industrial goods and that took fifty years.

It does not need emphasizing that moving forward on trade expansion will be even more difficult if the slow-down of Asian economies continues, and the predicted slow-down in Europe occurs. In addition, if the United States does not continue to be a source of economic good news, we will be looking at a very dark picture indeed. We could then expect trade relations among the great trading nations – the United States, Europe and Japan – to become more tense with negative implications for the rest of the world. Thus, it is likely that in the coming years we will have to make more efforts to maintain what we have already achieved, rather than advancing toward more liberalization.

Does this mean that there is nothing to do about trade growth, or the reduction of trade barriers, but sit on our hands and hope for the best? Obviously not. For example, there is much that can be done to ensure that quality standards are not used as trade barriers to developing countries seeking to enter the markets. While standards are necessary for expansion and making access fairer, at the same time they often function to deter market entry or to inhibit competition. In this regard, I should like to request the support of the multilateral community in organizing and setting up national or regional centres of quality certification and control in the developing world.

Similarly, a conflict has arisen between international trade and social norms over international labour standards. While the importance of this issue has been acknowledged, strong opposition has been voiced to dealing with it in the context of the market, under WTO rules. It is therefore encouraging to know that the ILO has now been charged with finding a consensus on international labour standards that are independent of trade concerns. Nor should it be forgotten that environmental issues have met with equally difficult stumbling blocks.

It is my opinion that developed countries have to further reduce tariff barriers for goods from developing countries, and also to make a concerted effort to prevent quality standards from being used unfairly. Activities such as dumping, countervailing duties and non-tariff barriers must be prevented from being used unfairly to stop trade by developing countries.

An important aside on this issue: I should like to make a plea for improved support for plans to set up a legal aid centre to advise weaker countries on the WTO rules and to help them prepare their cases for the disputes panel. Should these plans succeed, we in UNIDO would be more than willing to offer expert technical advice in cases involving manufactured goods. In a broader context, and complementing the technical cooperation programs of WTO, UNCTAD and ITC, our Organization has also recently embarked upon a series of exercises in developing countries designed to increase their awareness of the impact of the new world trade order on manufacturing industries.

Access to financing, always a problem for developing countries, has worsened since the onset of Asian problems in late 1997. Even trade financing, that was in the past one of the few reliable sources of credit, has become tighter. Any further financial crises, to say nothing of a deep market correction in the United States, are certain to turn the current incipient credit crunch into a rout for developing countries. In this critical area, it seems to me that multilateral organizations have an important role to play, a role that will require innovation and risk taking. Multilaterals should be freed from restrictions that overly limit their ability to leverage funds. This could be done by providing guarantees and collateral to stimulate and support private sector investment in developing countries, and especially in the least developed countries.

## PROSPECTS FOR DEVELOPMENT

However, as we know, all our efforts to develop and increase trade (what we have already done and what is still in the pipeline) do not necessarily add up to sustainable industrial development, or sustainable development in general.

The international development community has the knowledge and the tools to improve living conditions and to alleviate much of the world's poverty. But let us not be mistaken, or naive. Sustainable development is something else. What troubles me, as I travel more and more in the world's least developed countries, is the nagging doubt that we focus sufficiently on the alleviation of poverty. It is becoming increasingly obvious, if seldom admitted, that we don't know as much as we need to, or claim to, about how to create development that withstands the test of time.

In UNIDO we focus on small and medium-sized enterprises and we do it with great success; if, by success, we mean that certain sectors are enabled to improve their efficiency, their export record, their employment capacity and their technology incorporation. But one sector alone does not make a viable developing sustainable economy.

Let me be frank. If the multilateral development organizations do not make a concerted and rapid effort to work very closely together, and in cooperation, to develop new modes of thinking and new tools to strengthen the prospects for really closing the growing gap between developed countries and developing countries, and within developing countries, we are facing a very grim and, I would even say, a very dangerous scenario for our new century.

Perhaps the most fundamental assumption behind multilateral and bilateral economic aid is that, over time, the divergence between levels of economic activity and social well-being between developed and developing countries will be diminished. So far, this optimism has not been rewarded. The development gap continues to widen, even during one of the longest periods of sustained economic growth in history. Division of the world into a poor one and a rich one with some small grey areas in the middle is not just morally and socially objectionable; it threatens long term global stability, environmental protection and peace.

Evidence regarding convergence among developing countries and economies in transition is less than persuasive. Moreover, the case is even weaker with respect to advanced industrial countries. Between 1960 and 1990, per capita income in developing countries declined in relation to the developed world by almost half in South Asia and Africa and substantially deteriorated in Latin America.

As would be expected, the situation is most stark in the least developed countries. These LDCs are a group of 48 countries with a population of over 585 million people. Even though most of these nations have introduced far-reaching reforms since the late 1980s, they continue to show poor economic performance. The LDCs are suffering from premature de-industrialization. They are not on the world-wide technology train and so remain caught in the low-wage/low-productivity trap. A reversal of this trend is not in sight. In addition, when the world economy slows down, the LDCs face dire consequences: aid flows simply dry up. Aid to Africa is expected to decline from $8.4 billion last year to $4.2 billion this year.

Not only are most of these developing countries dependent on commodity exports at a time when forecasts are for continued price deterioration, they also have a very narrow manufacturing base. While the average share of industry in the GDP of the OECD countries is 21.5 per cent, in LDCs it averages just 9 per cent. It is only via the route of industrialization that the LDCs can aspire to join the "rich man's club".

Moreover, and this is problematic for all developing countries not just the least developed, when countries join trade groupings or sign trade agreements that theo-retically increase their export opportunities, they must also open their markets to imports. For many countries, as I need hardly explain here at this gathering, this can look very much like a "catch-22" situation. Open markets and a level playing field may well generate larger volumes of trade in theory. However, in practice, unless entrepreneurs in developing countries are equipped to enter the race and to compete on equal terms, the game is over before it starts.

This underlines the fundamental dilemma facing the LDCs. Productive sectors are handicapped because the state is unable to implement policies to strengthen them institutionally, to build the necessary capacities and to offset their failures. Yet the state cannot rely on an efficiently functioning market to make up for its failures.

## CONCLUSION

Multilateral organizations should and can contribute most to LDCs by working to break this double-edged vise. Although the international community recognizes the central role of multilateral aid in creating sustainable economic development, there is a growing awareness of the need to reconsider the framework in which multilat-eral organizations operate. New realities are demanding new approaches to devel-opment and new tools for implementing them.

There is clearly a move in that direction. The WTO's innovative Integrated Framework for Trade-Related Technical Assistance for the least developed coun-tries, as well as the United Nations Development Assistance Framework proposals and now the new Proposal for a Comprehensive Development Framework by the World Bank are indications of a growing awareness and willingness to consider new approaches.

Today, multilateralism is more valid than ever before. National governments are being pressured to devolve some of their power upward to supra-national entities and downward to sub-national entities, with the result that they have lost some of their room to manoeuvre. Developing countries face more severe restrictions: financial markets set limits to fiscal and monetary policy; the need for access to foreign markets limits the scope for trade policies; and international corporations decide on the location of their investments on the basis of tax regimes which reduce the latitude in tax policy. Although multilaterals are vital as never before, we must speed up the process of reform.

I won't try to be comprehensive, but I would like to risk making a few suggestions based on my experiences. First, let me tell you what I won't comment on: macroeconomic stabilization. I think we can all agree that this is a prerequisite for development. My only point in this regard is that, standing alone, it is not the full prescription. No matter what the debate on the Washington Consensus, we must move beyond it to the microeconomic challenges. Measures to remove micro-level constraints and improve institutional capabilities are where renewed efforts are required, and it is precisely in those areas that greater cooperation and policy and programmatic coherence among multilaterals is essential. It is to this imperative that I want to turn.

Trade and trade issues are seldom the stuff of headlines except when two major industrialized countries are slipping on banana skins. Trade is the quintessential example of the "devil in the details" that, by and large, makes it the domain of specialists like my colleagues in UNIDO who work on metrology and quality control.

While I believe the kinds of things that UNIDO is doing in technology and knowledge transfer give developing countries better tools to enter the trading system, it is also important to know why that needs to be done. I don't think it is an exaggeration to say that without trade a country may be able to grow, although even this is questionable; but without trade, sustainable development is not possible. Despite the difficulties involved in proving it, growing acceptance of this view explains why developing countries have been anxious to become members of the WTO where they now make up two thirds of the membership.

The adherence of developing countries to the WTO shows the perceived need of it and its predecessor, GATT, in overseeing the enormous expansion and liberalization of world trade. At the same time, the WTO extends the application and acceptance of rules-based trading. There is no doubt that these developments have been beneficial to developing countries. As we know, the developing world's share in trade in 1995 totalled just over 28 per cent as compared to 1970 when it was barely 19 per cent.

However, greater and freer trade, like macroeconomic structural reform, is not enough. More targeted efforts have to be made to level the playing field for developing countries, allowing them to improve their prospects for development. Let me provide unsolicited advice:

- As part of technical cooperation and knowledge transfer, multilateral organizations should set up special task forces to help developing countries to better understand their own interests in trade negotiations, and to help them prepare their strategies and positions, individually or collectively. They should also contribute to developing country efforts to be included in the preparations of trade talks.
- We would suggest that mechanisms be found for information on the benefits of the Generalized System of Preferences (GSP) to be better diffused to those countries that are eligible and, at the same time, we propose to expedite entry into the WTO of developing countries who have expressed a desire to join.

- We would like to congratulate the Government of Germany on the Cologne Initiative for improving and accelerating the relief of highly indebted poor countries.
- There should be a careful study of the timing, sequencing and degree of market liberalization, thus allowing developing countries to adapt individually to the consequences of open markets.

Let us bear in mind that the way to evaluate the progress of our society is not based on our capacity to add more to those who have enough, but rather on the capacity of our society to allow those who have too little to improve their living conditions.

# Chapter 39

# Part II. Trade and development

## 2. Trade and development prospects of developing countries

*Marcelo De Paiva Abreu\**

Whatever the outcome of present macroeconomic difficulties in emerging econo-mies and in the world economy, trade and development prospects will depend on factors which are mostly outside the influence of the World Trade Organization. Typically, the impact of macroeconomic policies on world economic growth and welfare can be much more intense than those arising from trade liberalization. Gains from the Uruguay Round, according to the most favourable scenarios, are estimated to have been in the region of 1 to 2 per cent of world GDP.

There is hidden, however, a dangerous asymmetry. While gains from comprehen-sive trade liberalization are bound to be modest, it should not be forgotten that the negative impact of a reversal of trade liberalization can be substantially more significant.

Let us stick with those aspects which can be affected by developments in the World Trade Organization. Prominent among these would be the results of a possi-ble new round of multilateral trade negotiations, and the way in which the specific interests of developing economies are likely to be affected.

Potential gains to developing economies would be partly related to the advan-tages of further liberalization of access to their domestic markets, building up on the very important liberalization which resulted from the Uruguay Round. It is difficult to exaggerate the importance of such developments.

In the case of my country, Brazil, the Uruguay Round resulted in radical change: an increase of bindings from covering something like 20 per cent of total trade to 100 per cent of trade, and a reduction of the tariff level on most products to 35 per cent compared to an average in the region of 60 per cent, plus many non-tariff barriers in the mid-1980s.

This was a sharp change of policy in a country which had had an outstandingly good performance until the 1970s, in spite of almost secular high protection. Brazil had no *laissez faire* tradition in contrast to other developing countries. Brazil was highly protectionist for 100 years and, in spite of this, grew rapidly until the 1970s, partly because of its market power concerning coffee – as higher prices of inputs entailed by higher tariffs could be passed through to coffee buyers. In contrast, more liberal policies made sense for some of our neighbours, at least until the European markets started to shrink, especially after World War II.

---

\* Department of Economics, Pontifical Catholic University, Rio De Janeiro, Brazil.

The Brazilian so-called outward-looking model, adopted in the mid-1960s was, in fact, "cross-eyed" since heavy export subsidization was combined with a closed market for imports; and since there was an important role for foreign investors who became major clients for subsidies and continuously clamoured for protectionist policies. The Brazilian case also shows how addictive protectionism is. There was no institutional basis to foster the abandonment of protectionist policies. The persistence of protectionism was helped by long-term growth success combined with a closed market.

When protectionism started to show fatigue in the 1980s, the role of multilateral trade negotiations proved to be essential in weakening the strength of protectionist lobbies – including multinational firms which had become addicted to high tariff walls and, in many cases, to absolute protection. That Brazil became a *demandeur* in the Uruguay Round was a major break with the past. Unilateral trade liberalization became a major pillar of comprehensive economic reforms which started to be implemented after the very early 1990s.

Even in the middle of the recent macroeconomic turmoil, with the successive financial crises in Asia and Russia ending by finally affecting Brazil in early 1999, commitment to a more liberal trade policy has been preserved on the whole. The liberalization process has, of course, raised severe problems related to the accommodation of conflicting interests. Problems arising out of the political economy of trade are not a monopoly of developed economies. After the reduction of high tariffs entailed by the Uruguay Round, further concessions by developing countries, such as the lowering of tariffs by Brazil, were bound to affect, even more severely, the established interests favoured by protectionist policies.

To circumvent such difficulties, Brazilian negotiators had to be able to show that the developed countries were willing to make significant concessions by opening their markets in all sectors.

However, efforts by developed economies to include a number of new issues – such as environment and labour rights which have not been traditionally dealt with by the GATT or the WTO – into the new Round's agenda, have introduced a new range of difficulties. The situation is not dissimilar to that before the launching of the Uruguay Round in the early 1980s, concerning trade-related intellectual property, trade-related investment measures and services. One important difference is that the economic arguments for the inclusion of such themes were sounder than those being used today in the policy harmonization debate.

In political terms, it is difficult not to associate this interest by developed countries in expanding the GATT/WTO negotiating agenda with a parallel interest in avoiding any consideration of the GATT/WTO backlog.

Much has been said about what developed economies may do in the next Round in terms of offers which may be of interest to the developing economies. The policy of putting everything on the table is of essential importance to developing countries. But it would have to contain no exceptions, and liberalization should balance both industrial and agricultural products. There is, for instance, no economic reason to limit offers to totally dismantle tariffs to industrial products only. Convergence in the direction of less distorted world agricultural markets may, however, require the international mobilization of resources to cope with the consequences of price rises on vulnerable food importers. In the same way that developing economies in the Uruguay Round were expected to, and did, fall in line with more liberal trade regimes affecting industrial products, now it is the time to remove the extremely severe distortions which still affect agricultural trade.

In my view, progress in relation to two other issues related to access is also essential if balanced results are to be obtained in the next Round of multilateral trade negotiations.

The first issue is related to the need to improve international disciplines concerning the application of anti-dumping duties, whose determination process is often crowned by the imposition of disguised voluntary export restraints. This seriously undermines the multilateral trading system.

The second issue relates to the core of the WTO activities. It involves strengthening the multilateral capacity to restrain the ability of specific countries to unilaterally adopt measures without recourse to the full possibilities of the multilateral dispute settlement system. These are difficult issues, but to ignore them is to leave the door open to protectionism and unreasonable use of political clout. Small economies – in a technical sense, developing economies – are especially interested in the reinforcement of a strong dispute settlement mechanism which would effectively dilute the market power of big players.

A new Round should also give high priority to the question of "special and differential" treatment. There is growing dissatisfaction amongst developing economies on how this question has been dealt with in the Uruguay Round agreements. Special and differential provisions have generally taken the form of extended adjustment periods in relation to newly-introduced disciplines. As such time limits start to become binding, dissatisfaction has become greater. Some of these special and differential provisions might be re-examined with an extended time frame in mind.

A crucial pending matter concerning "special and differential", is how to deal with the trade preferences related to the Generalized System of Preferences, and, in dealing with this system, how to give substance to the idea of graduation in the multilateral context. As in the case of tariff negotiations, a sound principle seems to be that the less discretionary the process is, the better. This applies to tariff cuts, as well as to concessions of full or partial trade preferences, and graduation of the more advanced developing economies.

Ambassador George Álvares Maciel led the efforts which resulted in the Framework Agreement, the General System of Preferences waiver and the recognition of the concept of graduation, back in 1978–79. The incorporation of such trade preferences in the GATT/WTO has been pending since then. Binding the full preferences entailed by the Generalized System of Preferences would reduce the role of discretionary policies in their distribution. Multilaterally-agreed graduation criteria may regulate levels of preference and their withdrawal. It would also generally define how, in the best scenario, a developing economy might receive progressively lower margins of protection as its GDP per capita increases and as it increasingly offers preferential market access to other developing economies.

# Chapter 40

# Part II. Trade and development

## 2. Trade and development prospects of developing countries

*Professor Arjun Sengupta\**

It has been argued that trade liberalization is not just a sufficient condition for growth, but that it is a necessary condition. I am afraid neither of these statements is true. First, it is not a sufficient condition, as has been pointed out very clearly by other speakers, because there are other policies that will have to complement liberalization without which growth may not materialize. Secondly, it is not a necessary condition because there are many examples of cases of closed economies which have achieved very high growth for long periods.

There are many theoretical models showing that freeing trade is not a necessary condition for growth – sometimes it can actually deteriorate growth, making a country considerably poorer. But all this does not mean that trade liberalization is not desirable. Trade liberalization is important because it gives countries a better opportunity to move ahead and implement other policies which would lead to development and growth. I would like to emphasize that without these complementary policies trade liberalization cannot work; while with such policies trade liberalization can be much more effective.

When you liberalize trade or markets there is a static efficiency gain; the resources are better utilized because there is an allocative efficiency. Output levels go up one time as a result. But that does not produce growth unless it increases the rate of savings, and the increased savings result in increased domestic investment. None of these are automatic, especially in an open economy. Even if your capital account is not convertible but your current account is, and you have liberalized trade, domestic savings will fly out if external returns are more lucrative. Even if you have an increased domestic saving because of an increased output and the marginal savings rates exceed the average, domestic investment may lag behind without raising the rate of growth.

Both the theory and the experience of investment in developing countries shows that the fundamental problem with investment is confidence. If investors do not have confidence that the country is following policies that can be sustained, they do not lock up their funds in irreversible investment. This means that these policies, in order to be perceived as sustainable, must be accepted by the people, which means that they should be associated with proper development policies – creating more employment, more equitable distribution of income, better provisions for health, nutrition and education – which people can support. Without such support, these

---

\* Professor of International Economic Organization, Centre for Policy Research, New Delhi, India.

policies can be unsustainable and, if they are expected to be unsustainable, investment will not come and trade liberalization will not increase either growth or development.

When we talk about launching another Uruguay Round type of new negotiations – whether we have completed the implementation of the results of previous negotiations or not – we have to seriously consider whether it would, as Fred Bergsten says, actually prevent protectionism and push the process of trade liberalization further. But even if it does happen – and we get a better negotiated result and more trade liberalization favouring the products of developing countries – unless these policies are supported by complementary policies of investment, trade and social security, they will not result in realizing the development objectives.

The IMF was created for a very simple purpose when the world was opened up to trade liberalization and the convertibility of the current account. Even in 1944 it was accepted that for countries moving towards the freeing of current account transactions, there could be a financing requirement because imports would increase first, exports would increase over time and the gap would have to be funded. Some activities will close down because of increased imports, and countries would need new investment in the new activities. This would require appropriate policies, time and, during this period, the countries would need assistance. When the IMF was created it was intended that adjustment support would be given to the members in need. Over a period of time the IMF has extended the nature of that support as its clientele has moved from three-year programmes to seven-year programmes including concessional assistance, admitting that the adjusting countries needed time. In the last twenty years these adjustment programmes have often failed, particularly in the poorer countries in Africa and Asia, mainly because of under-funding.

What I am suggesting is that if you are talking about trade liberalization programmes you must also talk about increasing the provision of finance for the countries which are adopting those programmes, and the related adjustment policies. Adjustment policies should be well designed, incorporating both macro-economic and micro-economic measures. Trade liberalization must be accompanied by policies for increasing investment, policies for improving infrastructure and, for confidence-building, policies for social development.

The World Bank and IMF have both got involved with the structural adjustment programmes built on such policies, but they don't have the required amount of money. Most of the programmes are under-funded. Financing has turned out to the most crucial requirement for any kind of trade liberalization programmes.

Connected to this is another issue raised by Professor Srinivasan. He said that the special and differential treatment was a wrong strategy for the developing countries because they should have negotiated with industrial countries on an equal footing. How can they negotiate on equal footing when their feet are not equal? If he was making a point of political strategy, he could argue that probably the industrialized countries would have been favourably-oriented towards giving more concessions to products of interest to developing countries. I am not quite sure of that.

On economic grounds, there is no reason why there should not be special and differential treatment for the developing countries. The IMF has adjustment programmes which are different for different countries, funded in different ways, with programme elements which are quite different. Why should we not have trade liberalization programmes, differently implemented depending upon the capacity of the country? So long as the implementation process does not reverse the process of trade liberalization, or in the name of special and differential treatment there is no policy roll-back, there is every reason why there should be differential treatment for countries at different stages of development.

Earlier in this seminar the point was made about special treatment for the least developed countries. That a group of developing countries should be given completely duty free, quota free access to industrialized countries' markets, would be a very major move which deserves full support. But why stop there? For instance, if there is investment coming from industrial countries to specific sectors in developing countries, perhaps they should be given special treatment, including selling such products in their own home markets. Industrial countries invest and subsidize the investment in their own regions. Why can't they subsidize investment of their own citizens in these LDCs, so that the capacities can be built up in these countries for selling in the industrialized countries' own markets? This is just one example of possible special treatment; there are other examples, such as exempting products – from joint ventures with investors from industrial countries – from anti-dumping procedures.

Fred Bergsten was very vocal against anti-dumping procedures. All economists have been vocal against anti-dumping procedures but nothing has happened. However, if there is sufficient pressure that, at least, the poor countries should be exempted from anti-dumping procedures, it will be an effective special and differential treatment. We also cannot do away with the GSP. The European Union was the prime mover of the GSP and they should promote that further. A number of countries derived a lot of benefit from the GSP, and it can be extended today incorporating special treatment of non-tariff barriers and investment subsidies for joint ventures.

When we open up negotiations for further trade liberalization they should be seen as leading towards genuine development of the poor countries, provided: (a) trade liberalization becomes a part of a package of policies that are implemented through programmes which are fully funded; and (b) the treatment given to the developing countries is special and differential.

# Chapter 41

# Part II.  Trade and development

## 2.  Trade and development prospects of developing countries

*Professor John Whalley\**

I will focus on the environment for developing country trade over the next few years, stressing the changes in the world ahead relative to recent decades, and emphasizing how trade-based development strategies in developing countries may need to adapt. Discussion of the participation of developing countries in the trading system over the next few decades cannot be based simply on the experiences of the past. I will then conclude with the issue of special and differential treatment for developing countries in the trading system.

Back in the 1930's Ragnar Nurkse, an eminent economist of his day, posed the question of whether trade is the engine or handmaiden of growth. Does trade drive growth, or does trade simply increase because of growth? That question has never been adequately answered by the research community but, in the post-war years and particularly in the last ten or so years, many people have become convinced that trade is central to growth and, therefore, important for development. Since the 1940's we have had global trade growth which has been approximately double income growth. In the three years before the crisis of later 1990's we experienced trade growth at something like three times global income growth. So, a deeply held belief in certain circles is that, in some sense, trade is the key to global prosperity, and participation in this process for the developing countries is going to be the magic key that unlocks the door to rapid increases in their growth rates.

## CHANGING FACE OF WORLD TRADE

We all very much hope that is the case, but the world of today and the world of the 1930's are different. From the 1930's to today we have had sharp reductions in tariff barriers. In the 1930's, at the height of the Smoot-Hawley tariff in the US, average tariff rates were 50 per cent. Today, average tariffs on manufactures in OECD countries range between 2 and 3 per cent, and we have made great progress in reducing these barriers to trade. But how much further is there to go? Where can further barrier reductions come in manufactures which would drive continued growth? What is going to provide the motor for the global economy in the future?

There are, of course, other things beside trade barrier reductions which have been crucial to this trade growth; one is reduced transportation costs, another is

---

\* University of Warwick, UK, and University of Western Ontario, Canada.

technological innovation. But faced with current low barriers in manufactures, some have suggested that not only are these barriers likely to plateau in the next few years but, under a more negative scenario of linkage of trade to non-trade issues (environment and labour standards), the potential exists for there to be barrier increases. If there were barrier increases, how large would those be? And how would they impact developing countries?

In the years since the 1930's we have thought of trade barriers in manufactures as always coming down. It wasn't just that barriers were low and going lower, the strong expectation was that these barriers would continue to be lowered. In terms of a developmental strategy, development economists focused on a route of growing labour – intensive manufactured exports and outward orientation; that is a route of trade growth and integration into the trading system. But these barriers in manufactures may plateau. When one looks at upcoming negotiations on large existing barriers to trade in agriculture, it is not inconceivable over the next twenty years that we may get more significant barrier reductions in agriculture than in manufactures. In the past we have thought of development strategies as being linked to the global economy and based upon growing trade in manufactures, but trade in agriculture may turn out to be a more significant source of growth in the future than in the past.

Another area where there are issues facing developing countries, in the choice of development strategy, concerns what some economists call the fallacy of composition. In the 1950's and 60's there were two spectacularly successful developing countries in terms of trade performance – Korea and Taiwan. Many other developing countries at that time adopted import substitution developmental strategies, and their trade growth was relatively modest. But the success of these two countries was one of the things that was instrumental in changing opinions in developing countries in the 1980's that this was the best route to follow. Today we may have as many as a hundred countries that, in one way or another, are trying to go down this same route. Can all this work?

Some have argued that there is a limited trade absorptive capacity in the developed countries, and that it is not clear that this can continue, even if we still have rapid growth rates in trade as some of the lower income countries come into the system. Others argue that new potential for the developing countries lies in a change in trade structure. At the moment we have rapid growth taking place in South–South trade. If you look at the data in the UNCTAD Least Developed Countries Report, it shows that for the least-developed countries over 50 per cent of their import value has, as its source, other developing countries. This may provide sufficient capability to deal with any fallacy of composition, but the question remains.

There are also the trade implications for developing countries of factors outside the WTO. For instance, model-based calculations of the impacts of carbon emission quotas – looking at the implications of emission reductions needed to stabilize emissions at 1990 levels – have clearly showed an increase in the price of energy-intensive manufactures, in some countries reversing the pattern of their trade. Significant reductions in global trade volumes occurred and, under some model-based scenarios these trade reductions were larger than all the increases in trade attributed to the GATT liberalization processes since 1947.

On top of all these factors we also have the heterogeneity of the developing countries to factor in. The least-developed countries, for instance, are generally not barrier constrained, outside of maybe two or three countries who are significant exporters of textiles and apparel, such as Bangladesh and Nepal. For these countries, trade performance is more an issue of commodity prices and the pricing regime which they face, than barrier influenced.

In turn, the rapid changes which are now taking place add further complications. If you take, e.g., services, these are now estimated to be perhaps 30–40 per cent of world trade in services and goods combined, with service trade growing at maybe double the rate of growth of world trade. It is clear that for the developing countries there are opportunities in the services areas, but it is often difficult for them to pinpoint exactly what they are. They are there in software for countries such as India; but activities, such as airline reservation arrangements, which are relatively labour intensive but which can be executed through electronic means, are moving to developing countries. Credit card transaction processing is another example.

Other changes abound. In the mid-1980's, Hong Kong, Korea and Taiwan accounted for perhaps 60 per cent of developing country exports of textiles and apparel. Now China accounts for 50 per cent plus of these exports, and India perhaps another 20 per cent. Those countries that, in the mid-1980's, were large exporters now have quotas which are often no longer binding. In agriculture, there has been a large increase in high-valued agricultural trade (processed products) involving items that go way beyond basic commodities – typically niche products sold as new varieties of product into developed country markets. Such products are now well over 50 per cent of global trade in agriculture. So, when we think of trade and trade arrangements in agriculture and the impacts on developing countries, these involve less of a conventional discussion of basic commodities (such as grains), and more of high-valued products.

Developing countries face a complex changing world on the trade front. In trying to design an appropriate trade and development strategy for the decades ahead, all these other changes need to be factored in. Those of us in the research community also have an equal and on-going problem of trying to understand these changes. All these developments may suggest different approaches from current thinking to some key trade policy questions for developing countries.

## SPECIAL AND DIFFERENTIAL TREATMENT

I will now turn to the issue of special and differential treatment (SDT) in WTO disciplines – a central part of the discussion of how the growth and development of developing countries can be facilitated through the trading system. The classic approach to SDT going back to the 1960's was to focus on special rights to protect, in GATT Article VIII (b) and Article XXVIII, along with preferential rights of access. These have been embodied in GSP schemes, and the GATT waiver which facilitated them. The issue now is where does this discussion go, both in the light of a new Round and in the comments that I have just made.

Generally speaking, the evaluation from the research community has been negative on the significance of these arrangements for the growth and development of developing countries. GSP has been heavily conditioned. We have had substantial reductions in multilateral tariffs and so the margins of preference have become worth less. Also, because GSP is an unbound instrument with a threat that it may be withdrawn, it can be used as a vehicle to obtain other concessions in other areas.

This has again weakened its significance and its usefulness. The GSP has been given relatively little credence in research studies as a source of significant benefit to the developing countries, and many in the research community have argued that, being relatively small, developing countries should move towards more open trade regimes and simply unilaterally liberalize their domestic markets.

In the Uruguay Round, there are a series of new SDT arrangements in the form of delays, exemptions and best efforts undertakings, in areas such as Agriculture, TBT, SPS, TRIMS, Customs Valuation, Safeguards and TRIPS. Many of these arrangements were arrived at relatively late in the negotiation and, inevitably, were somewhat ad hoc. But they have changed the nature of the debate on special and differential, away from growth and development needs per se, and more towards what the special developing country needs are as their integration into the global economy occurs.

Implicitly there are two levels of argument. One is that developing countries face special adjustment costs and these have to be recognized; the other is that developing countries have limits on their domestic policy capability, and they need rights to use border measures in ways that developed countries do not require. To give one example from the November 1988 WTO paper from the Egyptian Delegation, in many developing countries it is difficult to implement and enforce policy directed towards environmental concerns. This may suggest that developing countries would need to have special rights which would allow them to screen investment in light of potential environmental impacts in ways that developed countries would not need, because of the inability of the domestic environmental policy regime to deal with these matters.

Another argument is that in many developing countries, particularly in lower income countries, there is no meaningful competition policy. Thus, if you have a situation of suppliers from outside the market who are thought to be colluding in their activities in the domestic market, no domestic policy response may be available to deal with this. A border measure which involves an increase in tariffs may have the effect of recouping some of the collusive rents which could be involved. This might motivate a form of anti-collusion duty as a special form of instrument reserved for the developing countries to deal with these situations.

Clearly there would be great difficulty in making determinations of collusion. Such duties would simply be the inverse of dumping duties, a situation where a determination was made that sales were being made above rather than below cost and an intervention would take place. I am not advocating such measures, but discussion of them logically follows from a focus on the special difficulties of developing countries in terms of their policy capability and adjustment problems. The Uruguay Round decisions on "special and differential" moved in that direction in an ad hoc way as a late response in the negotiations. Perhaps a way forward is to codify such arrangements.

Let me conclude by making two further comments on "special and differential".

First, the decisions on "special and differential" in the Uruguay Round also contained a component focused on technical assistance. Nearly all the technical assistance, as I understand it, was assistance to implement the decisions of the Round. Yet as you begin to discuss trade and development issues – in terms of the wider environment within which developing countries will formulate their negotiating strategies in the future – it seems logical to argue that there is an equal need in terms of capacity to negotiate.

Secondly, "special and differential", in its classic sense, is also seen by some in terms of "reverse special and differential". This relates to the adverse outcomes for developing countries in various areas within the trading system, such as textiles and apparel, voluntary export restraints, and some components of agriculture. The perceived need to deal with "reverse special and differential" is still there. It was a strong driving force in the Uruguay Round and, presumably, will also be a central component to a discussion both of a new Round, and what exactly will or will not happen in the year 2004 as the MFA is terminated.

Thirdly, I earlier raised the question of whether special and differential can remain as an overarching negotiating strategy for the developing countries. Special and differential, I am sure, will remain as a broad phrase used to justify different treatments for developing countries in trade rules but, at the end of the day, it would seem that for the developing countries, the specific details of each negotiation area are what is really of interest. Participation in detailed negotiations, rather than a hope that a generalized special and differential approach would suffice, would seem to be the way to proceed. Recognition that developing countries need help in achieving meaningful participation seems to me inescapable.

# Chapter 42

# Part II.  Trade and development

## 3.  Further integration of developing countries, including least-developed countries (LDCs), in the multilateral trading system

*Alec Erwin\**

## INTRODUCTION

The topic of this panel is really about something much more fundamental than the title suggests. It is still true that most economies are not fully integrated into – nor benefit from – the global trading system, and the majority of the world's people remain impoverished. We, governments and members of the WTO, run the risk of losing credibility because this is as true now as it was when we initiated the Uruguay Round negotiations. If we are going to progress, we must do something new.

I want to argue that it is time for some adjustment, some change, to the paradigm that has governed our actions in regard to development. What I am about to say is a simplification of a very complicated argument.

It seems to me that the basic premise governing much of our action is that, for development to take place, developing countries must reform their economies. While this is true, I would argue that it is now becoming a dangerously incomplete starting point.

The response from developing countries to the presumption that they must reform their economies is that protectionism – old and new forms – is still evident in developed countries. At the same time, we hear arguments that developing countries, and particularly the least-developed countries (LDCs), require technical assistance if they are to participate in the complex new rules of the WTO.

All these points are true in one or other measure, but they lead into a cul-de-sac and are dangerous. Indeed, such arguments risk "throwing the baby out with the bath water" since attacks will increasingly be aimed at the rules-based system as it is an easily identifiable symbol of a deeper malaise. We have already witnessed events demonstrating how the system is becoming a focus of the anger that emanates from the frustration of under-development in the developing world and, in Europe, of perceived over-development.

We need a new paradigm that disentangles this circuitous argumentation. There are many ways of approaching what I am about to say but let me choose a line of

---

\* Minister of Trade and Industry, South Africa.

argument that I think offers a guide to workable processes. It also uses the existence of the rules-based trading system, institutionalized in the WTO, as an essential achievement and essential starting point.

In my view, it is imperative that economic interactions in the world economy are governed by a system of rules, not by the interplay of economic or military power. At the same time, it is also imperative that rules are designed to achieve clear and equitable objectives. If there is no clarity and agreement on these objectives, or on the need for them to be equitable, then the real danger will be that the world system functions on the basis of the interplay of power, under the guise of rules.


## STRUCTURAL CHANGES NEEDED IN BOTH WORLDS

The next round of negotiations must ensure structural changes in both the developed world and the developing world. Why is this? In the next decades, in the coming millennium, the impetus for growth in the world economy will not come from the developed countries (the G7) as they cannot attain sufficiently high growth rates. If the developing world wants to penetrate the markets of the G7, we will inevitably end up with a zero sum game.

This would impel us toward structural protectionism in the G7. If the developed world is not growing rapidly, if the developing world does not offer a dynamic and growing market, and if the developing world seeks its markets only in the developed world, then we run the risk that developed countries will inevitably, on the basis of internal political processes, be pressured into seeking agreements that merely serve narrowly defined interests. The objective will be to create economic space for growth when, in fact, that space and growth is not achievable within the structure of the world economy I have just described.

In these circumstances, no matter the inherent quality of an agreement (for example, electronic commerce, TRIPs, multilateral investment arrangements), these can easily become mechanisms whereby the developed world seeks to reinforce its own advantages over developing countries at a point in time.


## WHERE IS GROWTH TO COME FROM?

So where is the possible impetus for growth? Where is the impetus for real development, for the spread of wealth across the world economy into the next millennium? Obviously, it lies in raising the *per capita* incomes of the majority of the world's people. This is particularly true of the giant economies – China, India, Brazil, Philippines, Indonesia – and for the whole continent of Africa. The rise of GDP in these areas offers the true prospect for global growth and wealth in the next millennium.

This would only be achievable if these economies are capable of reaching the levels of industrialization that currently exist in the developed world. This involves achieving the capacity to develop sophisticated industrial processes and widen the variety of products produced through such processes. If this is the case, what is the quickest way to achieving this objective? I would argue that it is necessary for the developing world to be able to develop, or add value to, their own natural resources.

What this means is that industries in the developed world that utilize a higher proportion of natural resources are, in a sense, grandfather industries. The natural competitive advantage for those industries has shifted to – and now lies in – the developing world. This natural advantage can be dramatically enhanced by the existence of the information technology systems where the dissemination of technology – of knowledge – is far easier than it was before.

Currently, in the developed world in sectors such as agriculture and resource-based materials (steels and alloys, for example), a range of measures are employed to continue to increase output. In the case of agriculture, it seems to me indisputable that the costs of attempting to increase output are very high, not just in fiscal terms but increasingly in environmental terms. The desperate need to increase levels of output is also reflected in the vast effort on genetic engineering.

This being the case, we need to think about considerable structural changes in the developed world. Is it viable for the world economy that these grandfather industries remain as prominent in developed economies as they are now? If they do, then the prospects for the developing world to promote such industrial development is reduced. Let me give you a simple example.

In Southern Africa – between South Africa, Zimbabwe, Mozambique, Malawi, Zambia, and Tanzania – we could quite easily grow another four or five million tons of sugar. To do so, however, would be suicidal because the sugar price would collapse. Nevertheless, sometimes at three times the cost of production, Europe is producing a much larger amount of sugar.

This means that a very quick route to industrial development in Southern Africa is foreclosed. We could open infrastructure, we could upgrade mills – in Mozambique's case we would be rehabilitating historical areas of sugar growth. The impact on hundreds of thousands of jobs and on infrastructure would constitute meaningful and real development for the sub-continent. At present, this option is blocked because of the pattern of production in the world market for sugar.

I think this argument could be extended to many other areas of resource-based materials. This argument, however, is not simply about the relationship between the developing and developed worlds; it is also about the sequencing of processes. It is very difficult, at this stage, for the developing world to rapidly begin trading with itself, despite the fact that increasing South–South trade is essential. We, in the South, need the capacity to sell into existing markets where there is purchasing power. That is why structural change is needed in the developed world.

As we open these possibilities – and it is up to us in the developing world to realize the possibilities of increasing trading amongst ourselves – we must conceive of liberalization of trade between ourselves and not just between South and North. Once we start trading with each other, and industrializing at the same time, we can repeat the phenomenal experience earlier this century when the now developed countries rapidly increased trade with each other. Indeed, the growth in trade within the developed world has been most dramatic, diverse, complex and beneficial to their people.

We have to repeat that process in the new millennium, otherwise there will be no development and it will be a futile exercise to talk about integrating the developing countries into the world economy.

In short, we are arguing that structural change is necessary in the developed world. There is also no doubt that we have to take steps in the developing world.

## CRUCIAL ROLE OF GOVERNMENTS

In a world of increased capital mobility, the essential role of government in the developing world is to mitigate the perceived risk of capital inflows. Risk accounts for developing countries' inability to attract the required quality and quantity of capital. More critical, however, is the need to manage our economies and societies in a manner that allows for domestic accumulation of capital since, as we all know, domestic accumulation far outranks international capital flows. We have an obligation, despite what anyone tells us, to manage our economic systems in a manner that allows for domestic accumulation, and we will have to start opening our economies to each other.

This means that government must play a role, exactly as governments played a role in the industrialization process in the developed world. The precise nature of that role has to be spelt out. To argue that governments have no role to play, as is currently implicit in some trade remedial action, is manifestly unjust and wrong.

It is governments' responsibility to alter the economic environment in favour of industrialization and accumulation. To do it with massive subsidies and high costs is, of course, suicide because industrialization cannot occur or be sustained in that way. Support has to be provided in a way whereby the outcome, the output, of government intervention is world-competitiveness. But exactly what the role of government is in today's world does not seem to be addressed any more. We seem to think we've solved the problem, and that what is applicable to the developed world must now apply to the developing world. This is wrong.

## HOW DO WE SET ABOUT ACHIEVING THIS?

First, it will require political leadership from developed and developing countries, and there may well be a paucity of that in the world at the moment. I would suggest that the best way of integrating the developing countries into the world trade system is for the developed countries to engage in a serious discussion in their own societies about the structural adjustments that their economies have to undergo.

Secondly, developing countries must develop a counter-weight capacity to the powerful influence that the G7 has on the world economy. This is not to be understood as an anti-G7 position but merely a reflection of the fact that the interests of any party are best represented by that party itself. Accordingly, the developing world must be capable of articulating its problems and positions more clearly, and it must be capable of engaging in a serious dialogue with the developed world.

We must also develop our capacity to negotiate. Quite frankly, in my view, none of us in the developing world has the resources nor the expertise to handle the complexity of the WTO. It is clear to me that developing countries must come together and specialize where their strengths lie. We should cooperate, we should work together and we should pool our resources and our expertise – otherwise we cannot match the developed world.

Then, of course, the relationship between the key multilateral agencies needs to be clarified. At present, there is duplication and a lack of coordination with the result that instruments utilized by various multilateral agencies may, at times, conflict. Some of the progress already made between the WTO, UNCTAD, ILO, IMF and the World Bank in regard to the integrated initiative for least-developed countries needs to be strengthened.

## WE NEED AGREEMENT ON WTO ISSUES

Within the WTO, it is crucial that we clarify the following.

First, accessions – it is untenable for the World Trade Organization to function effectively without the membership including all major trading countries. If we want to treat this as a matter of advantage in bargaining at the moment of accession we may do so, but it delays accession, to the detriment of the efficacy and legitimacy of the entire system.

Secondly, we argue that we in the WTO make decisions by consensus – but how is that decision-making done? Do we all have a sense of possessing fair access to that decision-making? This is a complex issue but we need to get greater clarity to construct a workable system.

Thirdly, on participation – is it possible, from a logistical and practical perspective, for member states to understand and follow in a sustained manner the full scope of issues and work in the WTO?

Fourthly, is it possible and feasible for us in the developing world to comply with the often extremely technical matters that are products of the world trade agreements? It is not easy and the capacity for compliance simply does not always exist.

## CLARIFY THE OBJECTIVES OF VARIOUS NEGOTIATIONS

There may be a need to explicitly disentangle different objectives of the various negotiations that are possible in the upcoming Round. What are the objectives, and where should they be located?

Some of these discussions, such as the workings of the world's financial system and the question of debt relief, are obviously not matters to be dealt with in the WTO. Nevertheless there are clear interlinkages that must be addressed if we are to achieve our overall objectives. We need to come to grips with the impact on the world's financial system on the ability of the developing countries to maintain a momentum of growth and industrialization.

We should treat the agricultural negotiation as a structural negotiation. This is a negotiation about the distribution of agricultural production in the world economy as a whole. It should not be seen as an argument between those in Europe, the USA, Japan and Korea against other countries. We should treat this as a negotiation about the structural location of agricultural production.

I suggest that the priority should be to focus on those industries where the developing world has the greatest natural competitive advantage. These would include such resource-intensive sectors as agriculture, agro-industries, natural fibres, textiles and clothing, metal and fibre products of all types; that is, where the natural advantage lies in the intensity of the resource use of the product.

We have to develop a structural system – not a hand-out system when we feel generous – that will allow the least-developed countries to get easy and automatic access to markets.

As a structural issue, we must resolve the exact and acceptable role for governments in promoting industrial and economic development.

We must retain the integrity – as a structural issue – of the rules-based trading system.

The next category of agreements, of negotiations, should be designed to create level playing fields; that is, to enhance compatibility, consistency and transparency within the system. These would include competition, government procurement, investment rules, etc. If these are perceived merely as attempts by the developed world to open up the markets of the developing world, we will inevitably encounter an impasse. If they are treated as ways of creating a level playing field, then we can have a more serious, systematic and appropriate discussion about precisely what special and differential treatment means. It will be needed in these level playing field type agreements.

Then, we require negotiations that facilitate new forms of trade and commerce not envisaged when the GATT was formed, and certainly the dimensions of which were not well understood even during the Uruguay Round. These would encompass such areas as electronic commerce, the ITA agreement, and agreements around genetic engineering, amongst others.

## EQUITY AND SUSTAINABILITY OF THE WORLD ECONOMY

Within the overall objectives of the world economy, we will have to deal with the fundamental questions concerning the systemic equity and sustainability of the world economy, though not necessarily in the WTO system.

None of us can step aside from questions of labour and labour rights as this is part of this fundamental equity and sustainability. None of us can ignore the fact that social rights and social development are fundamental for the sustainability of the system.

Finally, and obviously, none of us can ignore the fact that the environment, and the protection of the environment, is fundamental to the sustainability of our system.

These are matters of common interest. If they are perceived to be matters of negotiating advantage for the commercial or economic benefit of one group of countries against another, we will make the serious error of not achieving agreement on these fundamentally crucial aspects which underpin the very existence of the world trading system.

The need to disentangle different negotiations and their objectives is qualitatively different from arguments about whether we should or should not have a comprehensive round. We must spell these issues and objectives in greater detail through an ongoing dialogue in order to clarify what we mean. Then, we will be in a better position to enter negotiations where the common interests of the world's people are more likely to be addressed.

# Chapter 43

## Part II. Trade and development

### 3. Further integration of developing countries, including least-developed countries (LDCs), in the multilateral trading system

*Sir Leon Brittan**


There is nothing new about the idea of using the trade system to advance development policies. The basic objectives of the WTO include the raising of standards of living, and the progressive development of all the economies, of all contracting parties. What I believe we need to do is to build on those objectives and turn them into a reality.

One cannot, of course, look at the WTO in isolation. It is part of a network of international bodies which address development and other needs, and which include the World Bank, the International Monetary Fund and the specialized UN agencies, in particular UNCTAD. It is also clear that development, as a policy area, goes much wider than trade and includes debt relief, poverty eradication, health, education and, of course, the environment. The WTO cannot hope to address all these issues and solve them itself. It does, however, need to play its part in coordination with other bodies and with the bilateral efforts of its members.

My central message today is that we need to rethink the application of GATT and WTO rules in the context of development, and ensure that opportunities provided by the multilateral trading system are available to all members.


## DEVELOPING COUNTRY PARTICIPATION IN THE WTO

As a first step, I believe we need to address the constraints on developing countries in terms of integration into the multilateral system.

The EU is committed to provide effective trade-related technical cooperation, as part of an integrated strategy for development coordinated across the international community. In that context, the high level meeting on least developed countries held in Geneva in October 1997 made significant progress and, among other things, set up an integrated framework to assist those countries.

---

* Vice-President, European Commission.

I believe that we need to build on that in order to continue to help build capacity in developing countries. To that end, I suggest that the WTO Ministerial in Seattle should give a strong endorsement to capacity-building. In particular, I propose that it should develop a work programme, to be launched in Seattle, which would build on current initiatives. That programme could, for example, include ways to enhance cooperation between donors, avoid duplication, improve targeting of assistance and strengthen evaluation of it.

The EU has, as another contribution to capacity-building, put forward a proposal for a new WTO Law Advisory Unit within the WTO which would strengthen the Secretariat's existing capacity to provide advice and assistance for the developing countries on dispute settlement, without undermining its impartiality. In addition, the EU has proposed a programme of internships to help create WTO-specialized legal expertise in developing countries themselves. These ideas have been presented in Geneva and we are working to encourage support for them from our WTO partners.

## NEW WTO ROUND

Strengthening the capacity of developing countries to participate in the system is necessary and worthwhile but cannot, in my view, be the whole story. Some developing countries have already expressed concerns that the Uruguay Round agreements themselves have produced an unbalanced result. If that is so, it is clear to me that the only way to address the issue is through a new Round of negotiations. I would ask all WTO members, including developing countries, whether they are entirely happy with the present trading system. If the answer is no, it is clear that the only way of improving upon that system is in a new Round, the Millennium Round.

I strongly believe that such a Round of multilateral trade negotiations is necessary in the current economic climate, to stimulate trade and growth and to reduce the risk of protectionism. Let me describe why I believe the mechanisms of a new Round are of vital importance for the interests of all WTO members, including developing countries.

First, one of the key features of a comprehensive Round is the open-ended nature of the agenda-setting process. Any issue or area of concern to any WTO member can be put forward for inclusion on the agenda, which is itself agreed by consensus. For its part, the EU will vigorously support the rights of all WTO members to put forward items of concern to them for inclusion on that agenda (whether it is anti-dumping rules or anything else).

In that context, I can announce now, and I believe this is very important, that the EU will put all its current tariffs on the table for negotiation in the new Round. We will not simply put forward a series of carefully selected tariff sectors where we would be prepared to make changes, and regard others as no-go areas. Instead, we are prepared to negotiate tariffs across the board, and look to others to do the same.

Another very important feature of a comprehensive Round is the fact that the outcome must be decided by consensus. No one is forced to agree to a particular outcome. It is for each WTO member, including developing and least-developed countries, to negotiate in their interests during the Round and to weigh up at the end whether the final package is acceptable to them or not. This is not just a theoretical statement of the legal position. Look back to the Singapore Ministerial meeting. There, the meaning of the consensus requirement in today's world became very clear. A numerically small group of developing countries were able to succeed; insisting that their concerns were met, before an agreement could be reached. The developed world cannot today impose its wishes on the rest of the world. This is not only a constitutional feature of the WTO system, it is also a political fact of life.

In summary, therefore, a new Round guarantees that developing country concerns can be put on the agenda, and that nothing can be imposed against the will of individual WTO members, including developing ones.

Much of this year in Geneva will be spent preparing for Seattle. I think it would be a pity, in that process, if a feeling developed that there are certain items, such as agriculture, textiles and trade defence instruments which, in some way, constitute the priority demands of developing countries, and that on the other hand there are issues such as trade and competition, trade and investment and, indeed, trade and the environment which constitute a developed country agenda.

The reality is, I believe, more complex than that. First, it is clear that in areas such as agriculture and textiles, we all have what may be called offensive as well as defensive interests. Such subjects cannot therefore be divided neatly into areas of interest to one category of countries but not to another.

In others areas, such as competition and investment, I believe that we need to look for an approach which is of widespread benefit to the whole WTO membership, and not simply to any particular category. The key, it seems to me, is to seek WTO rules which establish a more open and predictable regulatory framework for business, which in turn will have benefits for growth and employment – particularly for developing countries which can only attract the investment that their citizens so clearly need by providing just such a framework.

As for the environment, domestic pressure for environmental protection will not go away, in particular, but not only, in developed countries. The environment clearly is important for all WTO members. It seems to me far better to seek agreed international disciplines on trade and environmental matters rather than allow protectionism and unilateralism to flourish.

I also think we need to continue to look for lessons from the past Round when drawing up our approach to the next one. One of the features of the last Round was the size and complexity of its outcome, and the sheer number of reporting and review requirements under it. Developing countries have rightly raised their concerns about the burden of implementing the Uruguay Round.

One answer to this is further technical assistance in order to help build the capacity in WTO developing country members to implement the results fully and effectively. On the other hand, I think it is also fair to take into account the lessons of the Uruguay Round in the next generation of agreements. I believe we should try to ensure, to the greatest extent possible, that new agreements have features which facilitate their implementation by all WTO members including developing ones.

Those features could include, for example, realistic transitional periods to bring new agreements into force, and notification requirements which seek to place the lowest possible burden on WTO members consistent with achieving the aims of the agreement concerned.

## SPECIAL AND DIFFERENTIAL TREATMENT

I have described why a coherent policy approach is important, and why I believe a new Round will help advance the interests of developing countries, as well as all WTO members, so far as trade and development is concerned. Let me look, finally, at the important subject of special and differential treatment for developing and least-developed countries, which pervades the whole trade and development debate.

When I asked my staff for a list of developing countries, I was surprised to be told that there is no agreed WTO definition of them. In addition, there are a number of GATT and WTO provisions relating to developing and least-developed countries, coupled with some existing waivers of WTO rules by individual WTO members. The picture as a whole is of a complex patchwork of rules and exceptions.

I believe there would be value in the new Round in seeking to rationalize all this into a coherent and defensible approach, combining the virtues of the non-discriminatory nature of WTO rule-making with special treatment where it is justified on economic and developmental grounds.

## LEAST-DEVELOPED COUNTRIES

I should underline the EU's strong commitment to special treatment for least-developed countries. The EU already offers duty-free access for 99 per cent of LDC exports. The EU believes that all industrialized countries should make a commitment at Seattle to ensure duty-free market access, no later than at the end of the Round, for essentially all products exported by the least-developed. This would, in itself, be a major contribution to ensuring preferential market access for the poorest countries.

I have also recently put forward a WTO accessions initiative. The objective should be to enable the completion of as many accession negotiations as possible before the end of this year.

Within that initiative, I believe that special flexibility should be demonstrated in favour of least-developed countries. We should try to offer them accelerated and simplified procedures for accession. We could, for example, agree between WTO members on a general level of tariff binding in the field of goods that least-developed countries joining the WTO would accept, if necessary after a transition period of a few years. In the field of services and agriculture, we should agree that these countries should implement a level of market opening comparable to other least-developed countries who are already members of the WTO.

And regarding respect for basic WTO rules in areas such as the implementation of legislation to protect intellectual property rights, we should be prepared to grant transition periods to applicant countries if they can single out the areas where they are facing special difficulties in meeting WTO disciplines.

## CONCLUSION

I see today very much as the beginning rather than the end of a process. I have set out ideas – on capacity-building, on the nature of a new Round, and on special and differential treatment – which I hope will help to point the way to a coherent and coordinated approach. I hope very much that all WTO members, whether developed or developing, can subscribe to such an approach. I believe that if we do, we can use the world trade system to enhance the lot of the millions of underprivileged people in developing countries, to help create and apply sound and effective measures to protect the environment that we all share, and to improve living standards and job prospects throughout the world.

# Chapter 44

## Part II.  Trade and development

### 3.  Further integration of developing countries, including least-developed countries (LDCs), in the multilateral trading system

*J. Denis Bélisle**

Let me begin by questioning a commonly-held view that developing countries do not exploit the opportunities of globalization because they have no products to export. We in ITC believe that this view is incomplete and often inaccurate. We hold that many developing countries, including LDCs, have the immediate potential to export more than they do. I do not mean to minimize the case for market access and investment, which should remain at the heart of our concerns, but I do want to make the case for national capacity building which need not wait, indeed cannot wait, particularly in LDCs.

Let me give a few specific examples to substantiate our view.

* Benin exports cashew nuts, cotton seed and lumber to Europe, Mexico and South Africa (around US$300 million in 1997). It produces enough to satisfy larger demand.
* Its neighbour, Burkina Faso, another LDC, exports agricultural produce to Europe and other countries in Africa and crafted wooden items to the United States, Japan and Europe (about US$200 million in 1997). Could it not fill a bigger share of world demand?
* In a different part of the world, Nepal presents an even more striking example. A preliminary assessment we have just conducted to identify areas with substantial growth potential singled out bio-trade. Nepal should benefit from the exponential growth in demand for plant-based natural products for cosmetic, medicinal, and agricultural uses. This alone should present an exceptional opportunity for Nepal to go well beyond the US$400 million it exported in 1997.
* Mozambique produces sugar, manufactured products, timber and copra. It has vast quantities of high-quality and high-value minerals and dimension stones for which there is a vast market in many industrialized countries. Its total annual exports remain under US$270 million.

The list can be extended but the message is quite clear. While demand exists for products which developing countries can produce, and in many cases are already

---

* Executive Director, International Trade Centre, UNCTAD/WTO.

241

producing, trade is not taking place to the extent possible. The question is why? Why are these countries not capitalizing on the opportunities the liberalized world economy is offering to them, and what can possibly be done to make trade happen?

Market access and investment aside, we see three principal bottlenecks to increased exports from these countries, namely: lack of knowledge of the multilateral trading system; lack of competitiveness and knowledge of trade opportunities; and limited practical experience of the export game.

Let me dwell on these three problems and suggest steps that can be taken to overcome them.


# LACK OF KNOWLEDGE OF THE MULTILATERAL TRADING SYSTEM

Readily understandable information on the multilateral trading system (MTS) has to be widely disseminated to policy makers. Exporters also need to know the business implications of the system. They need to develop a clear understanding of such issues as the technical barriers to trade and the sanitary and phytosanitary measures that can stop their exports. They need to have a grasp of standardization and quality issues. Developing countries have often secured export orders only to fail to deliver because of their ignorance of, or inability to meet, technical and other standards.

A survey conducted by ITC has confirmed that exporting enterprises in developing countries, and even some of their ministries and institutions, are not sufficiently aware of the rules of the MTS and how to apply them.

For instance, enterprises in the textile sector in some LDCs are very concerned about their future when the Agreement on Textiles and Clothing (ATC) expires on 1 January 2005, and many of them are considering divesting their interests long before that deadline, with adverse consequences for export earnings and employment. The appropriate way to deal with this problem would be to plan a sequence of government initiatives for supporting the sector using the special and differential treatment of LDCs allowed under the WTO rules. This again requires a good understanding of the rules, their interpretation and application.

To help develop such an understanding, ITC has produced a *Business Guide to the Uruguay Round* and is now about to release a sequel to it. This book and specialized training material developed with WTO and UNCTAD are being made available to networks of experts/advisers in developing countries to help them disseminate information to exporting enterprises and address MTS issues.


# LACK OF COMPETITIVENESS AND KNOWLEDGE OF TRADE OPPORTUNITIES

Having understood the rules, one has to turn one's attention to making trade actually happen. For this, developing countries have to develop competitive enterprises able to spot opportunities and exploit them. The enterprise sector in many developing countries, and in particular in LDCs, frequently lacks the capacity to undertake such a task on its own.

Joint public/private sector export strategies are needed. Strong support services are required to help enterprises in identifying markets, adapting products and securing orders. They also need help in developing better managerial skills. Entrepreneurs have to gain a better understanding of the requirements of key markets and evolving trends in order to prosper and even to survive in the ever more competitive arena of international trade.

To take advantage of opportunities and to make trade actually happen, a multi-tiered approach is needed, including the following.

- Trade information services have to be strengthened at the national level by building networks for information exchange. New information and communication technologies, such as the Internet and CD-ROMs, need to be harnessed in favour of developing countries.
- Enterprise cost structures have to be rationalized and input costs reduced. These input costs typically make up between 40 and 60 per cent of product costs of exporting SMEs. Aggressive use of best procurement methods can have a significant impact on their bottom line.
- Labour productivity has to be improved through suitable human resource development and judicious acquisition of technology at an affordable price.

These are all part and parcel of the capacity building Mr Ruggiero mentioned in his chapter, and of the learning and training obligations which Mr Ricupero so rightly referred to as the third key element for competitiveness.

## LIMITED PRACTICAL EXPERIENCE IN EXPORTING

Finally, we believe that more enterprises from developing countries can, and need to, participate actively in the exporting game. Here, the right choice of export markets is essential. In many instances, they should not begin by tackling the world's most competitive markets. They should start off with the markets in which they can compete more easily.

South–South trade is a suitable arena for learning. We have a methodology for this trade. It consists of computerized trade flow analysis, the identification of import–export opportunities among groups of countries, supply and demand surveys by product and by country through field research, and buyer–seller meetings. The use of this methodology has contributed to an additional US$500 million in intra-African trade since 1990. Intra-COMESA trade is now growing twice as fast as the sub-region's trade with the rest of the world.

More recently in South Africa, Minister Erwin will remember, three buyer–seller meetings for the food and beverage sector generated business valued at US$100 million according to the reports made by the buyers and sellers themselves. These meetings have benefited some 70 South African and Zimbabwean buyers, who were able to identify new competitive sources of supply in the region, and about 150 African sellers, who were able to find new customers. Exploiting South–South trade opportunities has the advantage of stimulating the improvement of production processes and marketing skills in exporting enterprises, thereby better equipping them to tackle the more demanding markets of the North.

There are other innovative ways to integrate developing countries, including the poorest, into the MTS. With the help of NGOs, ITC has had some success in facilitating the growth of exporting groups of micro-enterprises. Our export-led poverty reduction programmes secure the sustainability of the process and contribute to ensuring that the benefits of export earnings actually reach the poor.

Identifying and translating trade potential into business transactions for enterprises in developing countries is a challenging task indeed. It is the only way forward if low-income developing countries are to benefit from the economic growth expected from a liberalized multilateral trading system. We in ITC look forward to continue accompanying our partners on this path.

# Chapter 45

# Part II. Trade and development

## 3. Further integration of developing countries, including least-developed countries (LDCs), in the multilateral trading system

*Robert Sharer**

## INTRODUCTION

A main concern for the new global trade round is the integration of the Least Developed Countries (LDCs)[1] into the international trading system. This concern comes from the observation that these countries have lagged behind the rest of the world, with growth in trade falling behind that of other developing countries and the world in general.

This marginalization has occurred notwithstanding a degree of preferential treatment of LDCs' exports in developed country markets through the Lomé Convention and the GSP provisions,[2] and other "special and differential treatment" in the WTO.

Much of the LDCs' marginalization reflects the economic policy framework of the past two decades, as well as deficiencies in infrastructure and resources. Some also reflects the fact that their exports have been concentrated in commodities whose price has been declining. However, the global environment has also played a part – particularly by concentrating preferences on commodities; and maintaining significant barriers to trade in areas where LDCs might have potentially significant comparative advantage, notably agriculture and, to some extent, textiles. Moreover, the complexity and uncertainty of trade preferences for LDCs, and some of the special provisions in the international trading rules, do not foster their integration into the world economy.

Any solution to the marginalization of the LDCs in world trade must center on the ongoing efforts of the countries themselves. This will involve strengthening the policy framework to promote economic growth, and efforts to create a more favourable financial environment, including appropriate debt relief.

There are already encouraging developments in this area. Real GDP growth in the LDCs improved markedly between 1995 and 1998 compared with the first

---

* Chief, Trade Policy Division, International Monetary Fund, Washington, DC.
[1]  The term Least Developed Countries refers to the list of 48 countries classified by the United Nations as least developed, as shown in Annex 1.
[2]  These preference systems apply to a much broader array of countries than those classified as "least-developed".

half of that decade, while inflation declined and other macroeconomic indicators showed marked improvement. Events of the past 18 months have clouded the international environment:

- commodity prices are depressed;
- there has been some slowdown in economic growth reducing demand for LDC exports; and
- external financing conditions have tightened.

In these circumstances it is essential that countries not turn away from open markets, but further invigorate market-oriented reforms. The policy framework needs to be reinforced to sustain and strengthen the improved economic performance of the last few years.

However, it will also be important to institute reforms to the global trading system in favour of the LDCs. The starting point for these reforms should be the proposals put forward by Mr Ruggiero that LDCs be given bound duty free access for all their exports to developed country markets.

In what follows we review the trade performance of LDCs, assess the role of the global trading environment and explore the benefits of LDCs' duty-free access to industrial country markets.

## TRADE PERFORMANCE OF THE LEAST-DEVELOPED COUNTRIES

The LDCs as a group have not relied on trade as an engine for growth to the same extent as other economies and, as a result, they have become increasingly marginalized from world trade. While over the last decade trade has been growing more quickly than GDP for the world as a whole, this has not been true for the LDCs. Thus the share of exports to GDP for LDCs has been steadily declining and their share of world trade has also fallen (see Figure 1).

Furthermore, it is interesting to note that trade is a much smaller proportion of economic activity in LDCs than in the rest of the world, with total exports and imports (including merchandise and services) accounting for 9 and 16 per cent of GDP respectively in 1995, compared to 24 and 26 per cent for other developing countries as a whole (OECD, 1997).

A similar story can be told for capital flows. While net private capital flows to all developing countries rose dramatically from US$14.4 billion in 1980 to US$131.8 billion in 1997, flows to the LDCs rose only slightly, from US$1.6 billion to US$2.9 billion (see Figure 2). Another relevant trend concerns foreign direct investment (FDI), since there is little opportunity for portfolio investment in LDCs. In 1991, FDI to LDCs made up 4.4 per cent of total FDI flows to developing countries, while in 1996 this figure fell to 1.5 per cent (UNCTAD, 1998). Thus LDCs have grown more dependent on official development assistance to finance a growing share of their investment.

This is a worrying trend considering the well-recognized link between open trade regimes, economic efficiency and growth. Trade and FDI have been particularly important components of growth in industrial countries and much of the developing

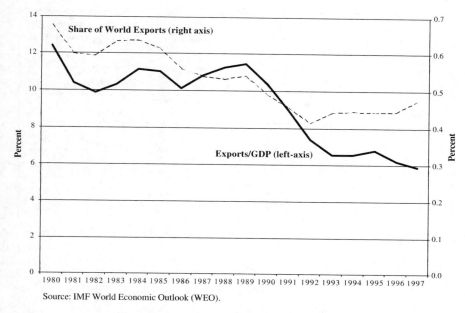

Source: IMF World Economic Outlook (WEO).

Figure 1.   Least Developed Countries: exports/GDP and share of world exports, 1980–97.

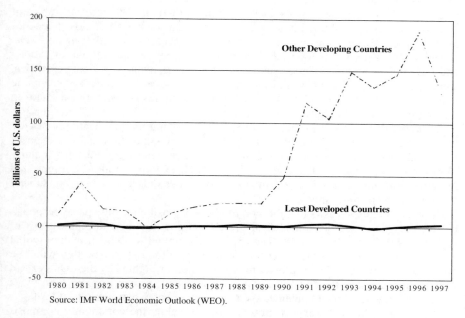

Source: IMF World Economic Outlook (WEO).

Figure 2.   Net private capital flows to LDCs and other developing countries, 1980–97.

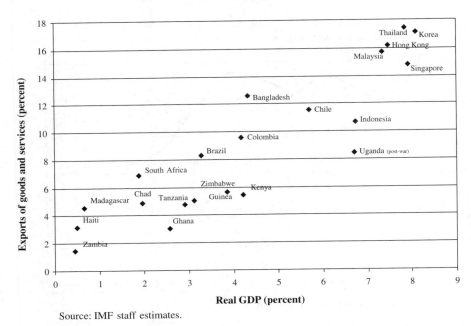

Source: IMF staff estimates.

Figure 3.   Growth of real GDP versus exports of goods and services, 1975–96.

world for decades. Export growth is consistently associated with economic growth in cross-sectional and time-series analysis. Indeed, there are no recent examples of countries achieving sustained high rates of growth on the basis of "closed" economies. Figure 3 shows the experience of some East Asian, Latin American, and LDC economies over the last two decades. From 1975 to 1995 annual growth of exports and real GDP averaged 15.7 per cent and 7.5 per cent in major East Asian countries, and 9 per cent and 4.5 per cent in Latin America. The greater openness of economic policies in Asian and Latin American developing countries is a significant factor in their strong trade performance.

A number of reasons have been given for the growing marginalization of LDCs from world trade. A common observation is that the composition of LDC exports, being concentrated in primary commodities, makes export earnings particularly sensitive to trade shocks. The composition of LDC exports is indeed concentrated in petroleum, raw materials and primary commodities (Table 1) which are subject to strong terms of trade shocks.

However, Figure 4 shows that this commodity composition is only partly responsible for the poor trade performance of these countries. It shows three measures of export growth from 1980 to 1996. The upper line is an index of the growth of global exports of all goods while the lower line is an index of the LDCs export growth. The middle line shows an index of growth in global exports weighted by the LDCs export composition. It indicates that LDC exports would have grown to more than twice their 1996 value had they maintained their share of global export markets in 1980.

The fact that the LDC export growth index is below the commodity composition index demonstrates that the LDCs weak export performance was due, to a

**Table 1    Leading exports of Least Developed Countries**

| | Value (millions of US$) | LDCs | As percentage of | |
|---|---|---|---|---|
| | | | Developing countries | World |
| All commodities | 16,318 | 100.0 | 1.4 | 0.4 |
| Petroleum, etc. | 3,398 | 20.8 | 2.3 | 1.8 |
| Copper | 1,010 | 6.2 | 9.2 | 3.3 |
| Pearls, precious and semi-precious stones | 854 | 5.2 | 9.5 | 2.3 |
| Cotton | 852 | 5.2 | 13.3 | 7.3 |
| Coffee and substitutes | 780 | 4.8 | 7.1 | 5.6 |
| Crustaceans and mollusks | 750 | 4.6 | 6.6 | 4.4 |
| Undergarments of textile fabrics | 644 | 3.9 | 7.4 | 5.3 |
| Outer garments, women's, of textile fabrics | 564 | 3.5 | 2.8 | 1.5 |
| Other wood in the rough ... | 472 | 2.9 | 14.5 | 5.1 |
| Radioactive and assoc. materials | 420 | 2.6 | 53.2 | 7.2 |
| Undergarments, knitted or crocheted | 411 | 2.5 | 3.5 | 2.0 |
| Outer garments, men's, of textile fabrics | 396 | 2.4 | 2.7 | 1.5 |
| Ores and concentrates of base metals | 385 | 2.4 | 4.7 | 2.3 |
| Tobacco, unmanufactured | 293 | 1.8 | 11.1 | 5.8 |
| Outergarments and other articles, knitted | 268 | 1.6 | 1.5 | 0.9 |
| Iron ore and concentrates | 267 | 1.6 | 7.6 | 3.2 |

Source: UNCTAD Least Developed Countries Report, 1998.

significant extent (about half the total) to a loss of market share in the goods they produce and export. Nevertheless, LDC exports have also suffered from being concentrated in low-growth products, as is shown by the fact that the commodity composition index is below the global export index. This illustrates the fact that for the LDCs, some measure of product diversification should complement policies to improve economic efficiency in order to foster export growth.

# ECONOMIC POLICIES IN THE LEAST-DEVELOPED COUNTRIES

The causes of the poor trade performance of the LDCs are complex. They include a lack of infrastructure and natural endowments, scarcity of capital, and other

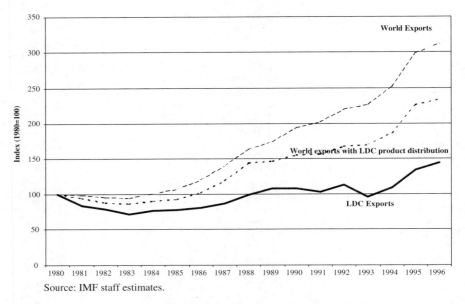

Source: IMF staff estimates.

Figure 4.    Commodity composition and export growth, 1980–96 (excluding petroleum exports).

exogenous factors such as geographic location. However, trade performance is also determined, to a very significant extent, by appropriate economic policies. In particular, a macroeconomic framework that emphasizes appropriate fiscal and monetary policies conducive to price stability, savings and investment, and a sustainable external current account position are critical in providing a stable environment for productive activities. These policies are a necessary condition to achieve a sustainable supply response. Macroeconomic stability must also be accompanied by structural policies and programs, designed on a country-specific basis, that enhance economic efficiency and productivity growth. Policy areas that are often particularly important to the promotion of productive trade and investment include:

- the removal of subsidies, excessive regulations, and exemptions;
- orienting public spending to the provision of essential public services, particularly health, education, and economic infrastructure;
- reforming the financial sector to mobilize savings and strengthen intermediation;
- privatizing state enterprises and economic assets in a transparent manner;
- institutional reforms to ensure that property rights are well defined and enforceable in an even-handed manner, and the general promotion of policies conducive to good governance; and
- adoption of liberal and open trade policies to promote trade and remove the anti-export bias.

Of these areas, trade policy is especially critical. Open trade regimes foster the development of export industries by allowing access to international inputs on a competitive basis, by fostering the importation and use of products that embody

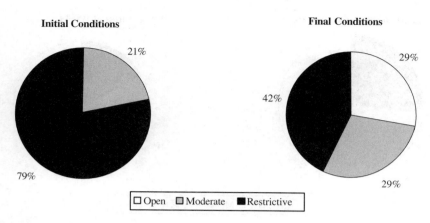

Initial Conditions         Final Conditions

21%

79%

29%

42%

29%

□ Open    ▨ Moderate    ■ Restrictive

Source: IMF staff estimates.

Figure 5. Trade restrictiveness of Least Developed Countries, 1990–95 (includes only those 14 Least Developed Countries with IMF programs during 1990–1995).

new technologies and production processes, and by allowing for larger production runs and the exploitation of economies of scale. Further, open trade regimes are also critical in attracting foreign investment, which also often brings new products, production processes and management practices. Complex opaque trade rules and regulations are anathema to good governance, transparency, and the creation of a level playing field which favours efficient foreign and domestic investment.

How do the LDCs compare in terms of openness of trade policy? A recent study of trade liberalization in IMF-supported programs has developed an index of aggregate trade restrictiveness that facilitates cross-country comparisons.[3] The index classifies countries into three categories based on a ten-point index of trade restrictiveness which takes into account tariff and non-tariff barriers. Countries with an index of seven to ten are considered restrictive; an index of five to six is considered moderate; while an index of one to four is considered open.

Figure 5 shows how trade restrictiveness has changed for a selected group of LDCs that had IMF programs from 1990 to 1995. In 1990 this group of LDCs was very closed, with 79 per cent having a restrictive trade policy and 21 per cent having a moderate policy. There were no countries with open regimes. By 1995 these countries had liberalized substantially, with 29 per cent having moved to an open policy and another 29 a moderate policy.

Figure 6 updates the analysis to 1998 and compares the aggregate degree of trade restrictiveness for the 48 LDCs to the rest of the world. It shows that the LDCs trade policy has continued the trend towards liberalization, but is still significantly more restrictive than the rest of the world. Indeed, the average unweighted tariff for least developed countries is above 18 per cent, compared to 14 per cent for other developing countries and 7 per cent for industrial countries.

---

[3] International Monetary Fund, *Trade Liberalization in IMF-Supported Programs*, 1998. Appendix I describes the IMF index of trade restrictiveness.

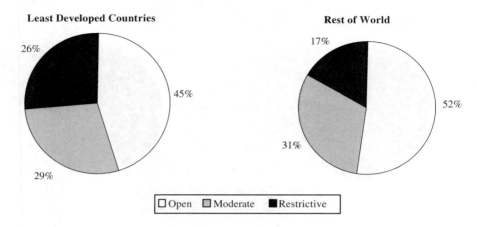

Source: IMF staff estimates.

Figure 6.    Trade restrictiveness of Least Developed Countries and rest of world, 1998 (based on the most recently available data).

## GLOBAL TRADING ENVIRONMENT FOR LESS DEVELOPED COUNTRIES

Although the main determinants of LDC export performance are macroeconomic and structural policies, particularly trade policy, the complementary global trading environment is equally important in setting the appropriate incentives for policy reform, and in establishing the conditions that allow reforms to result in rapid economic growth. As the LDCs integrate more fully into the world economy, the global trading environment (both economic and institutional) will be increasingly important as a determinant of their growth and development.

The global trading environment for LDCs is determined by two sets of policies that allow them special treatment under the rules of the WTO.

First is accelerated or preferential access to industrial country markets. The WTO allows industrial and other developing countries to move more quickly in implementing their commitments for liberalization towards LDCs than for other countries, even though this is a violation of the Most-Favored-Nation principle. In addition there are three trade preference schemes that allow LDCs special access to industrial country markets:

- the Generalized System of Trade Preferences (GSTP);
- the European Union's Lomé Convention; and
- the United States' Caribbean Basin Initiative (CBI).

Preferences have lowered trade barriers to some LDC exports into industrial country markets.

Secondly, there are a number of programmes and special provisions in the WTO regarding the LDCs. Recognizing the limited capacity for implementation of

Uruguay Round agreements, and the difficulties that LDCs encounter in multilateral trade negotiations, the WTO has only required these countries to undertake commitments and concessions in trade policy that are consistent with their individual level of development, financial and trade needs, or their administrative and institutional capacity. In practice this means that, in many cases, LDCs are not required to implement WTO provisions (for example in the case of export subsidies and domestic support measures in agriculture), or are allowed to delay the implementation of measures, sometimes for up to ten years (as is the case of Trade Related Intellectual Property Rights (TRIPS), disciplines on customs valuation and import licensing).

Yet these special provisions designed to benefit LDC exports have had little effect on their export growth. Studies of both the Generalized System of Preferences and the Lomé Convention find little evidence that preferences have resulted in higher trade flows, even in individual commodity groups. For example, a study by the US International Trade Commission (OECD, 1997) found that the GSP had led to increases in imports into the United States from developing countries in only 12 of the 650 commodity groups to which it applied. Perhaps this is not surprising considering the share of imports from developing countries into the European Union, the United States, and Japan combined – that benefit from the GSP is only 17 per cent (WTO, 1998). Indeed, this system of preferences may have inhibited export diversification and growth for a number of reasons.

First, important restrictions remain in areas where the LDCs have potential comparative advantage, particularly agriculture and textiles. In the area of agriculture, significant non-tariff barriers exist in the form of producer price supports, export subsidies and special marketing arrangements. These measures result in subsidies averaging 1.5 per cent of GDP in OECD countries which make it particularly difficult for LDCs to compete. In the area of textiles and apparel, LDCs face restrictive quotas in industrial country markets. There are also the industries where LDCs face the highest tariffs, in many cases the result of "tarrification" of quotas at extremely high rates under the Uruguay Round Agreement.

Secondly, these high barriers are accompanied by significant tariff escalation. Lower tariffs (or preferences) on raw material exports and higher tariffs moving up the production chain as value is added, discourage LDCs from diversifying into higher value-added exports. Figure 7 shows examples of the type of tariff escalation facing LDCs in industrial country markets for some agricultural processing and textile and apparel products where, as has been mentioned, they might compete.

Thirdly, access to industrial country markets is restricted by complex rules of origin and other administrative requirements, such as technical barriers to trade and sanitary and phytosanitary regulations that are difficult for LDC exporters to meet. For the US GSP system some 40 per cent of goods eligible for tariff preference do not in practice receive it, largely because of complex rules and exceptions (comparable data is not available for other OECD countries' GSP schemes).

Fourthly, the preferences granted LDCs in industrial country markets are not bound, apply only to particular products, and countries and may be removed at the discretion of industrial country authorities, depending on the level of imports from an individual country and its perceived level of development. Thus preferences are subject to an inherent uncertainty of market access which discourages long-term investment in export products and penalizes those that are successful.

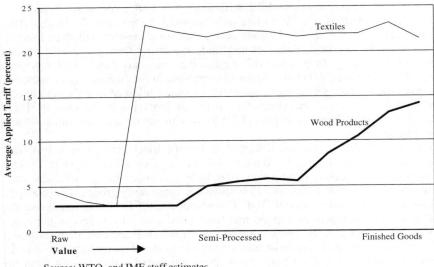

Source: WTO, and IMF staff estimates.

Figure 7.   Tariff escalation facing LDC exports in industrialized countries.

Finally, the system of preferences is designed to benefit all developing countries, not just the least developed. This means that in practice a large proportion of preferential access to industrial markets is taken up by large developing country exporters to the detriment of those from LDCs. For example, in 1996 Malaysia, Thailand, Brazil, Indonesia, the Philippines, and India accounted for 75 per cent of all GSP imports to the US. Imports from the 48 least developed countries accounted for less than 1 per cent of total imports entering under the GSP.

## REFORMS OF THE GLOBAL TRADING SYSTEM

We have argued that the way forward for the LDCs involves principally policy reform in the countries themselves, and especially in trade policy. But the success of this policy reform is conditioned on the existence of an open and vibrant international economy and a stable international trading system. Ideally, such an environment could be secured by moving to global free trade, including in the very sensitive areas of agriculture and textiles which are so important to LDCs. However, while the global trading system is moving towards such an objective, it is unlikely that it will be realized during the next round of multilateral trade negotiations. In our view, the next best alternative would involve reforming the unwieldy system of preferences that has not resulted in increased integration of LDCs into the international trading system.

The marginalization of LDCs in world trade and economic prosperity warrant extraordinary efforts on the part of the major beneficiaries of the global trading system in support of these countries. Amid increasing calls to focus on the interests of the poorest countries, WTO Director General Ruggiero has put forward a bold proposal for industrial countries to allow across-the-board bound, duty-free access into their markets for the Least Developed Countries. We endorse Mr Ruggiero's proposal, believing that it has a number of advantages for the development of the LDCs and their integration into the international trading system.

First, it provides LDCs with a substantial incentive to integrate themselves further into the international trading system in the WTO. At present, only 29 LDCs are members of the WTO, while another 9 have observer status. Gaining open access to industrial country markets would be a major improvement over the current preference system, and would allow LDCs to diversify their trading relations by country as well as by product. Thus it would provide substantial incentive for all LDCs to join the WTO. By integrating these countries into the WTO this proposal would strengthen the rules-based international trading system by making it more comprehensive and representative.

The binding of access to industrial country markets in the WTO is important to ensure the supply response in LDCs. Unlike the present systems of preferences, which is discretionary and can be removed by industrial country governments, bound duty free access would provide a stable incentive environment which would give security to investors in exporting industries in LDCs. If market access were also not subject to safeguard or antidumping measures, then it would be fully secured, giving the maximum incentive to investment. Such exceptional actions by the industrial countries to enhance export and investment incentives in the LDCs should, in our view, be matched by appropriately ambitious trade reforms in the LDCs, also bound in the WTO, with a similar foreswearing of recourse to safeguard and antidumping actions. The LDCs would also have to undertake complementary reforms to attract foreign direct investment into their exporting sectors, since domestic investment capacity might not exist to take advantage of new market opportunities.

Bringing the LDCs into the global trading system would also give them an incentive to develop the institutional and administrative capacity to implement trade and macroeconomic reforms, with the help of technical assistance from multilateral organizations and bilateral aid programs. However, in this connection the treatment of LDCs as "separate and different" in the Uruguay Round should be revised to ensure that these countries meet the same standards for policy reform as other countries. Policy proposals that are considered beneficial should be implemented by all. For the global system to simply exempt a large proportion of its membership from application of the rules contributes to the marginalization of those members. Instead of exempting or postponing reforms for LDCs, these countries should be given special access to technical and financial assistance to raise their capacity to implement reforms. Moreover, ways should be found to lower the cost of LDC access to the dispute settlement mechanisms within the WTO.

Proposals for duty free access are not sufficient, however, since in addition to duties there are significant non-tariff barriers for LDCs in important industries, especially agriculture, where their potential comparative advantage is most significant. Markets for agriculture in the world's richest economies remain highly distorted by import restrictions and export and production subsidies. The Uruguay Round made major advances in this area, and these should be followed by further ambitious reforms. Only with open market access in these areas can LDCs attain some measure of export growth and diversification. Full liberalization of textile markets would also contribute significantly to allowing LDC to exploit their comparative advantage.

Some concerns have been voiced that the proposal for duty free access for LDCs will be distortional because it gives preferences to LDCs that would be denied to other countries. While it is true that such preferences might lead to a degree of trade diversion, the amount of trade involved is not sufficient to warrant concerns about misallocation of resources in industrial country markets. On the side of the LDCs, since bound duty free access would be across all industries and across all major markets, it would provide them with a uniform pattern of price incentives that would allow them to begin to exploit their comparative advantage in relation to industrial country markets. This is in sharp contrast to the present system of preferences which, as we have mentioned, distorts incentives for LDCs.

The costs for industrial countries of allowing LDCs duty free access would be negligible. In 1995, LDC exports amounted to less than half of one per cent of industrial country imports. Of these, over a third are made up of commodity exports (such as fuel and petroleum) that enter into industrial country markets already duty free. Thus, assuming a generous supply response for LDC non-fuel exports as a result of the removal of trade barriers, their share of total industrial country imports would still be negligible. Moreover the proposal would improve consumer welfare in the industrial countries through improved resource allocation and lower prices to consumers, particularly in agriculture.

## CONCLUSION

Despite special concession and trade preferences, the Least Developed Countries have remained largely marginalized from world trade and economic prosperity. To some extent this is the result of LDCs economic policies, which have until recently not promoted a pattern of openness and links to the international economy. The global trading environment has not helped, however, since it has discouraged export diversification and exempted LDCs from necessary economic reforms. The new round of WTO negotiations that is likely to be initiated later this year represents a unique opportunity to bring the LDCs into the global trading system and establish the external conditions that will allow them to diversify exports and use trade as an engine for growth and development. Offering LDCs duty free access to industrial country markets in exchange for their participation in the global trading system will give them the incentives to implement domestic reforms, especially a more liberal trade policy, that will also enhance their prospects for growth. Further, while potentially significant for the LDCs, this proposal would not involve significant costs for industrial countries. Past schemes to help the LDCs integrate into the international trading system have not worked. It is time to try something new.

## ANNEX I

### Least Developed Countries

Afghanistan              Benin
Angola                   Bhutan
Bangladesh               Burkina Faso

Burundi
Cambodia
Cape Verde
Central African Republic
Chad
Comoros
Djibouti
Equatorial Guinea
Eritrea
Ethiopia
Gambia, The
Guinea
Guinea-Bissau
Haiti
Kiribati
Lao, PDR
Lesotho
Liberia
Madagascar
Malawi
Maldives

Mali
Mauritania
Mozambique
Myanmar
Nepal
Niger
Rwanda
Samoa
São Tomé and Príncipe
Sierra Leone
Solomon Islands
Somalia
Sudan
Tanzania
Togo
Tuvalu
Uganda
Vanuatu
Yemen, Republic of
Zambia
Zimbabwe

# REFERENCES

International Monetary Fund (1998), *Trade Liberalization in IMF-Supported Programs*, World Economic and Financial Surveys (Washington DC: International Monetary Fund).
Organization for Economic Cooperation and Development (1997), *Market Access for the Least Developed Countries: Where are the Obstacles?*, OECD document TD/TC(97)19 (Paris: OECD).
United Nations Conference on Trade and Development (UNCTAD) (1998), *The Least Developed Countries 1998 Report* (Geneva: United Nations).
World Trade Organization (WTO) (1997), *Market Access for the Least Developed Countries*, WTO document WT/LDC/HL/14 (Geneva: WTO).

# Chapter 46

# Part II.  Trade and development

## 3.  Further integration of developing countries, including least-developed countries (LDCs), in the multilateral trading system

*Anna Kajumulo Tibaijuka**

My task is to add the perspective of a person charged with overseeing and advocating the interests of the relatively disadvantaged countries in international development cooperation.

These are developing countries which are least developed in terms of specific qualifying criteria, including: GDP per capita below US$765; an augmented physical quality of life index of 47 or less; an economic diversification index (EDI) of 26 or less; and population below 75 million. LDCs are not a club that a country joins by choice. It is an economic grouping of the United Nations for the poorest nations. However, a country recommended to be included on the list by the UN could choose not to be included if it so wishes. I have also to advocate for the interest of countries disadvantaged by geographic location, namely, land-locked countries and island developing countries. As I will elaborate shortly, in the present international trading system, such a geographic location is a disadvantage, and leads to high transport costs.

The official views of UNCTAD on the whole question of trade and development have already been elaborated by Rubens Ricupero, the UNCTAD Secretary General. Mine are personal reflections on what I believe needs to be done to further integrate developing countries and LDCs in the multilateral trading system.

I have decided to narrate, at the end of this chapter, a list of international support measures which could be instrumental in the economic development of LDCs and their progressive integration in the world economy. But before that let me, for the sake of clarity, revisit some basic definitions. My premise is to define development to mean attainment of a broad-based improvement in living standards for a country or community. From this perspective, economic growth, as measured by GDP per se, is a necessary but not sufficient condition for development. It means economic development policies which promote economic growth but lead to increasing inequality are defective, and must be rectified or complemented by effective re-distributive policies.

You might say that this is straightforward. I say it is not because it has consistently proved very difficult to achieve. Practically all developing countries,

---

* Special Coordinator for the Least-Developed, Land-Locked and Island Developing Countries, UNCTAD.

including LDCs, have spent the last twenty years trying to improve the economic performance of their economies by pursuing export-led growth and structural adjustment policies and programs prescribed and supported by the Bretton Woods institutions. While these policies have assisted to secure more stable macroeconomic policies and environments, they are not known to have led to equitable economic growth. Poverty and inequality in developing countries, particularly LDCs, continue to stand out as a challenge, not only for the citizens of these countries but for the entire international community that aspires for international solidarity and cooperation.

One key element of Structural Adjustment Programmes (SAPs) is the liberalization of the domestic trade regime to allow free national and international trade. Thus, in most LDCs the most important factor leading to trade liberalization is not the WTO agreements but the conditions of trade liberalization prescribed by the IMF and the World Bank in order to access loans. In other words, LDCs quite often are pressured to liberalize their economies beyond the WTO undertakings. Provision of special and differential treatment in the agreements does not necessarily mean that LDCs have sufficient space to phase the opening up of their economies. For poor countries, issues of WTO agreements are secondary, at least in the immediate term.

Although, out of 48 LDCs, 29 are members of the WTO, at present only 17 have representative missions in Geneva. The absence of a mission in Geneva means, in practice, that the country has limited scope to participate in WTO negotiations. Even those who have missions in Geneva are constrained by inadequate staff to cover the major trade issues confronting these nations. It must be remembered that, besides covering the issues relating to other UN agencies such as WHO, ILO, UNHCR, WIPO, etc., mission staff also have to attend to the WTO (which I see as the referee in a rule-based international trading system), as well as UNCTAD (which, in my opinion is the coach in the trade game), which makes it virtually impossible for them to pursue issues comprehensively. I do not have to tell you what will happen to a player who enters the ring to face a referee without adequate coaching. The meaningful participation of poor countries in the multilateral trading system requires adequate preparation and resources.

## INTEGRATION

This brings me to the next issue that I would like to address – the issue of integration. Integration is an ideal and, like all ideals, will not come out accidentally but has to be worked for. The standard Oxford dictionary defines integration as "combining two things in such a way that one becomes fully a part of the other". It elaborates that it is about making somebody fully a member of a community, rather than remaining a separate group.

This means that, in discussing integration, we are confronted with the challenging task of identifying strategies that will facilitate the process of integrating developing countries, including LDCs, into the multilateral trading system.

The implications then are obvious. We are concerned with integration because we recognize that these countries are, at the moment, not key actors but rather spectators in the multilateral trading system. We would like their integration because we believe, or know, that their situation is not desirable, and we aspire to change it.

But are we ready to do the work and make the sacrifice that is required to achieve our ideal, that of integration?

## WHAT THEN NEEDS TO BE DONE?

There are three inter-related areas. Overcoming underdevelopment is one of the key factors in integrating developing countries, including LDCs, in the multilateral trading system. Trade is about the exchange of goods, services and, increasingly, ideas. You cannot be in the marketplace unless you have something to exchange. I need not recite what has been said before and in a number of our official publications. I can only refer you to read our Annual LDC Report on such issues. The conclusion is that most LDCs have not been able to exploit the opportunities offered by the special and differential treatment contained in the Uruguay Round Agreements, partly because they are not in a position to do so. While there is a case for the international community to respect their commitments and to refrain from the use of non-tariff barriers, so as to further improve the access of developing countries and LDCs to their markets, it is also a fact that the biggest challenge facing LDCs is overcoming their supply response constraints.

In particular, we need to assist LDCs to restructure their production systems to adapt to new market opportunities. The fallacy of composition, whereby LDCs are encouraged to increase traditional exports of the same kind, has been pointed out on numerous occasions. But most SAPs have not been prepared to go beyond addressing the issue of fair market prices. They have, however, not been very successful in eliminating, or perhaps are not meant to eliminate, structural bottlenecks which limit LDCs opportunities to trade. Most of these countries are faced with structural constraints that are not easy to overcome without the intervention of the international community – offering both development finance through ODA and debt relief, and expertise through technical assistance. Let me elaborate.

## STRUCTURAL AND SOCIAL DUALISM

The LDC economies are typically dual economies characterized, on the one hand, by a modern sector – comprised of government network and export enclaves often dominated by transnational corporations – and, on the other, by a traditional rural sector of semi-subsistence peasant farmers using rudimentary technology with very low productivity. The modern sector is favoured when it comes to access to capital in that it can often get finance at relatively low interest rates in modern financial institutions; while the peasant sector has no access to such services, and exists as a labour reserve for the enclave export sector. This economic model is not suited for enhancing performance as it bypasses the majority of the population, and is therefore incapable of reducing, let alone eliminating, poverty.

What is more, this economic structure also has reinforced gender biases within this social dualism. The rural sector is dominated by poor women peasant farmers who are often discriminated against by factors such as access to land, employment (in terms of being kept poorly educated) and capital (since lack of property rights for women means they have no collateral).

Economic and social dualism has to be overcome because it limits the ability of a country to compete in a global economy where national borders are increasingly disappearing and the free flow of goods and services is on the rise. This is not surprising. How can a country that is bypassing more than half of its human resources (i.e. women) compete with one that has decided to put all able-bodied hands to work?

The integration of LDCs in the MTS has implications for the design of economic policies that will result in the full mobilization of all domestic resources according to comparative advantage. This is a challenge for the LDCs and the international community alike.

## AREAS FOR INTERNATIONAL SUPPORT AND TECHNICAL ASSISTANCE

### Infrastructure

The importance of developing, establishing and expanding domestic infrastructures, and of ensuring their efficient functioning and systemic wide availability is obvious, but what is being done about it? Vital infrastructures include roads, potable water, electricity installations, health care delivery, communications, telephone, information technology and the use of computers and computer literacy. Advocates of SAPs and trade liberalization always assume that these things are in place. They concentrate on creating an incentive system for the entrepreneur.

In most LDCs, however, these basic infrastructures are often not in place because there is a problem of market failure. No trader will send a truck into a rural area if the road is so bad that the truck will break down and, if so, the price will be exorbitant. In a number of LDCs that used to depend on the now discredited public trading enterprises, national trade, which must be seen as a component of international trade, has been adversely affected. It can be argued, of course, that this has led to a restructuring of production patterns such that regions can produce products for which they have comparative advantage.

But there is the other side of the story. In Tanzania, for instance, the shift in the production patterns of key food crops – such as maize from remote regions with comparative advantage in production from the point of view of weather and more reliable rainfall, to more arid regions nearer to the market – has meant that national level food security has worsened. Besides, comparative advantage of location is nothing but a factor of infrastructure development. We are in a world where it is cheaper to transport low value food crops from distant continents than to move them a few kilometres inside an LDC.

### Expanding productive capacity

This is a key challenge of transforming the production function through technological improvements. But how does one achieve this in a poor country when we are pushing to liberalize everything except technology? While the need to protect and reward innovation is indisputable, it is also true to say that trading in ideas cannot be left entirely to the market. We need regulations to protect the greater public interest. For example, a trade agreement that would prevent small farmers from saving seeds for the next season is difficult to comprehend, let alone defend, when we are talking about trade and development.

## Increasing capacity utilization

Considerable scope lies in getting rid of a number of inefficiencies in trade facilitation by eliminating illegal tolls and tariffs and other cross-border constraints to trade. Also, privatization of previously state-owned productive assets such as go-downs, farm land, factories, etc., is progressing very slowly, all leading to low-productivity and trade. Some of the problems are within the means of national governments to solve. For example, the leaders could adopt more friendlier attitudes to local investors instead of favouring foreign investors, even in areas where this might not be attractive.

## Human capital, knowledge and learning

Without knowledge, training and education, including the use of information technology, LDCs will fall further behind.

## Regulatory environment

Domestic trade liberalization is a prerequisite for successful integration in international trade. Competition legislation, and fair trade anti-monopoly institutions with statutory enforcement powers, are important. But these will not come about without support from development partners. Their establishment, and for quite some time their efficient management, will require technical assistance and a host of other international support measures.

## Finance for development

There is no short cut to investment for development. Who is going to pay the bill? I would like to end my contribution here by reiterating the importance of honouring the commitment to LDCs and urging all donor countries to contribute the agreed share of 1 per cent GNP to ODA. Also, the debt burden is well known but little progress is being made to solve it. While I leave it to my IMF colleague to elaborate, it should be obvious that a country which is spending 40 per cent of export earnings to service debt cannot develop sustainably.

# Chapter 47

# Part II. Trade and development

## 3. Further integration of developing countries, including least-developed countries (LDCs), in the multilateral trading system

*H.E. Ambassador Moussa Toure**

Although they go back to the 1960s, in particular to the aftermath of the wave of declarations of independence, the development problems of the African continent are now taking on an extra dimension following the emergence of a new aspect of the international environment, namely globalization.

For some years, through the structural adjustment policies supported by the International Monetary Fund and the World Bank, the African countries have been implementing reforms intended to expedite their integration into the world economy, which would enable them to profit from the increased volume of world trade and to attract the capital necessary to finance investment and growth. The example of the Asian economies has often been used to justify this approach, as the Asian countries have generally succeeded in taking good advantage of their integration into the world economy.

However, since the international financial crisis, often referred to as the Asian crisis, even the stoutest believers have begun to shade their views. In the light of the harmful consequences of globalization which the crisis has revealed, is the strategy of opening up the African economies and integrating them more closely into the world market still justified? More generally, can the inherent risks of globalization be offset by its anticipated advantages?

At WAEMU we believe that the developing countries must start out from the assumption that globalization is inevitable and frame their development strategy accordingly. Thus, the African countries must make globalization a factor in their development, or risk seeing the continent further marginalized and the income gap between rich and poor countries further widened.

In order to explore this subject, I have divided my chapter into two main parts.

In the first part, I will share with you some personal reflections on the challenges which the African countries must meet in managing their integration into world trade.

In the second part, I shall define a number of ground rules on which to base the development strategies that must be put in place in order to take full advantage of globalization.

---

* Chairman of the WAEMU Commission, Burkina Faso.

# THE CHALLENGES OF GLOBALIZATION

In order to take the new element of globalization into account as a factor in the take-off of the African economies three major challenges must be met:

- the challenge of the evolution of the world trading system;
- the challenge of a new approach to direct investment; and
- the challenge of the mastery of technology and information flows.

## Challenge of the evolution of the world trading system

The multilateral trade negotiations of the Uruguay Round and the establishment of the WTO have complicated Africa's integration into the world economy. These agreements extended the scope of multilateral trade disciplines to services, intellectual property, investment and agriculture. The generalized reduction in customs tariffs and the lowering of certain non-tariff barriers will lead to erosion of the trade preferences which Africa enjoyed under the Generalized System of Preferences (GSP) and the Lomé Convention.

However, these new arrangements are also bringing opportunities for market expansion resulting from the partial roll-back of protectionist measures on a global scale. This expansion will only benefit those countries which have been able to improve their competitiveness by attracting foreign investment, thanks to the existence of a stable macroeconomic and institutional environment together with an adequate infrastructure and a skilled workforce.

It follows that governments must have at their disposal a critical mass of qualified personnel familiar with the multilateral agreements and determined to support companies in their efforts to exploit the opportunities resulting from the liberalization of world trade.

## Challenge of a new approach to direct investment

The trend in direct foreign investment must be reversed. The big challenge is to create the conditions for fruitful symbiosis between Africa's public and private sectors. An UNCTAD study (1995) has shown that investment in Africa can be very profitable. However, certain factors, such as the level of development, political instability, market size, the quality of the physical and telecommunications infrastructure and the productivity of labour, are tending to discourage the flow of direct investment into the continent.

The continent's performance in terms of attracting investment must be improved through regional integration.

## Challenge of the mastery of technology and information flows

The rapid progress in telecommunications and information technologies is offering new marketing possibilities. Africa should seize these new export opportunities, in particular for long-distance and relatively labour-intensive services, such as data processing, software programming, professional services, etc. The fall in telecommunications and IT costs should enable Africa to skip certain stages of technological development and tap new sources of competitiveness. For example, Swissair's invoicing system is managed from Bombay. Nearer home, the reforms undertaken within the framework of WAEMU have aroused the interest of a firm of European accountancy consultants. In order to take advantage of the area's comparative advantages, this firm has recruited young Burkina Faso accountants who for several months, under expert management, have been handling European customers' accounting operations at Ouagadougou. In Senegal, too, young companies are springing up in the same sector.

Meeting the technological and information challenges calls for the establishment of a programme to strengthen African technological capabilities involving, for example, the creation of scientific and technical databases and the introduction of information technology into the educational and research systems and into business enterprises.

# CHOICE OF DEVELOPMENT STRATEGY IN THE FACE OF GLOBALIZATION

In order to exploit the promise of globalization, the African States should seek inspiration in the example of the emerging countries of South-East Asia in order to define a development strategy that will enable them to overcome the obstacles which their development has faced so far.

As the basis for the definition of such a strategy, I would recommend the following four courses of action:

- regional integration;
- the training of human resources;
- the construction of an efficient industrial sector; and
- the strengthening of democracy.

## Regional integration

Regional integration can make a useful contribution to the global integration process, though it cannot replace it.

Regional arrangements open to the outside world help to overcome the disadvantages due to the smallness of the economies of the member countries, strengthen the competitiveness of exports, minimize adjustment costs and provide a framework for reform of the financial sector and legislation, investment promotion and sectoral policy-making. They can also help to promote transparency in macroeconomic management.

Finally, regional integration can be a powerful means of preventing or settling disputes, thus contributing to the establishment of the stable environment needed for economic development.

For their part, the Member States of the West African Monetary Union (WAMU) became aware of the issues and challenges of globalization at a fairly early stage.

This is why, at a meeting in Dakar on 10 January 1994, they established the West African Economic and Monetary Union (WAEMU), which was conceived as a common strategy for obtaining the advantages of harmonious integration into the world economy with a view to ensuring the sustainable development of the sub-region itself.

It is worth noting that, even in the preamble to the Treaty establishing WAEMU, the Heads of State who signed the Treaty affirmed "their determination to comply with the principles of an open-market, competitive economy favouring the optimum allocation of resources". This choice followed from the realization that where integration is concerned it is better to be outward-looking than inward-looking.

The WAEMU Treaty goes further since several of its provisions stress compliance with the principles and rules of the GATT/WTO.

As the eight Member States of WAEMU are also WTO Members, in designing the Customs Union (the Union) the Commission took particular care to ensure that the institutions established were consistent with the legal system set up by the WTO to govern free trade areas and customs unions.

Thus, overall, the structure chosen for the Common External Tariff corresponds to an external tariff-cutting process since the average duty rate, which was 13.2 per cent for the Union as a whole, has been reduced to 12 per cent.

## Training of human resources

In Africa, human resource training should be a basic component of any development policy. The training should be aimed not only at the acquisition of technical skills but also at promoting a culture which places greater emphasis on rational choice in the everyday behaviour of the individual.

These measures, which should lead to the transformation of the mentality and social structure of the African countries, should also act as a spur to development. They are therefore inseparable from the structural changes that need to be introduced into the economy, which they should closely reflect.

A person who has been trained to promote development must be deeply imbued with the desire to succeed, to move ahead, to exert an influence on nature, to improve his environment and to make his contribution to world progress.

In this connection, the Union is implementing a programme of joint action to make the most of its human resources. This is centred on:

- identifying and promoting centres of excellence in higher education, vocational training and scientific research to ensure that the sub-region's managers receive high-quality training;
- improving health; and
- enhancing the role of women in the integration process and in the economic and social development of the member states.

## Construction of an efficient industrial sector

This is an option which involves breaking away from primary specialization and confronting the vulnerability of economies based on the exploitation of raw materials. Accordingly, it goes beyond the structural adjustment policies which, in most African countries, are still proposing the development of export crops or services.

It is obvious that the most highly developed countries are also the ones which are most industrialized. The causal relationship could, of course, be debated, but this observation applies both to the big economic powers and to the emerging powers usually known as "newly industrialized countries" (NICs). It is therefore a matter of urgency for the African countries also to embark openly and resolutely on the path of industrialization. The objective of industrialization will have to be made consistent with the policies being applied in other sectors of the economy.

Additional Protocol No. 11 concerning WAEMU's sectoral policies includes a chapter devoted to industrial and mining policy. The provisions of the Protocol stress the emergence of efficient enterprises, equipped to meet the domestic demand under competitive conditions, taking on the international competition and furthering social progress.

Consequently, the Common Industrial Policy being drawn up for the Union rules out approaches of the "industrialization by import substitution" type, whose limitations are well known, and lays the stress on export-led industrialization. Within this context, various initiatives referred to as "accelerators of the industrial development process" have been developed, namely:

- the harmonization of standards at regional level;
- the upgrading of the Union's enterprises;
- the strengthening of regional consultation and the role of the private sector in common sectoral programmes;
- the setting up of an economic and technological information system; and
- the promotion of investment and joint ventures.

This latter initiative has been backed up with a common investment code.

It should be pointed out that the WAEMU Regional Consular Chamber, established under Article 40 of the Treaty, has been in place since 1998. Its main role is to ensure the effective involvement of the private sector in the WAEMU economic integration process.

## Strengthening of democracy and good government

It may seem unnecessary to mention the strengthening of democracy as the basis for a development policy, but an analysis of the economic situation in Africa and the world reveals that, whatever their ideological persuasions, undemocratic regimes have, in the end, led only to economic disaster.

In fact, economic prosperity depends on taking care of the interests of the different groups that make up the nation: the businessmen, workers, civil servants, farmers, etc. All these meso-economic interests cannot be satisfied without increasing productivity, itself the basis for a competitive economy. Only democracy can ensure a broad distribution of national wealth and enable each group to defend its economic interests as effectively as possible, so that the economic situation is in equilibrium between the various pressure groups. Moreover, it is only under these conditions that the ruling circles will be compelled to manage the economy responsibly, on pain of being voted out at the next elections.

The Inter-Parliamentary Committee is the main channel for involving civil society in WAEMU's economic integration process. The existence of this body, which brings together the Union's members of parliament, should help to strengthen democratic principles and good government in the Member States of the Union.

## CONCLUSION

The African continent is at the crossroads. It has failed to profit from the economic, technological and institutional changes which have marked the end of the century, mainly due to a lack of foresight. In the face of globalization, it is essential to obtain a better grasp on the evolution of the increasingly complex external environment in order to lay the foundations for a strategy of anticipation and constant adaptation based on the control of information (a strategic raw material of the third millennium) and know-how and their systematic dissemination among decision-makers and enterprises.

At the dawn of the 21st century, Africans must understand that human resources, much more than raw materials, are the key to the success of an enterprise.[1] Thus, the integration of the continent into the world economy will have to be based on the promotion of human resources in order to reduce the asymmetry which characterizes its relations with the rest of the world.

I would like to conclude my remarks by stressing the vital importance for WAEMU of the sectoral and structural policies to be applied with a view to strengthening and maintaining the competitiveness of the economies of its Member States. The implementation of these reforms will generate heavy transitional costs, the absorption of which will require the support of the international community and the international organizations. This applies in particular to the thorny problem of the external debt.

---

[1]    Countries such as Singapore and Korea have neither oil nor gas nor tropical products such as coffee and cocoa.

# Chapter 48

# Part II.  Trade and development

## Conclusion

*Rubens Ricupero*\*

I would like to summarize the main points covered on trade and development prospects of developing countries, starting with highlights from the chapter by Carlos Magarinos. He said that trade and development prospects are not rosy but they do present developing countries with the opportunities to undertake structural reforms and increase exports. He mentioned MERCOSUR as an example that brought about prudent fiscal policies, tariff reform, privatization, stable microeconomic policies and reduction of public sector expenditure. He stressed the importance of outward-looking policies and opening opportunities.

A central point in his presentation was that trade liberalization is important and a necessary condition for growth and development, although not a sufficient condition. Other elements are also necessary. He mentioned that non-tariff barriers constituted a pernicious source of protectionism. To address the problem, liberalization should contain specific measures that could assist – such as establishing national and regional centres for quality standards and certification, more specifically in terms of the technical barriers.

He said that trade financing was difficult for developing countries, and that multilateral institutions should assist developing countries to leverage funds. He also stressed the need for a strong industrial base as a necessary element for trade liberalization as it will condition the supply capability of countries to offer goods in the market place. He made several proposals regarding debt relief and trade related technical assistance including: capacity building; the importance of timing and sequencing of trade liberalization; and above all the role of new technology as absolutely decisive in an economy that is fast becoming knowledge and technology intensive.

I will not try to repeat all the points made in the chapters but some of the points were repeated again and again. For instance, that global macroeconomic trends are critical in determining whether developing countries benefit from trade reform measures and trade liberalization. It was felt that trade policies must be integrated into a wider set of development strategies including microeconomic sectoral and structural reforms, while it is important that such strategies receive international support.

I should mention here, in connection with these points, the need for increasing coherence in international economic policy-making. Trade liberalization must be

---

\* Secretary General, UNCTAD.

supported by efforts in other areas, in finance and in debt relief. In general terms, the need was expressed for improvements in the financial sector in the global architecture, to make sure that there was coherence between trade and other important elements in this increasingly interdependent world.

Technology was repeatedly mentioned in the interventions as a means to enable developing countries to take advantage of liberalization. Assistance is necessary in making use of this technology. It was felt that future negotiations should seek to integrate developing countries, and particularly the least developed countries, more fully into the multilateral trading system. Continued progress in market access, particularly in the areas of textiles, clothing and agriculture, is essential for these objectives to be reached. Of course, the areas that were mentioned are the areas where we have the hard core of protectionism, where tariff peaks and tariff escalations are concentrated.

Access by developing countries to the dispute settlement mechanism must be strengthened and made less costly – tougher disciplines and anti-dumping are necessary. Many writers stressed that technical assistance is essential in strengthening the capacity of developing countries, particularly the least developed countries, to participate in trade negotiations and the work of the WTO in general, and in their capacities to formulate negotiating positions.

The importance of continued and thorough on-going trade liberalization in areas of interest to developing countries was stressed. There were many different opinions about special and differential treatment. I can't say that there was agreement in terms of substantive content of those provisions, but I could say that many writers were in agreement with the need to update, to modernize, to take into account the necessity of giving special and differential provisions, and of giving the conditions to fulfil potential and avoid distortions.

Finally, there was general agreement about the need to take a very proactive position in future negotiations. What came across very strongly was a pragmatic approach in terms of looking at opportunities of liberalization, or flexibility in rules that will really make a difference in the situation of developing countries. I have the impression that there is a strong desire to participate more actively, though many recognize the limitations in terms of their capacity to fully participate in the coming negotiations.

In concluding, I really believe that it was an extremely lively and important debate. What made it so was the opportunity for everybody to speak.

# Chapter 49

# Part II.  Trade and development

## Conclusion

*Renato Ruggiero\**

I will conclude this second symposium on trade and development in the same way in which I concluded the first one on trade and the environment. That is, by stating that we have had a very positive and very important meeting. I think we have shown our human face – we have demonstrated that, as people, we can meet together to examine and discuss how to improve the world in which we live. It should be noted that our discussion has shown strong support for the priority of the least developed countries.

I cannot pretend to be able to sum up all the ideas, opinions and proposals expressed here. If there have been differences of opinion, sometimes important differences, there have also been expressed many positive lines of action which have shown convergence of views, even the possibility that we could reach consensus.

But I do want to underline a few basic points. First, on trade liberalization, I particularly liked the ideas of Alec Erwin, especially the notion that trade liberalization, to assist development policy, requires adjustment, not just on the part of the developing countries but also, and maybe more, on the part of the developed countries if we want to avoid protectionism.

There seemed to be wide support for trade liberalization, for what it can contribute, for its usefulness, but most agree that it is not sufficient by itself. Development is a very complex objective and needs a complex strategy. There was agreement that international institutions must work together if we are to reach that goal. It seems essential that these institutions must work together, even when preparing for the new Round.

What we need for development strategy is an integrated framework for development, beyond a merely financial architecture. We must move towards an improved global architecture.

There has been some discussion of goals, and I repeat Alec Erwin's "need for more social equity" in any future negotiations.

In talking about the benefits of the Uruguay Round there emerged a theme of difficulties of implementation. This is a serious problem which we have to face with an open mind in any future negotiations. It seems as though there was general agreement that there have been benefits, but that they have not been well distributed. In the next Round, many call it the development Round, some say that there

---

\* Director-General, World Trade Organization.

should be delay of the initial phase while others say there is a need for meeting the agreed-upon deadline.

I would urge the developing countries to have more confidence in themselves, in their roles, in their leverage. I paraphrase the words of Rubens Ricupero, that they have to face a positive agenda with a more aggressive state of mind to try to meet and defend their interests.

It was generally agreed that the new technologies are an essential element of any new negotiations. I was very impressed, for instance, by recent meetings on liberalizing telecommunications. It did not seem so difficult for the developing countries, though more difficult for the big players. The developing countries understood that there was something interesting for them, that they could receive investment that way, that it would increase their capacity to compete. An ambitious programme was concluded in just a few weeks.

The idea of electronic commerce was positively received in the developing countries. Entering a new field of action, we must not just look at the past but look towards the future – in this case, how to use these new technologies to accelerate integration for the developing and least developed countries.

A major success in this symposium was the expression of full support for the need to give priority to the integration of the least developed countries into the trading system. The developed countries have to open their markets, have to give free access to the LDCs beginning in the next Round. We, i.e. the international trading system, and the international institutions, must show our human face.

We are already giving wide support to an integrated strategy for capacity building, an initiative which stems from the LDCs themselves. There seems to be full support for quick decisions to existing proposals, such as legal and financial assistance to the developing countries, and the LDCs, in their participation in the Dispute Settlement Mechanism.

There have been concerns expressed that the system excludes some developing countries, that it is not very transparent, that there are too many informal meetings, and that the ratification procedures are too rapid. I do not pretend that we have a perfect system. I know that there are problems of participation, but I stress that this is not a policy of exclusion. There are just too many meetings. Many of the smaller countries have difficulties with adequate representation. So this is an objective problem which we must tackle, but again I say that it is not a deliberate policy of exclusion.

A parallel problem is the notion that the WTO is not working in the interests of some countries, that some developing countries are obliged to accept what others dictate. I can only say that the developing countries, and the LDCs, play a very important role in our work. I would point to the Singapore meeting where it was trade ministers from the developing countries, from the region, who brought about the agreement, not representatives from Europe or elsewhere.

I will conclude by saying that we know that we have to help many developing countries to help themselves. We all need to know each other better if everything is to be improved. Finally, I declare this second symposium, like the first, to be closed; but a new dialogue to be opened.

# INDEX